Educating Young Children with Diverse Languages and Cultures

This comprehensive textbook prepares early childhood educators to effectively work with and support young children (ages 0–8) with diverse languages, cultures, and learning needs. With a multipurpose, multilevel format, this dynamic resource focuses on the central role of language development and culture in all aspects of learning. Adaptable chapters cover curriculum, family involvement, co-teaching, classroom environment and more, and feature both brief and deeper study versions of the material, alongside a wealth of case examples and implementation strategies. Accompanied by an online instructor's manual, this ground-breaking text is an ideal resource for students and educators in early childhood and second language education, and all fields that work with young children.

Karen N. Nemeth is an author, speaker, and consultant specializing in improving early childhood education for children who are dual language/multilingual learners. She is the founder and president of Language Castle LLC, providing resources and guidance for early childhood educators and organizations in the U.S. and other countries.

Educating Young Children with Diverse Languages and Cultures

Karen N. Nemeth

NEW YORK AND LONDON

First published 2022
by Routledge
605 Third Avenue, New York, NY 10158

and by Routledge
2 Park Square, Milton Park, Abingdon, Oxon OX14 4RN

Routledge is an imprint of the Taylor & Francis Group, an informa business

© 2022 Karen N. Nemeth

The right of Karen N. Nemeth to be identified as author of this work has been asserted in accordance with sections 77 and 78 of the Copyright, Designs and Patents Act 1988.

All rights reserved. No part of this book may be reprinted or reproduced or utilised in any form or by any electronic, mechanical, or other means, now known or hereafter invented, including photocopying and recording, or in any information storage or retrieval system, without permission in writing from the publishers.

Trademark notice: Product or corporate names may be trademarks or registered trademarks, and are used only for identification and explanation without intent to infringe.

Library of Congress Cataloging-in-Publication Data
A catalog record for this title has been requested

ISBN: 978-0-367-54421-8 (hbk)
ISBN: 978-0-367-53508-7 (pbk)
ISBN: 978-1-003-08921-6 (ebk)

DOI: 10.4324/9781003089216

Typeset in Sabon
by Taylor & Francis Books

Access the Support Material: www.routledge.com/9780367535087

To Jan Greenberg. Not all early childhood educators know her name, but chances are their work has been informed by things she has written or elevated for the field. I am grateful for the insights and expertise she provided for this book.

Contents

List of tables viii
List of boxes ix

1 Introduction   1
2 Language Development   8
3 Getting Started   28
4 Curriculum   40
5 Meeting Individual Needs   60
6 Environment and Materials   82
7 Family and Community   103
8 Co-teaching, Collaborating, and Working with Specialists   118
9 Professionalism   132
10 What Administrators, Supervisors, and Instructors Need to Know 150

Index   158

Tables

2.1	Learning interaction questions	19
6.1	Items to request from homes	88
6.2	Culturally responsive learning materials by age	91
6.3	Actionable literacy supports in different settings	97
8.1	Suggested topics for collaboration	126
8.2	Cross-discipline conversation starters	130

Boxes

Top Tips for Language Development	8
Top Tips for Getting Started	28
Top Tips for Curriculum	40
Top Tips for Meeting Individual Needs	60
Top Tips for Planning Environment and Materials	82
Top Tips for Partnering with Families and the Community	103
Top Tips for Collaborating, Co-Teaching, and Working with Specialists	118
Top Tips for Fostering Professionalism	132
Top Tips for What Administrators, Supervisors, and Instructors Need to Know	150

1 Introduction

Follow the Chapter 1 Roadmap with These Headings

The Focus of this Book
Important Terms
Features of this Book
Early Childhood Educator Competencies for the Future

This chapter introduces the premise of this book as a comprehensive, multidisciplinary textbook for anyone studying to work with young children from birth to 8 years. It identifies the core focus in the study of language development and its connections to all of the chapter topics. Important terms used in this text are explained. The format and features of the chapters are described. The chapter concludes with a listing of competencies identified by researchers as critical to the successful work of early childhood educators. All of these competencies are addressed in the content of this book to form a complete resource for college and university study as well as a support that belongs on the shelf of every early childhood educator.

The Focus of this Book

Language is the center of nearly everything that is human. When you begin your study with language, you will learn how the brain works, how learning works, and how social interactions work. Language serves us on the outside where people can read and hear what we say, as well as on the inside as it allows us to process our thoughts and feelings. Centering your study around language prepares you to understand what happens when things don't go as expected. Your deeper understanding of language empowers you to interact with diverse children, families, and colleagues. So this textbook starts with language at the center. This approach makes it possible for you to gain deeper insights into all areas of development and teaching that will make you a better educator in any position working with young children ages birth through 8 years.

Language as a general concept is the system of communication based on a structure that all humans use. It allows us to receive information, express information, and think about information. We use the same word to refer to the particular system developed and shared by people in a country or region. We identify a language as "Spanish" or "English" or "Vietnamese," but recognize that there may be many dialects or versions of each language. While language is the central focus of this book, diversity is always part of the discussion. Linguistic diversity is rising in many countries, particularly the United States, where language diversity is growing fastest among the youngest children in the population (Park,

O'Toole, & Katsiaficas, 2017). In both the United Kingdom and the United States, there are many indigenous languages in addition to languages from other countries.

In England, more than 20% of primary students use English as an additional language, according to the Statista website. This number has increased steadily since 1997 when the count was just under 8%. London is one of the most linguistically diverse cities in the world. In the United States, close to 1/3 of young children live in homes where a language other than English is spoken (Park, O'Toole, & Katsiaficas, 2017). The Office of Head Start began using the term "dual language learner" (DLL) to refer to children who are developing two or more languages (U.S. Department of Health and Human Services & U.S. Department of Education, 2016). This includes children who are learning two languages simultaneously as well as children who are adding a new language because they've moved to a new school, community, or country. In either case, children under the age of 8 are still learning about language and they have two (or more) language systems, so they know some things in one language, some in the other. This means that all young children who are growing up with two or more languages need support in all their languages. And one key point to recognize is that this increase in language diversity means that most people entering early childhood education fields will encounter children who speak another language in their work. For example, Head Start found that more than 85% of their classrooms have at least one child who is a DLL (Administration for Children and Families, 2008).

There is a great deal of science to support the way we work with children who are DLLs, but we still need so much more. Even so, many services, classes, and programs that serve children who are DLLs are affected by factors far removed from this science. From year to year, public opinion about early childhood care and education funding may change, as will attitudes about teaching young children with diverse languages. The languages that appear in our programs change with shifts in population. Additional factors such as poverty levels, housing stability, and cultural acceptance also impact the early experiences of children who may enroll in your program. Being prepared for early childhood education requires you to be ready to understand and meet the needs of children from diverse experiences, cultures, abilities, and languages (Nemeth, Brillante, & Mullen, 2015).

Being prepared for all children is the most important step in building equitable access to early education. Not every early childhood educator needs to be an expert in everything, but they do need to have the confidence to deal with every child. Our shared goal in the field should be to ensure equitable access to learning to all young children. We need more than an "equity lens" as some people call it. We need to establish a full equity foundation on which all our work is built. This does not mean *providing* equal education. It means providing flexible, proactive, and responsive education that each child *receives* in ways that meet their needs. You will read more about how to achieve this goal with research-based, inclusive strategies for addressing experiences, cultures, abilities, and languages throughout this book.

Important Terms

The language we use when talking about young children influences their feelings about themselves and others and influences your own attitudes and behaviors. For example, it is important to use "person first language" in speaking and writing about young children. This expresses respect for the person primarily and makes descriptions second to recognition of the value of each individual. We might say "a child who loves to build with blocks, has a favorite kind of pizza, and uses a wheelchair" rather than "a disabled child." We might say "an infant who loves to notice pets in stories and on walks, and who is growing up in a home with English and Polish" rather than only calling them "a dual language learner." We should also avoid labeling children as belonging to a group. Why say "African American boys" when we know they are not all alike? Even with good intentions, this kind of group labeling can lead to stereotyping and interfering with your ability to see each child as an individual.

Children who are growing up with two or more languages may be identified as needing language support services. These services may be called English as a Second Language (ESL) or English as an Additional Language (EAL), which may be full time, partial schedule, or via consultation with the classroom teacher. There may be bilingual education (BE) that is conducted in two languages and may be considered transitional (to help children learn in their home language until they are ready to transition to learning in English) or maintenance (designed to help children continue learning and developing in their home language and English). Two-way dual language immersion classes are a version of bilingual education. Some children are assigned to English language development services, which just provide a bit of learning support, not as extensive as BE or ESL/EAL. A teacher may be bilingual without being certified to teach an official bilingual education class. Being bilingual is a great asset for an early childhood teacher, but this brings up another issue: language matching. A teacher who speaks two languages may not be fluent in all of the languages of children in her work. So educators may be monolingual, bilingual in the language that matches the children, or bilingual in non-matching languages.

Children should not be identified by their educational services. In other words, it is not appropriate to call a child "a special ed kid" or "an ESL." The most widely used terms for young children who are learning in two or more languages are dual language learner (DLL) or multilingual learner (ML). Some people use the term "emergent bilingual," but this term assumes that all children learning in two or more languages would be heading toward bilingualism. This is not always the case. Some children have language learning experiences in the early years that expose them to other cultures and languages without plans for becoming bilingual. Some funding sources may refer to students with "limited English proficiency," but we know that young children who are learning English and more languages have extra assets, not limitations. We see many educators who work with older students use the terms "English Learners" (ELs) or "English language learners" (ELLs), but these terms are not ideal for early childhood. The research has made it clear that young children are still in the process of learning in both of their languages and that growing up bilingual will be beneficial for them. The term "English learner" gives the impression the goal is to learn English while leaving the first language behind, and this is not the goal for young learners (NASEM, 2017). It is also important to note that some children start life in the U.S. or U.K. in an English-speaking family, and begin learning their heritage or indigenous language when they go to school.

Keep in mind that a group can be diverse, but a child is not. We refer to a linguistically diverse school or class, but each member is a child who is a DLL or ML. Children who have moved in from another country are immigrants. But many children who are new to English were born in the U.S. or the U.K. to non-English speaking families. Rather than drawing attention to languages spoken or countries of origin, some people refer to "people of color" but there is another term you can use, Black Indigenous People of Color (BIPOC), to ensure all are included.

There are lots of options for talking in the languages spoken by or learned by young children. In this book, the most used term for the main language a child learns at home is "home language." Other times you will see mention of children learning their Tribal, native, indigenous, or heritage language, which may be the home language or the language of the family's culture. ESL teachers often refer to L1 and L2 meaning first and second language. Globally, the term "mother tongue" is widely used. Culturally, we talk about the majority language spoken by most people in a region or country, and the minority languages that might be a child's first or new language.

Culture and language are closely tied across all ages. When you are not aware of cultural similarities and differences, you might engage in unspoken or implicit bias. When you make the effort to learn about the cultures of the adults and children around you, you are less likely to be influenced by stereotypes. This willingness to learn is often called "cultural humility." You may also see terms such as "cultural competence," but this phrase may not always be interpreted as an ongoing process. You will also see the term "cultural and linguistic responsiveness" which implies a willingness to use the languages of the children in teaching and learning and to embed authentic representations of each child's culture. Many children and families experience prejudice against them due to the color of their skin or the sound of their language. This may take the form of barely noticeable "micro-aggressions" or the "hidden curriculum" of unwritten practices that may unwittingly cause discrimination. The more you reflect, discuss, and learn about those around you, the more you can understand their values, strengths, and needs to approach early education equitably.

Features of this Book

This book is organized with features that will set you on a path to success in your work with young children now and in the future. In addition to the focus on language as the basis for the book content, each chapter includes:

- An abstract that serves as a roadmap to the content and highlights of the chapter.
- A brief version introducing "Top Tips" from the chapter.
- Deeper learning on the key components of early childhood educator preparation.
- Choose Your Own Path Check-In to guide planning across disciplines.
- Social media messages and discussion starters to facilitate engagement with your personal learning network.
- References which are also resources for further study.

This book was designed intentionally to support interdisciplinary learning for those preparing to work with young children birth–age 8 in various capacities and in various settings. To simplify language, we use the following terms:

- "Class" and "classroom" indicate groups of children and learning environments in child care, nursery, family child care, schools, and other settings.
- "Early childhood educator" encompasses many practitioners in the field, including teachers, caregivers, assistants, therapists, and specialists.
- "Specialists" include people with specialized degrees, licenses, or certifications who work with young children on a regularly scheduled or occasional basis.
- "Family" includes parents, guardians, and other family members as well as diverse family structures.

At the time of this book's writing, the field of early education is facing upheaval due to several key trends, including school shutdowns in a pandemic. Here are some key topics that are covered in the rest of the chapters.

- Supporting linguistically and culturally diverse learners through remote learning.
- Two new position statements by the National Association for the Education of Young Children: Advancing Equity in Early Childhood Education and Developmentally Appropriate Practice (both found at www.naeyc.org/resources/position-statements).

- Focus on interdisciplinary coordination of learning for adults and children.
- Implementing proactive Universal Design strategies.
- Anti-bias focus on equitable access to early education and the importance of building a diverse early childhood workforce.
- Trauma-informed and assets-based practices.

Early Childhood Educator Competencies for the Future

Research summarized in three of the most important reports in our field has given us a clear list of competencies that early childhood educators need to succeed in their work with young children. These will be addressed throughout this book. Early childhood educators need to know:

- The development of first and multiple languages.
- The role of culture in early development and language learning.
- Effective strategies for engaging with diverse families of young children.
- Teaching strategies and resources to help children learn and grow with two or more languages.
- How to adapt formal and informal assessments to work with children's languages. (NASEM, 2017; U.S. Department of Health and Human Services & U.S. Department of Education, 2016; Institute of Medicine & National Research Council, 2015)

In addition to the subject area knowledge and skills early childhood educators need to work with diverse young children, their attitudes and beliefs play a significant role in education choices and practices. Garrity et al. (2018) found that teachers with negative views about supporting children's home languages tended to approach teaching with deficit-based assumptions about children who are DLLs. This happened even though they had degrees and had learned about the research showing multiple languages are a strength for young learners. As you progress in your studies, your ability to acknowledge and question your own assumptions will be crucial to your ability to follow the research toward high quality early childhood education.

The National Association for the Education of Young Children updated their position statement about what all early childhood educators need to learn in higher education programs: Professional Standards and Competencies for Early Childhood Educators (NAEYC, 2020).

The standards are described as:

1 Child development and learning in context …
2 Family–teacher partnerships and community connections …
3 Child observations, documentation, and assessment …
4 Developmentally, culturally, and linguistically appropriate teaching practices …
5 Knowledge, applications, and integration of academic content in the early childhood curriculum …
6 Professionalism as an early childhood educator.

(NAEYC, 2020, pp. 9–10)

NAEYC's first standard highlights the importance of understanding how children develop and learn in all of the contexts that they experience. This is covered in our Chapters 2 ("Language Development") and 5 ("Meeting Individual Needs"). Chapter 7 of this book is titled "Family and Community," and it corresponds with NAEYC's second standard that emphasizes the importance of partnerships between families and teachers as well as connecting with the general community outside of the school or program. The third of NAEYC's standards looks at what teachers should know about child observation, documentation, assessment, which are topics covered in this book's Chapters 4 ("Curriculum") and 5.

Another standard from NAEYC focuses on ensuring teachers are prepared to implement developmentally, culturally, and linguistically appropriate practices. These topics are woven throughout this book, with notable content in Chapters 5 and 6 ("Environment and Materials"). The NAEYC standard that focuses on content and curriculum corresponds to this book's Chapter 4. Finally, NAEYC closes with a standard that describes all aspects of professionalism that should be addressed in higher education programs for preparing early childhood teachers. This book provides a great deal of depth on this topic, covered in Chapter 3 ("Getting Started"), Chapter 8 ("Collaboration, Co-teaching, and Working with Specialists"), and Chapter 9 ("Professionalism"). All of these standards are incorporated in the guidance for administrators that is provided in Chapter 10 of this book.

There is no field more important than early childhood education. Everyone who works with young children will have an effect on the future for all of us. As you look around your college or university, you can begin to realize that high quality early childhood education made every major and specialty possible. Every professor in every department of your college or university got their start in an early learning environment. As a field, we know we cannot afford to leave anyone out, or to leave anyone behind. All early educators need to be ready, confident, and informed to work effectively with children from diverse experiences, cultures, abilities, and languages. Your dedication to this work is appreciated.

Social Media Discussion Starters from this Chapter

- What is one thing that all educators need to know about working with children from birth to 8 years?
- What is your favorite term to refer to young children who are growing up with two or more languages?
- In early childhood education, all teachers are teachers of English learners. What does this statement mean to you?

Resources for Further Learning:

NASEM website with additional resources to support use of the Promising Futures report: www.nap.edu/catalog/24677/promoting-the-educational-success-of-children-and-youth-learning-english

NASEM website with additional resources to support use of the Transforming the Workforce report: www.nap.edu/catalog/19401/transforming-the-workforce-for-children-birth-through-age-8-a

NAEYC Position Statements: www.naeyc.org/resources/position-statements

References

Administration for Children and Families (2008) *Dual Language Learning: What Does It Take? Head Start Dual Language Report*, retrieved from https://eclkc.ohs.acf.hhs.gov/sites/default/files/pdf/dual-language-learning-what-does-it-take.pdf

Garrity, S., Aquino-Sterling, C., Van Liew, C., & Day, A. (2018) Beliefs about Bilingualism, Bilingual Education, and Dual Language Development of Early Childhood Preservice Teachers Raised in a Prop 227 Environment, *International Journal of Bilingual Education and Bilingualism*, 21 (2), 179–196.

Institute of Medicine & National Research Council (2015) *Transforming the Workforce for Children Birth through Age 8: A Unifying Foundation*, Washington, DC: The National Academies Press.

NAEYC (2020) *Professional Standards and Competencies*, Washington, DC: NAEYC.

NASEM (2017) *Promoting the Educational Success of Children and Youth Learning English: Promising Futures*, Washington, DC: National Academies Press.

Nemeth, K., Brillante, P., & Mullen, L. (2015) Naming the New, Inclusive Early Childhood Education: All Teachers Ready for DECAL!, retrieved from www.languagecastle.com/2015/08/decalfor-inclusiveearlyed/.

Park, M., O'Toole, A., & Katsiaficas, C. (2017) *Dual Language Learners: A National Demographic and Policy Profile*, Washington, DC: Migration Policy Institute.

U.S. Department of Health and Human Services & U.S. Department of Education (2016) *Policy Statement on Supporting the Development of Children who are Dual Language Learners in Early Childhood Programs*, Washington, DC: U.S. Department of Health and Human Services & U.S. Department of Education.

2 Language Development

Follow the Chapter 2 Roadmap with These Headings

Introduction	Research to Practice
Language Development	Language Learners are Not All the Same
Developing Additional Languages	Speaking One Language Does Not Make Us the Same
Language Across Learning Domains	Language and the Future

Chapter 2 focuses on the role of language in all aspects of early childhood teaching and learning. It provides background knowledge in first and second language development as well as specifics about language across learning domains. Strategies for implementing research to practice are provided. Descriptions of the various experiences and categories of children who are dual language learners help readers view language in the context of individual learning and development.

Top Tips for Language Development

- Supports for language development must address all of the three purposes of language:
  - To receive and comprehend information.
  - To communicate thoughts and feelings.
  - To organize learning and thinking internally.
- The human brain is prepared to learn in two or more languages from before birth and this does not cause confusion or delay.
- Young children need to vocalize and talk in order to learn vocabulary and concepts – conversations are key to early learning for long term results.
- Children learn a new language for informal use very quickly, but it may take about 7 years to develop full academic fluency in a new language to rely on it for all learning without home language supports.
- Whether you believe early childhood education should focus on play-based learning, a focus on social interactions, or academic rigor, language is at the core of all of it.
- Understanding how language develops informs your understanding of how all learning happens.
- Small groups and individual interactions provide the most effective learning environments for linguistically diverse young children.

DOI: 10.4324/9781003089216-2

Introduction

Language is what makes us uniquely human and what makes each human unique. Our brains begin to process sounds and patterns before we're born, and children use their developing language in all aspects of experience and learning. As we see rapid growth of language diversity across the globe, it becomes more important for educators to understand how language develops, how children acquire more than one language, and how this understanding is critical to effective teaching in the early years. Children's brains are prepared to learn one, two, or more languages right from the start. By closely studying the language development of dual language or multilingual learners, you will gain the greatest insights into all aspects of child development and learning that will help you succeed in your work.

Language Development

The Three Purposes of Language

Language takes many forms in different places and at different ages. In your work with young children, you might focus more closely on particular components of language development at times. Supporting a specialized area of child development effectively depends on your deep understanding of language as a whole. To understand how language works and how to support it, you need to keep in mind the three purposes of language:

- To receive and comprehend information.
- To communicate thoughts and feelings.
- To organize learning and thinking internally.

The human brain is prepared to do all these things with increasing variation and effectiveness as we age. The greatest growth and change happens in the early years (NASEM, 2017) and early years educators have the privilege and responsibility for facilitating that development. The brain doesn't work in silos the way schools often do. For example, a teacher might present a lesson on writing, but to learn how to express thoughts via writing, a child has to listen and understand the instructions, then think internally about how to implement those instructions and decide what to write. The three components are always working together, even if the educator is drawing attention to a portion of this work.

Language Begins before Birth

A fetus's brain is exposed to sound and movement sensations as it develops. Several studies have demonstrated that newborn infants respond differently to familiar speech sounds than they do to unfamiliar speech sounds (May et al., 2011). This can only happen as a result of information about environmental speech being remembered by the developing brain. Scientists explain this indicates that the human brain is pre-programmed to gather data about speech sounds automatically. They have also found that infants can catalog and respond to sounds from more than one language that is heard regularly while they are in the womb.

This sets the stage for a predictable pattern of language development for all children, in all countries, in all languages. The linguistic environment of the child provides the fuel for this development by exposing them to words and nonverbal communication and by providing responses that guide the child's continuing language development. But much of language development is controlled by the inner workings of each child's brain. These patterns may occur in one or more languages at the same time if the child is born into and growing up in a multilingual language environment.

First Six Months

In the first few months of life, babies communicate by crying and cooing. You can observe them playing with moving their mouths and making different sounds. You will hear the tone of their sounds begin to get more intense, sounding more urgent, as they experience the stress of discomfort or hunger until they start to cry. Scientists, parents, teachers, and caregivers report being able to tell the difference between the kinds of crying infants do under different circumstances. The hunger cry sounds different than the sleepy cry or the hurting cry. This is a fascinating time to watch the way the newly developing brain uses the tools at its disposal to get the baby's needs met. What you might not realize is how much the infant is taking in during this time. The language children understand is called "receptive language," which develops faster than their ability to say words, or "expressive language." In the first six months they are not ready to say words, but research shows they are beginning to notice words and recognize patterns of sounds that they hear regularly in their environment (Gibson, Peña, & Bedore, 2014). For the most part, the sounds an infant hears will be the sounds of their home language.

Language is an important part of every infant's day. Teachers should be ready to narrate what's happening and describe what infants see, hear, touch, taste, and smell. Even though they might not say a word, we know their brain is already recognizing speech sounds and some words, so there is value to interacting with infants using their home language or familiar songs they hear at home.

Another amazing skill we see developing in the first six months is the ability to have back-and-forth interactions with a responsive adult or older child. This activity is a precursor to communicative conversations. The infant will make eye contact with the adult and make some sounds, then be quiet while the adult speaks, then make sounds or movements again when the adult is quiet. This shows the infant is ready to engage in turn-taking patterns and this is a good thing to practice with them. They are able to detect the nonverbal components of these interactions as well. Research shows this serve-and-return pattern is critical for language learning, but depends on appropriate responses from adults (Center on the Developing Child, 2021).

In the first 6 months, most babies enjoy being close to an adult and interacting briefly with baby-safe books. This is a great time to introduce words, and the repeating patterns of children's books while you engage in joint attention and begin pointing to and naming pictures. Sustained interest will come later, so it is important not to expect too much time from the baby at this age.

We describe infant sounds as "cooing" when they mostly make vowel sounds like "oooooh" and "aaaaaaaaah" and funny screeches. During this stage, babies generally sound the same regardless of what languages are spoken around them. Even children with hearing loss sound like their hearing peers. Keep in mind that the baby brain needs language stimulation even if the child has hearing impairment, so their day should be filled with nonverbal communication and sign language that provides the same level of repetition and pattern.

Six to Twelve Months

Sometime around 6 months, the infant will begin to shift from cooing to babbling by adding consonants to their experimentation with sound. Now you might hear "bah bah

bah" or "goo." Something new is happening in the baby's brain. They are gaining more control over choosing and approximating sounds they hear in the language around them. Bit by bit they begin to weed out sounds that are not used in their language environment. As children get closer to a year old, you will be able to hear a different sort of babbling from babies, depending on the sounds of the language they hear around them (Sundara et al., 2019).

Infants benefit from frequent, focused interactions with attentive, responsive adults during this time (Kuhl, 2010). As children develop, you will observe them responding accurately to things adults say. They show anticipation when you mention bath time or they giggle when you say, "Here comes the teddy bear!" They need adults to model understandable and increasingly complex words and sentences and they need adults to respond to their speech attempts. Babies as young as 9 months may begin to approximate words, or make sounds that seem like words, or make the same sound every time they want a drink. It is very important for babies to receive feedback and encouragement to help them learn they are on the right track and their utterances have impact. When infants are cared for by someone who doesn't know their home language, the child may be saying real words or communicating clearly but their attempts get ignored by the unsuspecting adult. Consulting with family members about the child's vocalizations is vital at this stage.

The responsive adult helps the child to focus on language cues. Another important component of this process is the infant's ability to direct their attention to the adult's face to detect language cues. Several researchers learned that, between the ages of 8 and 12 months, babies often focus on the mouth of the speaker as they are beginning to learn and remember words. As they get closer to 12 months, when they have started to develop receptive language, they shift their focus to watching an adult's eyes when communicating. But, when an adult speaks to the 12-month-old in a new language, they are likely to change their gaze and watch the speaker's mouth to get more cues about unfamiliar language (Lewkowicz & Hansen-Tift, 2012).

Research shows that children under a year learn almost nothing from passively listening or passively viewing TV or videos. There are studies showing that these young children do respond when adults interact and respond to them via video chat (Kuhl, 2010).

> A wise grandmother made up a little song for each of her grandchildren who lived in another country. She sang each child's special tune to them from the time they were born and started every video chat with that tune. She captured the infant's attention with a familiar tune and a little game of "peek-a-boo" that happened the same way every time. With this pattern, she was able to build meaningful relationships with each child even when they weren't together. The parents reported their children asked for the grandmother when she was not online with them – indicating that the responsive and repeating interactions had helped them make a lasting connection. When the grandmother was able to travel for a visit, she knew the infants might react with fear as if she was a stranger. She entered slowly and started singing the baby's song, then played a couple of turns of peek-a-boo. This helped the child's brain make the comfortable connection between the sound of the familiar voice and the real person in front of them.

When early intervention services are provided to an infant due to significant delays, the home language is just as important. Regardless of the child's progress in producing sounds and words, evidence shows their brains are still hard at work cataloging the sounds they hear. Connecting to them by using and building on familiar words and phrases can be helpful and is worth the effort.

Another important development at this stage is the explosion of gestural and nonverbal communication as part of expressive language. Babies start pointing to things that capture their attention or that they want to bring to your attention. Experts at Zero to Three tell us there are about 16 meaningful gestures we can expect most children to develop between 9 and 14 months (MacLaughlin, 2019). In addition to picking up visual cues, infants begin to use and recognize other cues such as volume and tone of voice. They can tell the difference between a sad adult and a happy adult. They know how to make an angry voice or a silly voice. They know how to shout to you when you are in another room. Being aware of these developing components of language will help you be a better language model and responsive language receiver.

Twelve to Eighteen Months

Sometime around the first year, most babies will say their first word. They also start to walk. New research has shown a connection between a spike in language production and the onset of independent walking. Children who walk later may also be children who are slower to add vocabulary and progress toward combining words (He, Walle, & Campos, 2015). By the time they reach 18 months, children should be able to say about 10 words, and begin to put two-word sentences together after 18 months.

During this period, children understand a great deal of what is said to them and near them. For example, you might be telling your co-teacher you need a ball for an activity and be surprised that a toddler has heard you and brought you a ball. Their receptive language is growing at a rapid pace, so it is increasingly important that they are exposed to high-quality language models in their home language as well as English.

There may be some uneven progress through these stages of language development when children are growing up with two or more languages, but this does not indicate problems for the future. This may be attributed, to some extent, to the added processing time it takes for emergent bilingual children to recognize and respond to words in their two languages. This does not seem to be a cause or result of confusion (Paradis, Genesee, & Crago, 2021).

One surprising area of controversy is around the way adults speak to babies. There is a lot of confusion about terms like "baby talk" and "motherese" or "parentese." There is a significant body of research that supports the particular way most adults, and even older children, adjust their speech to interact with infants (Ramírez, Lytle, & Kuhl, 2020). It is certainly simpler, but it is not babyish. Research shows that some level of simplification is helpful as the brain is making sense of the input it receives. Consider the following example from an adult's perspective: If you are new to the Japanese language, you would not want a waiter at a restaurant in Japan to speak to you at the same speed and complexity as he speaks to native speakers – you would ask him to slow down and use simple sentences so you could make sense of what he is saying about the menu. This is a helpful strategy for the brain to be able to recognize key words and build meaning. It's the same for young children. Short sentences, repeating vocabulary, recognizable words help the child begin to make connections and respond accordingly. Once you see the child demonstrate they know the word "big" several times, then you might add words like "huge" and "gigantic." It's not that babies are delayed by simple language. The opposite is true: Simple language is like stepping stones that help the child build understanding and confidence to make connections with ever more complex language.

Eighteen to Thirty-Six Months

This is the period of development when young children begin to narrate their activities, tell little stories, and engage in symbolic and pretend play. Providing them with high-quality, authentic, and culturally relevant materials at this age gives them plenty to talk about as they build their receptive language and their expressive vocabulary.

It is also important to have high-quality, multi-turn conversations with children at this age. Their early attempts at speech can be entertaining and endearing, but they are also evidence of impressive brain power. It is a vital component of early learning and development that establishes a foundation for all future learning. Language interactions with young children should promote thinking and problem solving, and help them talk about their ideas and feelings. If you ask them one question, you should be ready to ask a follow up question to keep the conversation going.

Children need plenty of time to practice oral language in any of the languages they are learning. It is important to remember that any oral language practice builds language understanding and language use as children at this age are just beginning to understand how language works – this is called metalinguistic awareness. What children know about how language works will help them build skills in all of their languages (Paradis, Genesee, & Crago, 2021).

Whether developing a first or second language, when children are beginning to speak in one- or two-word utterances or phrases, the following speech strategies are very effective for educators and families to use with their child.

- *Echo* – Repeat the sounds or words the child produces to let them know you hear them and those speech attempts bring results and are worthy of your attention.
- *Expand* – Add to what the child says to provide a broader context for their utterance. For example, if the baby says "sock," you might say "Oh! You lost your sock!"
- *Self-talk* – Adults build receptive language experiences into the child's environment by narrating what they are doing as the child observes them. For example, you might say "I am wiping off the table. I want to make the table clean for lunch."
- *Parallel talk* – Adults narrate the child's activities to give them words they can learn to use to express their own thoughts and actions. For example, "You are building a big tower right now!"

Three to Five Years

As children approach their third birthday, they are no longer referred to as toddlers. They are preschool-aged children who are learning at an extraordinary pace. They may be able to talk and understand in two or more languages, and they may also understand and use words in additional languages to interact with friends and neighbors. They can tell intricate stories and funny (or not so funny) jokes. They can even tell you something they know is not true. All this takes very sophisticated brain activity. They are learning to hold a thought in one language while they switch to another language, then jump back to the original thought and proceed with talking about that.

We have a lot of research to support the practice of code-switching (NASEM, 2017) or translanguaging (Garcia & Wei, 2013). This happens when the child switches between two languages in the same utterance. For example, "Can we have leche and cereal esta mañana?" Researchers explain this happens when the child has a clear idea of the message they want to convey, but they're not sure of the words in one language so they add words from their other language to get their point across. This is not indicative of confusion – it is a sign of effective use of brain resources to support communication. Adults should strive to provide complete sentences in one language or the other to provide high-quality language modeling that children can begin to adopt as they progress.

Children need to hear high-quality language models in both or all their languages. They need to know multiple uses of words and appropriate sentence construction in each language as a whole. They should experience meaningful conversations, stories, and playful learning in each of their languages.

As children learn the rules of grammar and usage, they often begin making errors that result from overgeneralization. They may even change from saying something correctly to making a mistake before going back to the correct form. For example, a child might tell you one day that they went to the zoo. Soon after, you might observe the child saying, "My dad goed to the store" or "I didn't goed home." This is a constructed error as the child starts to be aware of the rule for using the "ed" ending to indicate past tense and overgeneralizes to use it in places it doesn't belong. This is also an interesting development since we might guess the child does not hear that phrase from the adults in their environment, so it comes from the way their brain is demonstrating its mastery of the language. There's no need to correct the child because their continued oral language and conversational practice will give their brain lots of data to use to refine their understanding of when/when not to use that grammar rule.

> My own experiences over the years have always brought me to the wonders and wonderfulness of language and young children (the Migrant children from Texas, New Mexico; the children in inner-city communities; the children in rural farms and agriculture countries). They loved to talk, to share, to giggle, laugh and as teachers recommended, "use your words."
>
> William H. Strader
> Ed.D. Professor, Early Childhood Education,
> Coordinator, New England Symposium on Play,
> Facilitator, Student Interest Forum of NAEYC
> Shelburne Falls, MA 01370

Six Years and Up

When children enter primary school, the demands on all aspects of language increase greatly. Children need to work on their abilities to take in information by reading and listening, and they need to work on producing information by talking and writing. When children have already gotten off to a good start in their first language in those areas of learning, they are much better equipped to add a new language. We want children to be ready to learn in school, but this can be accomplished by building a strong foundation in the home language with some introduction of English, then gradually adding English as each child is ready.

> Learning a new language does not have to be at the expense of another. Create and protect the space for students to use their home language at school. When students are free to use their home language, we get to see a fuller picture of the magic they are capable of.
>
> Tan K. Huynh
> Educator/subject matter expert EmpoweringELLs.com

Developing Additional Languages

Phases of Second Language Development

From before birth, the human brain develops language skills that enable the child to produce language, comprehend language, and use language to organize thoughts, in one or more languages. Many children encounter new or additional languages sometime later in this process. There are advantages to learning a second language as early as possible while the brain retains its neural plasticity (Kuhl, 2010). On the other hand, there are different advantages to learning a new language and literacy after the child has developed the cognitive ability to understand how language works and how to connect the meanings of words (Paradis, Genesee, & Crago, 2021). There is no right or wrong time to learn additional languages. Since this can occur at any time in a child's development, the patterns of second language development are not as clear and predictable as the patterns of first language development. When the content and structure of a new language are added after the child has already progressed through stages of first language development, their understanding about how to use language will influence how they learn the new language. Other factors that have an impact on second language learning include social-emotional factors such as the level or stress or comfort associated with the new language experience, as well as practical factors like the quality and quantity of input of the second language and the child's basic language ability. With so many variables, this process is much less predictable, and does not fit the expectations associated with the term "stages." Some theorists describe the development of a new language in phases (Tabors, 2008):

- *First language only* – When a child first enters care or school, they may only be able to understand or speak their first language. They often try to use it even when it becomes clear that it won't work in the new situation. You may observe young children urgently repeating a message in their language, or saying it louder and slower. As they realize their language is not helping them communicate, they will reduce or stop using it for a while.
- *Silent period* – Many children enter a silent period as they begin to observe the language around them and try to make sense of it. It may last a few days or weeks or even months. Not all children enter a silent period so they can progress in learning the new language. Some move quickly from using their first language to trying new words in the new language. But it is also important to realize there are many reasons a child might not talk in childcare or school. For example, the child may have a hearing problem, so do not hesitate to talk with the family about having their child's hearing tested. Ask family members to send in audio or video recordings of the child talking or singing at home so you can get a sense of the child's overall language development that might contribute to the silent period or that might indicate a need for further screening for possible delay. You want to make sure you don't take for granted that a silent period is natural for every child learning a new language – it is not.
- *Telegraphic speech* – When children begin to learn the new language, they learn to say whole chunks or phrases to communicate. Generally, when a child is already talking in their first language and is now adding a new language, they are beyond the one-word-at-a-time stage. A child in kindergarten/reception might start by saying, "Whatisthis" as one word, not realizing there are three words in that utterance that could be used for other purposes. As they try using various phrases to interact with adults and peers and to get their needs met, they will gradually add words and vary their messages with increasing confidence.

- *Informal or playground speech* – In a high-quality language environment where their home language continues to be supported while they learn English, many children learn quickly how to talk with their English-speaking friends and adults, and how to express themselves in multiple ways. While this might happen in less than a year, it may still take up to seven years or more to develop full academic fluency in the new language (Cummins, 2000). A child at this stage can tell you about what's on their mind and what's happening right now. But, if you challenge them to talk about different meanings for one word, or to talk about something that they did not bring up or that didn't happen right in front of them, you may start to see that they are not fluent enough to use decontextualized language.
- *Full academic fluency* – According to Cummins (2000), after as many as seven years, children will likely become fully fluent in their new language, at which point they can compose essays, read fiction and nonfiction books, and learn across all domains and subjects without relying on their home language.

Language across Learning Domains

Typically, we see language and literacy highlighted as one of the most important learning domains for young children, and often it is the domain that gets the most coverage in standards and curricula. At the same time, it is also true that language plays a major role in every other learning domain. This is a good time to recall that children use language for three purposes and those three purposes are at work in every learning domain. No matter the domain, including motor development, children need to develop language that allows them to understand the terms and concepts for that domain, allows them express what they know and can do within that domain, and that helps them make strong and appropriate learning connections that make sense to their thinking processes and prior knowledge. Now, let's take a look at some specific examples of the role of language in each of these domains for infants through primary years.

Language and Cognitive Development

Topics related to science, technology, engineering, and math (STEM) have their vocabularies. While you are likely to use lots of hands-on activities and demonstrations to teach these subjects across all ages, teacher talk is needed to introduce, explain, and build skill learning. The language aspects of these lessons can create a barrier to learning for children who do not comprehend. The accessibility of language used in lessons is often referred to as "comprehensible input." When it is used in high-quality, two-way interactions between teachers and children, learning grows.

Science involves the knowledge of words and concepts about living things and non-living things as well as skills of observation and experimentation.

> Miss Piña brought in some monarch butterfly chrysalis sets for her class of 4-year-olds. The group watched a brief video about the butterfly life cycle. They drew pictures of the chrysalis and its changes. They talked about what would happen when the butterflies hatched, what they would eat, and where they would go. Miss Piña met with her assistant and volunteers to go over how they would add to this learning by discussing in the home languages of the children.

Technology is the study of how things work. You might use digital technology like computers and tablets, or simple technology like ramps, hinges, or funnels. Explorations of technology are fascinating for young children and provide many opportunities to build language skills as well.

Engineering focuses on the how to make things work – what works and what doesn't work to accomplish a goal or task. This is another fascinating subject for young children that involves a lot of rich language. Keep in mind that children in the early years find everything new. Before they learn about large or distant objects like bridges, help them connect with familiar objects in their environment.

> Learning how to make funnels and how they work can be an interesting study from toddlers through primary school. How can you make a funnel out of paper? How do funnels help us pour dry things and liquids without spilling? What fits in the funnel?

Math(s) covers a broad range of topics including number names, counting, order, comparison, and geometry – but all of it is learned along with the appropriate vocabulary (Méndez et al., 2019; Dumas et al., 2019). Math vocabulary and concepts should be taught with strategies and adaptations to be sure that all children can understand and use the full range of math skills.

Language and Social/Emotional Development

Learning social skills, empathy, and emotional expression are all vital components in early childhood development. There are formally developed Social-Emotional Learning (SEL) curricula available for early years as well as many informal strategies for fostering this kind of learning. For the most part, language plays a central role.

> Mr. Avin helped his group of 2-year-olds learn to identify and talk about their feelings by taking photos of their faces in different circumstances. He used the photos to create a picture communication board posted at the children's level. He invited family members to add the words they used with their children in their home languages (some had to help him learn the pronunciation). And he also used the photos to create simple puppets for interactions with the children.

Language and Motor Development

Indoor and outdoor play that focuses on fine and large motor development is enhanced when you use them as opportunities to talk about action, movement, and safety. Playgrounds, parks, and water table areas should be filled with the sounds of self-talk, parallel talk, echoing, and expansion of language in English and the home languages of the children.

> The year 2 students at Primrose School talked about important safety rules for their outdoor play area. Then, they made some simple signs with words and pictures to remind their younger schoolmates about being safe outdoors. Their teacher encouraged them to use both English and home languages on their signs.

18 Language Development

Language and the Arts

Visual arts in two and three dimensions, as well as music and drama, all provide a rich backdrop for lots of language and learning. Instead of labeling the "art area" or "music area" in your classroom, consider posting conversation starter labels about the different materials and techniques that might be used when children gather there.

> Miss Liz brought some picture books with award winning illustrations to her kindergarten/reception class. The 5-year-olds observed the different ways artists had created artwork to tell a story and Miss Liz gave them a variety of art tools so they could try to use similar techniques as the artists. They all discussed new words in English and home languages for the different colors, textures, brushstrokes, and styles they were seeing.

Language and Approaches to Learning

How young children learn to learn is just as important as what they learn. Approaches to learning is the domain that covers curiosity, persistence, and problem solving. Language support is needed so all children have the words to describe their interests and their approaches to learning.

> When planning to introduce new sensory materials to the infants in her group, Maria learns some words for the materials and for explorations in the home languages of the children. In addition to identifying the lime, banana, and mango they will use for today's fruit salad, she also learns to say "you are smelling" and "does that smell nice?" in the home languages of the babies.

Language and Health and Wellness

Messages about health and wellness are so important in the early years as you help young children develop lifelong healthy habits. Being able to talk about what is healthy and why will be even more valuable for the children. Making content about health and wellness comprehensible in English, home languages, and with visual cues is necessary for all of the children in your group.

> Mr. Bertrand's first grade created a classroom book with pictures of their visit to the recycling center and they each wrote a caption about why it is important to recycle and what kinds of materials can be recycled. Each child worked with a family member to write the caption in English and the home language.

Literacy and Language

Literacy is built on a foundation of skills that are learned years before a child is able to read or write. These components of preliteracy should be part of many conversations at home and in programs.

> - *Alphabet knowledge and early writing* – Knowing how an alphabet works, learning the names of letters and characters and trying to write them.

- *Background knowledge* – The content and concepts children have to learn to understand the meanings of written and spoken language.
- *Book knowledge and concepts of print* – Learning how a book works, the parts of a book, and how the markings on a page convey meaning.
- *Oral language and vocabulary* – Speaking in meaningful ways and developing the ability to comprehend and express increasingly sophisticated words.
- *Phonological awareness* – Noticing the sounds of speech that make meaningful differences between words.

Research to Practice

Teaching that Works for All Languages

Teaching strategies that support language and literacy are the same for all languages. However, children who are DLLs need additional supports for both or all their languages. According to research, the following strategies have been successful for children from preschool through primary school:

- Small group instruction allowing more responsive feedback for each child and those important multi-turn conversations.
- Explaining the meanings of words.
- Vocabulary bridging by explaining and demonstrating the connection between familiar words in the home language and new words in English or other new language (Lugo-Neris, Jackson, & Goldstein, 2010).
- Reducing teacher talk and increasing opportunities for student talk.
- Hands on, collaborative, project-based learning (López & Páez, 2020; Paradis, Genesee, & Crago, 2021).

The types of questions you ask and model for children make all the difference in the effectiveness and sophistication of conversations. Table 2.1 shows some examples. Imagine the kinds of responses you might get to each of these types of questions. Which ones lead to more high-quality teaching and learning interactions?

Another way to think of the kinds of questions you would ask children to begin and sustain conversations would be to consider the purpose – what do you need to know or what do you want the child to think about? In her description of a "conversation compass," Stephanie Curenton (2016) categorizes questions using who, what, when, and where to inform

Table 2.1 Learning interaction questions

Closed-ended questions (Limited response)	Open-ended questions (Expanded response options)	Analysis and prediction questions (Higher level responses)
What color is this?	What is your favorite color?	What will happen if we mix these colors together?
Did you build a tower?	What are you building?	Why do you start your tower with bigger blocks on the bottom and smaller on top?
Do we need an umbrella on a rainy day or a cloudy day?	What do you need to keep dry on a rainy day?	How could you use some of these materials to stay dry If you go out in the rain?

the conversation. Questions starting with how and why support analysis. Questions that ask "what if" can lead to brainstorming. There are times when a closed-ended question can be useful. For example, when a child is just learning to speak in one or more languages, simple questions with simple answers are easier and help them build confidence in their ability to join a conversation. Simple open-ended questions build in more options, respect a child's choices, and build the conversation. Analysis and prediction questions engage the child in critical thinking and problem-solving that facilitate high-quality interactions for learning outcomes.

BICS and CALP

Researcher Jim Cummins (2000) has focused on teaching English as a second or additional language for primary grades. His work identified two levels of language proficiency that provide helpful clarification about what we can expect as children learn additional languages. BICS means Basic Interpersonal Communication Skills – the more casual language that children learn with relative ease through playing and interacting with adults and peers. This offers a successful experience for the emergent bilingual child because they can communicate their ideas, needs, and feelings, and form meaningful relationships with children and adults outside their home/home language community. But, learning this informal language does not provide a complete picture of how quickly or well they can learn academic subjects in their new language. CALP is Cognitive Academic Language Proficiency and Cummins found that it can take up to seven years for students to develop this fully. The key finding here is that developing BICS is a wonderful asset for any young child and enables them to communicate, comprehend, and enjoy relationships. It does not mean that the child is ready to give up home language supports in their learning environment. These continuing home language supports allow the child to build on their existing knowledge and make important learning connections.

30 Million Words

In 1995, researchers Todd Hart and Betty Risley were highly celebrated for the study they published in *Meaningful Differences in the Everyday Experiences of Young American Children*. Although it was based on a relatively small sample size, the findings were striking:

> Many news articles and media releases were focused on this short phrase: The 30 million word gap. Funding initiatives arose throughout the country. We now realize there are more nuances than were reflected in this research at the time.
>
> (Williams, 2020)

The study ignited many discussions about how to support young children's early language in more equitable ways so all can enter school ready to learn. After this study was published and publicized, new research clarified that families with more economic advantages provided many more words when communicating with their children than families with fewer advantages. But researchers also learned that children need more than a flood of words floating around them. Young brains thrive when lots of interesting words are used with them in engaging conversations that encourage children to think about new words and practice using them in authentic ways. This is why acting out a story or doing a puppet show after reading can be so valuable. Even when families fill an infant's environment with language, they have the most impact when they also pause and listen to the sounds the baby makes and practice that all-important serve and return pattern that helps prepare children for conversations later on. Always remember that listening to children is just as important as talking to them.

We repeat: Listening to children is just as important as talking to them. But this means truly, actively listening. In their work *Powerful Interactions*, Stetson, Dombro, and Jablon (2012) describe the valuable practice of pausing, making eye contact, clearing your mind and just being truly present with the child. By making time to show the child they are the most important thing to you for a few minutes, the authors believe you can observe the child's interests to further their learning, get to know them as individuals even if they don't have the language yet, and contribute to the child's sense of belonging and confidence. So, amid the effort to say millions of words, you have to make time to be quiet and pay attention to each child.

Your knowledge about language development will help you recognize what each child needs. We know that young children do not learn the features of language in isolation. They learn best in the context of meaningful interactions. Research on the development of phonemic awareness (the role of sounds in making the meaning of spoken words) shows that children don't learn passively from just listening to teachers tell them about phonemes. They learn about phonemes by saying them in meaningful ways and getting support from adults. So, a child who is new to English may not benefit from memorizing sounds that have no meaning for them. But they will easily learn phonemes based on familiar content in their home language. This understanding can easily be transferred to English. For example, you might play a game in Spanish identifying "un zapato, dos zapatos." Once the child can articulate the difference between the two words, modified by plural "s," they can easily understand that you might have one shoe or two shoes. This is much harder to learn when using nonsense words or new words that are not yet meaningful to the child as in nonsense rhymes or words children don't yet know.

Language Transfer

One thing we know about the science of early learning and literacy development is that young children with a strong foundation in their home language can readily transfer knowledge to their new language and experience ongoing success in that new language as they progress through the school years. In other words, students who know the alphabet in their home language will understand how an alphabet works and what it is for – so they can easily learn a new alphabet. Research supports the intuitive conclusion that this is easier for children learning two languages, with similar alphabets like English and Spanish, German, or French (NASEM, 2017). When children have a home language with a character system that is not similar to the English alphabet, spend additional time with all the children on working on careful listening to speech sounds and meanings to help them connect to alphabetic knowledge.

This research leads us to believe there is no need to rush the teaching of a new language. There are advantages when learning two languages happens naturally for a child growing up with parents who speak different languages (Paradis, Genesee, & Crago, 2021). But when learning a new language is tied to going to childcare or preschool and being with people who are not the child's family members, it is better to provide that broad and deep foundation of knowledge with as much home language support as possible (Banse, 2021). The new language, such as English, can be added in gradually and intentionally over the first five years.

Cognates

Cognates are words that sound and are spelled nearly the same in two languages. This similarity makes it easier for young children to learn new words connected to their familiar home language words (Paradis, Genesee, & Crago, 2021). With this foundation and confidence, children become ready to broaden their learning to less similar words. Some languages share many cognates with English, while others have few, if any. In addition to bilingual dictionaries and online resources, ask family members or volunteers if they can provide a list of cognates their child might know. Learning words in a new language with confidence and clarity gives children a social/emotional foundation as well as a cognitive foundation on which to do the harder work of learning words that don't sound similar to what they know.

> Mrs. Ramirez and her assistant teacher taught her bilingual preschool class about some animals they would see on their trip to the local zoo. They began by showing them "animals/los animales." When the children understood the connection between these two words, they were able to understand similar pairings like "elephant/elefante" and "lion/el león" then "kangaroo/el canguro." Once the children were able to understand and use both the English and Spanish words because of these similarities, they were then ready to learn "frog/la rana" and "pig/el cerdo."

Importance of Supporting the Home Language

In a review of the research, Linda Espinosa (2013) summarized the important factors that are impacted by learning the home language while also learning a new language. Especially for young children, their language is part of who they are. They are not able to think of their language as separate from their identity. When they enter a setting where their language is belittled or ignored, the child may feel belittled or ignored. Settings that include and embed home languages along with English can also build children's social connections and sense of belonging. This is important for children from birth to primary years in any type of program

Home language support also has cognitive benefits. Using the home language to teach concepts and skills can help children comprehend and remember more. This lays the groundwork for a strong knowledge base that enhances transfer to English. "English proficiency cannot be seen as a prerequisite to meaningful participation in the curriculum because this limits engagement" (Nordmeyer, Boals, MacDonald, & Westerlund, 2021). In the longer view, helping children grow and learn in both home language and English helps them grow up bilingual, possibly developing assets like stronger executive function skills. Growing up bilingual also helps strengthen family bonds by allowing children to communicate with and receive support from parents, siblings, grandparents, and any family member speaking the home language(s). In a review of research on early learning for children who are DLLs, Holland Banse highlighted one conclusion that is clear across the board: Helping children learn in their home language has no downside (Banse, 2021).

Using Sign Language

Sign language can add visual representations of words that young children from a variety of language backgrounds and abilities can all understand. Research has shown that children as young as 6 months, both hearing and hearing-impaired, can begin to learn simple signs, such as "more" and "milk" that they can use to get their needs met. Toddlers and preschoolers can learn signs for "help," "eat," "all done," "play," or "toilet" that they can use to augment communication with adults and peers while they are in early stages of spoken vocabulary. This can be especially helpful in a group with several languages. For example, an adult might ask one child if she needs the toilet in that child's home language, but if they also use the sign for toilet, everyone in the group can understand and be included. Studies show that use of signs to add to expressive vocabulary builds children's language and communication abilities (Daniels, 1994). For children who are slow to speak, this can be a great benefit. For children who speak different languages, signs offer a way to equalize communication and bridge communication gaps.

Sign language is a distinct language. It is not a word for word representation of spoken language, It has its own syntax and informal rules. British Sign Language (BSL) is used in England and American Sign Language (ASL) is used in the United States. If you use sign language to expand communication in your work with young children, you will be giving them the added benefit of learning an additional language that can be used in the community as well.

Language Interactions in Digital Environments

Some early childhood educators have concerns about exposing young children to screens – TVs, tablets, smartphones, and computers. In her exploration of what happens to children's brains when they are exposed to two languages in infancy, Patricia Kuhl (2010) found that children learned the sounds and words because they were engaged in responsive interactions. When exposed to a passive experience listening to audio or viewing video did not result in learning.

Other researchers took this question further. Now we have a solid and growing body of research showing that young children actually do learn language when they interact with responsive adults over video chat (Roseberry et al., 2013). This piece of research is important as many preschool and primary programs had to rely on online learning in 2020, and some report they plan to continue this option for some time. Success with children's learning depends greatly on the choices made in planning for remote learning. The interactions have to be developmentally appropriate, real time, and interactive. Small groups or one-on-one activities will work best to encourage conversations. Making sure children have something to do with their hands while learning and interacting is also important. Don't overlook the importance of highlighting home language and English during digital activities. Use technology features like recording children's talk for later translation or using voice translation apps to support communication.

Children today are growing up as digital natives. They have a lot of experience interacting with live or recorded language, and language in games on their devices. Adults – both educators and parents/other adult family members – will need to serve as media mentors to guide appropriate use (Garcia & Nemeth, 2017).

Language Learners Are Not All the Same

Children who are growing up with two languages from birth or early in their lives are called simultaneous bilinguals. Children who have made progress in one language and begin to learn one or more additional languages after they are about three years old are considered sequential bilinguals (Paradis, Genesee, & Crago, 2021). However, there are many children who learn some of an additional language, but not enough to be considered bilingual. For example, children who attend a language immersion preschool may learn to sing and recite in a new language but won't become bilingual or retain much of what they learned if there is no continuing use of the language beyond school. Children who grow up in a neighborhood with lots of exposure to a language not spoken by their own family might gain significant informal language, but they might not be exposed to enough sophisticated language to build academic fluency. Children of international adoptions may arrive with some home language, either expressive or receptive, but this will not last if no one in the new family can keep using the first language with the child.

When an older child or adult is fully fluent and able to read, write, speak, and understand in two languages, they may be considered a balanced bilingual. When a young child begins to learn an additional language, they might be called emergent bilingual. Many children and adults develop fluency in a new language on certain topics, rather than a balanced development. We don't have a specific term for this common condition. For example, a child from a German-speaking family might learn to talk about soccer in English because their whole family has started following European matches on TV in the U.S. A 7-year-old might seem bilingual, but is unable to talk about their science project with their Arabic speaking grandmother because they only know the science words in English. A fully bilingual speech therapist may remember all their Vietnamese language from childhood, but find it difficult to communicate with a Vietnamese family about their child's language issues because all of their professional vocabulary was learned in graduate school in the U.S. These examples describe variations in bilingualism. Being bilingual does not have to mean the child or adult knows every word in two languages. Real situations reveal all kinds of differences. The more you get to know children and families, the more you will understand their language experiences. In turn, this will help you communicate more effectively with them.

Where you live can also influence how you progress in two or more languages. Learning a minority language when you already speak the majority language of your community is very different from the experience of living in a community where you speak a minority language and have to learn the majority language. For example, in San Francisco or London, a child who speaks English but attends a Chinese language playgroup may have positive language learning experiences. A Gujarati-speaking child who is away from home for the first time in a London or San Francisco preschool where mostly English is spoken may experience several kinds of stress. We actually have far more research about dual language learning for children from minorities in learning the majority language. But across the world, we see many families sending their child to preschools or activity groups to learn an additional language and there is little research to tell us what method works best to make that happen.

The term dual language learner (DLL) has been used in the early childhood education field in the United States since about 2008. While the official definition initiated by the Office of Head Start includes all young children who are growing up with two or more languages, some groups of families and preschool programs have resisted using that term. They may think that DLL refers only to immigrant children who are learning English. You may have opportunities to teach children in the U.S. or U.K. who are native born in a family or community that speaks mainly a non-English language. You may teach children of immigrant families who speak only English. In many parts of the United States, American Indian and Alaskan Native families speak English at home but are depending on preschool and primary school to teach their child their native or heritage language. In Chapter 5 we will talk more about strategies for teaching and caring for children from this wide array of language circumstances. The most important balance for you as an educator will be to honor the research about what's best for early childhood learning and development while also respecting the circumstances and wishes of the families.

Speaking One Language Does Not Make Us the Same

Even when a group of children or adults speak the same language, there are many factors that make the ways they learn and use language unique. For example, English speaking children may speak different dialects depending on what part of the country they are from. Even children from the same city may speak different versions of English depending on their neighborhood, the language spoken by their families, and their prior experiences. Families who come from Spanish-speaking countries may use different words for the same item, concept, or idea. For example, the word palomita means little bird or dove to some Spanish speakers and popcorn to others.

These differences mean not every speaker of a particular language is going to be a good interpreter or translator for the language you need in your program. The French you learned in college might not be easily understood if you try to use it on your next visit to Montreal, Canada. We need to be aware of the ways that culture and tradition can impact the way a language is spoken and understood.

In many cases, there are biases for and against people who sound a certain way, who speak with certain mannerisms or accents. Families may worry their child will be bullied or held back in school due to their home language, so they may insist the child be taught in English only. As we have described, this goes against research on best teaching practices, but you will need to respect the family's right to voice their concerns, then offer information that will help them support your work.

In other chapters of this book, we talk about language equity and language justice.

> English proficiency cannot be seen as a prerequisite to meaningful participation in the curriculum because this limits engagement. Instead, language must be viewed as something that is developed *in the process of learning* when students are supported and have access to the richest curriculum our schools have to offer.
>
> (NASEM, 2017)

In reviewing the vast array of international research about dual language learning, Paradis, Genesee, and Crago (2021) found there were a multitude of factors that influence language development, making it difficult to separate out the effects of learning in two languages. These factors include:

- Education level of parents.
- General language and academic ability of child.
- Family income.
- Health.
- Experiences of stress or trauma.
- Age when adding new language.
- Dosage and quality of language input.
- Similarities of the two languages.
- Social status of each language.

Language and the Future

We have a lot to look forward to as we watch for the evolving roles of language. Language diversity is increasing all over the world. The chances that an early childhood professional will work with children who speak other languages keeps growing every year. The career and social options for those young children who are supported as they grow up to be bilingual as well as biliterate will be exciting and limitless. Technology tools that can help us all communicate across and within languages are already taking off. How are these advances changing the way you use language? How might these factors change the way you will interact with the families in your work? How will they change how you pursue continuing education? You are preparing today to be part of the diverse early childhood workforce tomorrow. Take some time to reflect on where you are in this process and where you want to go. Language will always play a role in your work and your decisions.

Choose your Own Path Check-In

Age/setting	*What is a key language fact that a professional needs to know in each of these kinds of work?*
Infant care center	
Toddler play room	
Outdoor learning environment	
Family childcare home	
Open preschool/nursery classroom	
Kindergarten/reception classroom	
Academic primary classroom	
Space for individual or small group therapies	
Family education space	
Virtual learning	
Remote learning home environment	

Social Media Messages and Conversation Starters

- Observe teachers working with different ages of young children. Who does most of the talking or vocalizing – teacher or child?
- How do you modify your speech when communicating with someone who is not fluent in your language?

References

Banse, H. (2021) Dual Language Learners and Four Areas of Early Childhood Learning and Development: What Do We Know and What Do We Need to Learn?, *Early Child Development and Care*, 191 (9), 1347–1360.

Center on the Developing Child (2021) Serve and Return, retrieved from https://developingchild.harvard.edu/science/key-concepts/serve-and-return.

Cummins, J. (2000) *Language, Power, and Pedagogy: Bilingual Children in the Crossfire*, Clevedon, U.K.: Multilingual Matters.

Curenton, S. (2016) *Conversation Compass: A Teacher's Guide to High-Quality Language Learning in Young Children*, St. Paul, MN: Redleaf Press.

Daniels, M. (1994) The Effect of Sign Language on Hearing Children's Language Development, *Communication Education*, 43 (4), 291–298.

Dumas, D., McNeish, D., Sarama, J., & Clements, D. (2019) Preschool Mathematics Intervention Can Significantly Improve Student Learning Trajectories Through Elementary School, *AERA Open*, 5 (4), doi:10.1177/2332858419879446.

Espinosa, L.M. (2013) *PreK-3rd: Challenging Common Myths about Dual Language Learners: An Update to the Seminal 2008 Report*, New York: Foundation for Child Development.

Garcia, A., & Nemeth, K. (2017) Family Engagement Strategies for All Languages and Cultures, in C. Donohue (Ed.), *Family Engagement in the Digital Age*, New York: Routledge.

Garcia, O., & Wei, L. (2013) *Translanguaging: Language, Bilingualism and Education*, New York: Springer.

Gibson, T.A., Peña, E.D., & Bedore, L.M. (2014) The Relation Between Language Experience and Receptive-Expressive Semantic Gaps in Bilingual Children, *International Journal of Bilingual Education*, 17 (1), 90–110.

Hart, B., & Risley, T.R. (1995), *Meaningful Differences in the Everyday Experience of American Children*, Baltimore, MD: Paul H. Brookes.

He, M., Walle, E.A., & Campos, J.J. (2015) A Cross-National Investigation of the Relationship Between Infant Walking and Language Development, *Infancy*, 20 (3), 283–305.

Kuhl, P. (2010) The Linguistic Genius of Babies, TED Talk, retrieved from www.ted.com/talks/patricia_kuhl_the_linguistic_genius_of_babies.

Lewkowicz, D.J., & Hansen-Tift, A.M. (2012) Infants Deploy Selective Attention to the Mouth of a Talking Face When Learning Speech, *Proceedings of the National Academy of Sciences of the United States of America*, 109 (5), 1431–1436.

López, L.M., & Páez, M.M. (2020) *Teaching Dual Language Learners: What Early Childhood Educators Need to Know*, Baltimore, MD: Paul H. Brookes.

Lugo-Neris, M.J., Jackson, C.W., & Goldstein, H. (2010) Facilitating Vocabulary Acquisition in Young English Language Learners, *Language, Speech, and Hearing Services in Schools*, 41, 314–327.

MacLaughlin, S. (2019) *What Are You Pointing at, Baby?*, Washington, DC: Zero to Three.

May, L., Byers-Heinlein, K., Gervain, J., & Werker, J. (2011) Language and the Newborn: Does Prenatal Language Experience Shape Neonate Neural Response to Speech?, *Frontiers in Psychology*, September 21.

Méndez, L.I., Hammer, C.S., Lopez, L.M., & Blair, C. (2019) Examining Language and Early Numeracy Skills in Young Latino Dual Language Learners, *Early Childhood Research Quarterly*, 46 (1), 252–261.

NASEM (2017) *Promoting the Educational Success of Children and Youth Learning English: Promising Futures*, Washington, DC: The National Academies Press.

Nordmeyer, J., Boals, T., MacDonald, R., & Westerlund, R. (2021) What Doe Equity Really Mean for Multilingual Learners?, *Education Leadership*, 78 (6), 60–65.

Paradis, J., Genesee, F., & Crago, M.B. (2021) *Dual Language Development and Disorders: A Handbook on Bilingualism and Second Language Learning*, 3rd ed., Baltimore, MD: Paul H. Brookes.

Ramírez, N.F., Lytle, S.R., & Kuhl, P.K. (2020) Parent Coaching Increases Conversational Turns and Advances Infant Language Development, *Proceedings of the National Academy of Sciences of the United States of America*, 117 (7), 3484–3491.

Roseberry, S., Hirsh-Pasek, K., & Golinkoff, R.M. (2013) Skype Me! Socially Contingent Interactions Help Toddlers Learn Language, *Child Development*, September.

Stetson, C., Dombro, A.L., & Jablon, J. (2012) *Powerful Interactions: How to Connect with Children to Extend their Learning*, Washington, DC: NAEYC.

Sundara, M., Ward, N., Conboy, B., & Kuhl, P. (2019) *Exposure to Second Language in Infancy Alters Speech Production, Bilingualism, Language, and Cognition*, Washington, DC: University of Washington.

Tabors, P.O. (2008) *One Child, Two Languages*, 2nd ed., Baltimore, MD: Paul H. Brookes.

Williams, C. (2020) *New Research Ignites Debate on the "30 Million Word Gap"*, Marin County, CA: Edutopia.

3 Getting Started

Follow the Chapter 3 Roadmap with These Headings	
Introduction	Things to Address in the Early Days
Before you Graduate	Setting Up a New Classroom
Getting a Job	Planning for Students to Get Started
Beginning a New Position	Preparing to Greet Each Child

Chapter 3 helps you prepare to become an early childhood educator, with an eye toward success and resilience in a changing field. There are strategies for you to take on before you graduate and ideas to help you find a job. Once you have been hired, you will want to use the sections on beginning a new position and things to address in the early days. These sections are followed by topics that prepare you to begin your work with students by setting up a new classroom, planning for students to get started, and preparing to greet each child.

Top Tips for Getting Started

- Preparing to teach linguistically and culturally diverse children begins before you start your career.
- Pre-service coursework and in-service professional development for early childhood educators should represent the diverse populations they'll be teaching.
- New educators in any position should learn about how diverse languages and cultures should be addressed in their work.
- Early childhood educators need specific information about the language backgrounds and home literacy practices of each and every child.
- Every teacher needs to set up their own classroom before they welcome children, bringing a combination of school-supplied furnishings and personal belongings, but there should be plenty of opportunity for the children to have input when they arrive as well.
- Early childhood classrooms include many kinds of technology, and teachers need to be prepared to use them properly and know where to get help when needed.
- A top priority for beginning each new teaching job is getting to know other staff and resources so you'll know where to go for help.
- Emergency procedures should take into account that many children and families will not have English as their strongest language.

DOI: 10.4324/9781003089216-3

Introduction

Your work as a teacher begins well before you get your first position. Language plays an important part in how you will prepare as a job candidate and a new teacher. Make it part of your professional responsibility to plan ahead for the kind of teaching job you wish to experience. What can you do to prepare to teach linguistically and culturally diverse children? Have you had hands-on experience working with children and/or adults who speak different languages? How might you add that experience to your resumé before you start applying for jobs? These are all considerations for anyone planning to work with young children.

Learn more about what is expected in the field by reading NAEYC's Professional Standards and Competencies for Early Childhood Educators (NAEYC, 2020b).

1   Child development and learning in context …
2   Family–teacher partnerships and community connections …
3   Child observations, documentation, and assessment …
4   Developmentally, culturally, and linguistically appropriate teaching practices …
5   Knowledge, applications, and integration of academic content in the early childhood curriculum …
6   Professionalism as an early childhood educator.

(NAEYC, 2020b, pp. 9–10)

Before you Graduate

Look for ways to set yourself apart from other job candidates by taking extra courses, attending special events, joining clubs, volunteering, and taking on leadership or organizing roles. Seek out opportunities to give yourself more practice working with children and adults who speak languages that are not familiar to you. Research shows home visits with diverse families enhance cultural awareness for pre-service teachers (Vesely, Brown, & Mehta, 2017). Find bilingual friends or mentors at school and in the community who can give you insights into the experiences of being bilingual and who can partner with you as you strengthen your confidence in building productive relationships across language differences. Identify the strategies you use to work with culturally and linguistically diverse groups or individuals so you can describe the benefits of your experience during the application and hiring process.

If you are bilingual, reflect on your own language skills, background, and experiences. Find out if your college or university offers certification or endorsement for bilingual education to add to your credential. You may have to take a language test to qualify. It is possible for adults to be confidently bilingual in some areas of knowledge, but not fully bilingual in all areas to pass the required language test. Even if you don't get that certification, add your language to your resumé. Your multilingual skills can be valuable in many ways, such as building relationships with diverse families, providing feedback on translated school resources, and supporting high-quality interactions with young children who are dual language learners (DLLs). With these goals in mind, it is a good idea to continue learning and practicing your language(s) in addition to English with a focus on education-related vocabulary.

Your ability to articulate your experiences, expertise, and approach to teaching is another way that your language skills support your success. Whether you are monolingual or multilingual, you can be more effective when you are able to explain what you think is important, what you've practiced, what you want to learn as a professional, and where you need support. Your practice at taking good notes in classes and meetings, drafting your lessons and presentations, and keeping anecdotal records of student learning are all ways that your language skills support your work as an educator. As a teacher candidate, you need to do more than learning about teaching – you need to learn to talk about teaching. Don't assume that interviewers or observers know why you are doing what you are doing. As you fine-tune your ability to communicate about your work, you will find you can also make it more clear to families and the community.

Learn a new language. It is a great way to build your understanding about how languages work and how your brain responds to learning a language. It also looks great on a resumé. Is there a language you enjoy? Have you noticed a growth in the speakers of a particular language in the area where you want to teach? Have you often thought about trying sign language with young children? American Sign Language and British Sign Language are both good options depending on your location. Keep in mind you don't have to be fully fluent – but as you learn a new language, consider how you will use it with children and families and how you will use it in teaching. Ask questions and engage in practice work that will help you connect with children who speak the language. This is helpful even if you are not fully fluent in the additional language because it helps to bridge vocabulary between a child's two languages (Lugo-Neris, Jackson, & Goldstein, 2010).

Reach out to students and professors in fields related to your future work. Sometimes they take courses that seem similar to the ones you take but are taught by faculty in other departments. Librarians, speech pathologists, English as a Second/Additional Language (ESL/EAL) teachers, bilingual educators, special education teachers, and general education teachers all claim expertise in early literacy, but they rarely read each other's books and research and they don't attend the same professional development events or conferences. You can bring the various disciplines together in your own work by exploring possible connections while still in college. Some colleges/universities have already established this type of interdisciplinary collaboration, but more needs to be done. The more we all coordinate and unify our work as educators, the more seamless and effective our work can be with young children and their families.

Getting a Job

Successful applicants for positions in early childhood education do more than tell their own story. It is also important to be familiar with each potential employer and show an interest in something unique about the people, the program, or the location. Prepare a strong resumé and personalized cover letter with help from staff at your college or university. If you plan to work with young children in a specialized aspect of the field, highlight any coursework or practical experience you have with each age group.

When preparing for an interview, keep in mind some strategies suggested by a blog post from the National Association for the Education of Young Children (Franco, 2015). They suggest you summarize the background you submitted in your application, describe exactly how you would teach a literacy or math lesson, or interact with toddlers around some outdoor insects, talk about how you plan to guide the behavior of your students, and how you plan to communicate with families. Here are some additional suggestions:

- Be prepared to talk about why you want this particular job. What have you learned about this school or program that makes it seem like the right fit for you? This shows the interviewer that you have done your homework and you are a desirable

candidate who is more likely to succeed. This would be a good time to mention something you know about the diversity of languages and cultures in this school and how you are prepared to support them.
- When you talk about the specifics of a lesson you might teach, include the ages of the target children in your description and give specific examples of how you would adapt your lesson to make it accessible for children from a variety of languages, cultures, and abilities. Use examples from the curriculum model currently being used by the school.
- Many interviewers want to know how a candidate would handle conflict or challenging behavior. Ideally, you should try to find out if the school uses any published methods for classroom management so you can be prepared to talk about the methods they are already using. Of course, being able to talk about how you will communicate with children who speak different languages to uphold a positive learning environment will be important to answering this question. More information on strategies and models on this topic can be found in Chapter 5.
- Be familiar with the newest version of NAEYC's position statement on Developmentally Appropriate Practice (DAP) as this is the leading document in the field of early childhood education in the United States and is generally created with significant buy-in from members. The statement was updated in 2020 with lots of details that can inform anyone who works with young children in the U.S. or in the U.K. It will guide you in planning your career and help you answer questions in a job interview. No school or program follows every bit of the DAP guidance, but every educator should be aware of its recommendations before entering the field (NAEYC, 2020a).
- Chapter 7 will give you lots of creative ideas to include in responding to questions about how you will communicate with families. Interviewers want to know that you consider this a valuable part of your job as an educator and that you will not be overwhelmed by working with diverse families on behalf of the children you teach (Franco, 2015).

Beginning a New Position

Starting a new position in early childhood education is so much more than just setting up your classroom. Request at least one contact from the new school that you can call upon to help you prepare for your first day. Some information will be meant to help you feel comfortable in your new position. Other points have major impact on how and what you teach. But, together, the compilation of this information can help you get off to the right start as a professional, colleague, and teacher. Here are some questions to ask at your new place of employment as you get ready to be an early childhood educator or specialist.

- What languages will my students speak? What is your expectation about when and how I will use English and my other languages? Will you support me in learning a new language?
- What are the language resources in the school and community? What languages are spoken by colleagues? Teaching partners? Volunteers? What paid services for translating and interpreting are available to you and how do you access them?
- What kinds of language software/websites/apps are we able/allowed to use? How can I learn about them before I start?
- What is the dress code for adults and children?
- What are some school traditions and unwritten expectations such as when to start and end the day, what you're allowed to eat and drink in the classroom, how to make copies of classroom materials, how to call in sick, and how to prepare for substitutes?

32 *Getting Started*

- What are areas of flexibility in school policies and process that will support me in navigating between your own beliefs and the school's requirements.
- What are the rules and consequences regarding my participation in social media for school or personal purposes? Many schools have very strict rules about how you can use social media – even for personal use – so that is important to learn when getting started. What are the pros and cons of using various social media platforms to communicate with the school community?
- How can I prepare for high-quality teaching? What are areas of flexibility? Can I choose the books and music you use with the children? Assignments? Assessments? Prepare for this discussion by reading *High-Quality Early Childhood Programs: The What, Why, and How* by Colker and Koralek (2018).
- What is the daily schedule assigned to me? What aspects of the schedule allow me to make changes as you need to? How much time will be spent outdoors and with whom?
- How does the school or program handle holidays? Are there optional or required performances? Celebrations? Or am I expected to celebrate more inclusive non-holiday events such as the beginning of spring?
- What books, articles, websites, checklists, webinars, or other professional learning resources would be best for me to study before starting? How will the school support me in participating in professional development? How does the school follow up and support implementation?

Things to Address in the Early Days

Ideally, your new employer would provide you with a coach or mentor right away. This person can be a great resource as you learn, plan, and get ready to teach. You might also benefit from connecting with an ally or informal mentor. Getting to know a formal coach and an informal mentor takes some time, so it is best to start these relationships as soon as possible. It will also be helpful to have a clear understanding of the roles of each participant in these relationships. Ask about formal communities of practice and informal professional learning networks that might be available where you work, such as book discussion groups, or curriculum studies.

Another thing to consider in the first few days will be how you can arrange your schedule to allow you to get involved with school committees, special projects, additional coursework, volunteer work, or professional activities outside of your employment. Be especially mindful of the policies your employer has about outside activities such as babysitting, tutoring, blogging, presenting at conferences, and outside employment. You will also need to determine how much time you will spend outside of school hours to prepare lessons, take care of paperwork, and manage recordkeeping and assignments.

Learn about emergency procedures, conduct during fire drills, and field trip policies. Many schools are making this information available for families via video examples that families can then explain to their children in their home language.

> Miss Elly described an emergency that happened when she was a toddler teacher at a private childcare center. One of the little ones became ill and vomited during a time when Miss Elly was alone in the classroom with 6 children under age 3. She knew she had to take the ill child to the office to be sent home, but she couldn't leave the other children in the classroom. No one answered the office phone and other teachers had taken their groups outside. So, Miss Elly coached all the children to hold hands and

> march in a parade with her while she carried the ill child to the office for help, all while singing a marching song. She tells this story to remind new teachers to never assume that policies and procedures are in place and it's always best to ask.

Establishing positive, mutually beneficial relationships with each family should be a priority within the first few days of school to be sure you know everything you need to know about each child. Read Chapter 7 to learn a variety of methods for this purpose.

Make the best use of planning periods, mealtimes, children's rest times, or other provisions for getting schoolwork done during school hours. When you have time allotted for planning during the working day, it is likely to be shorter than you wish. Knowing how to make the best use of this time will be a big help in your work. Talk to other teachers about how they use this time. For example, do they use the time to meet with others, share lesson ideas and materials, or confer about particular students? You'll need to allot time for that activity. Whether you use planning time solo or with colleagues, you will be using the time on your own – always be prepared to use your time by having a to-do list and the necessary materials ready. Work with colleagues and mentors to develop a strategy for identifying work that has to be done during this planning or preparation period and work that can wait until after hours. Teachers often report that their planning periods or children's nap times can be unpredictable with lots of possible interruptions. Always plan ahead.

Build relationships with specialists and learn how your school allows/expects you to interact with them. What is the referral process for special services? Who are the therapists who might be assigned to visit a child in your class or pull them out? What is the plan for exchanging information or co-planning? What do you know about early childhood education and/or specialties that you can share with each other to enhance your work? Share information about your language background. Let people know if you are fluent in more than one language and whether there are languages you are trying to learn. Find out if there are others in the school community who might help you learn a language or who might need help from you, especially when communicating with a child or family.

Setting up a New Classroom

Getting ready for the first day of school means setting up a new classroom. You can read about choosing and arranging materials and displays in Chapter 6. In this section, we will consider the ways classroom environments affect how you approach your work. Languages will be woven throughout the visual environment as well as the practices you put into place.

The learning environment should welcome diverse languages, cultures, and experiences. This should happen at the entrance to the classroom to establish positive first impressions. It should also be embedded in the ongoing spirit and practical work of the children and adults who work there. The environment must be set up to provide equitable access to learning for all children. It must be welcoming and respectful of the adults who join in. Keep these goals in mind to guide the choices you make.

Clear communication helps to support an inclusive environment by making it possible for visitors and children to find what they need and communicate with each other. Post policies and announcements in multiple languages for visitors. Make them visible in easily accessible space with QR codes allowing families to access the information on their phones or copies to take home. Leave a suggestion box or other container with paper and pens for families who want to leave a note. Be ready to use a quick-response digital translator such as Google Translate mobile app if an impromptu conversation is called for.

Children also need accessible communication from the moment they enter the classroom. They need some confidence that there's a way for them to understand what's happening and for them to make their needs known. This is important in helping them feel like equal participants in their school or program. For example, when working with infants and toddlers, offer them simple choices about toys or places to play that allow them some control over their participation. Post picture communication boards to help preschoolers and school-aged children express themselves. Create a comforting setting that protects different kinds of work and play, such as keeping loud block play separate from the quiet reading corner. And make labels and images around the environment that help adults use the home languages of the children.

Colleagues, family members, and children may feel respected, seen, and heard in an environment with space for private conversations with adults and children. Design space that supports thoughtful work such as recording observation notes. Consider the space from the perspectives of adults who will visit the room. Where can observers sit or stand? What space is available for volunteers? It is also important to represent the authentic languages and everyday cultures of the children and adults.

Establish and post classroom rules so students are supported by structure. Post and explain in their home languages and use images to help children remember rules. Ideally, children should participate in deciding on some of the rules when they are old enough.

With the onset of pandemic-related school shut-downs and the rise of hybrid models of instruction, your classroom should be designed with in-person and virtual learning in mind. Each school handles hybrid and remote learning differently and many experts say these new models and combinations of models will continue to be used now that they have been established. Ask for help to set up equipment and learn how to create effective lessons that work in any situation.

Get to know what technology is available and what's expected of you to use it. You will need to know how to get help with any unfamiliar technology. Learn the rules, including what you are allowed to send, receive, or download and what websites are blocked. Use this checklist to identify which types of technology are familiar to you, which you are ready to use effectively with children at different ages, and which you need to learn more about before you start teaching. Look for ways to use these tools to support diverse languages of children and adults.

- computers
- laptops
- tablets
- digital cameras
- software
- text messaging apps for school communication
- websites
- Smart boards
- document cameras/overhead projector
- Intercom
- videos and photos
- recorded stories
- smart pen
- televisions or DVDs
- closed circuit TV
- observation cameras for families to observe
- color printer
- 3D printer.

The 2020 U.S. National Teacher of the Year is Tabatha Rosproy (2020), a preschool teacher from Kansas. She rose to national attention during the COVID-19 pandemic and used many of her speeches and interviews to talk about how she kept teaching young children successfully via screen-based connections. When asked how she keeps young children engaged in remote learning, Ms. Rosproy advised teachers to "go all in" and not to be afraid to seem foolish or silly. She also talked frequently about how she involved families to support learning at home, "... alot lot of what I did was help parents create schedules and visual aids for kids to know what to do and when. This was especially helpful for parents who were also working from home."

What are some things you remember about teachers and classrooms on the first day of school? Do you have preschool memories too? How can these memories inform your point of view about what makes a welcoming learning environment?

Planning for Students to Get Started

Beginning in 2020, most school and childcare programs were closed for many months. Getting started as a teacher, getting started in the new school year, and getting started with new students meant preparing for remote learning. Some schools blended some time with online learning and some in-person time. As circumstances changed, the use of technology to welcome and engage young children also changed and will continue to change. The main point here is that all teachers need to be prepared to support digital learning that is synchronous or asynchronous, as well as in-person learning in a physical classroom, or any combination of these elements that we call "hybrid learning." Many teachers are finding themselves back in a classroom with some students present and some still participating from home via video chat links. This means the teacher has to be prepared to conduct lessons and learning activities that work for children in the building as well as children who are participating on a screen. There has been hybrid learning for young children before, but it remains to be seen how much this will grow in the future.

Be prepared to have your first encounters with some students over video chat. If you know this will be the case, you will need to be in regular contact with family members who must be present to help their young child sign on and use the features of their computer and the programs you plan to use. Also, plan at least some one-on-one time with each child (together with a family member if needed) so you can get to know them as individuals and begin to build a relationship with them. This will help you find ways to engage them in learning when you welcome them into the group. Your school is likely to have guidelines for when to turn on the video chat with young children, and for how long. They will also have rules about what must be done and what should be done. Many teachers and programs are delivering materials and books that families with young children can use at home at any time or during specific learning activities for a hands-on experience. How might your interactions with young children be different on screen than in-person? Do you have both kinds of experiences with young children so you can plan accordingly? If not, this is a good time to gain some practice and see how you might need to adjust your teaching for online success (Nemeth, 2015).

There is an interesting body of research showing that young children learn very little when viewing information passively on screens, but they can learn quite a bit when they have responsive interactions with others on screens. What does this mean? It turns out that screen time is not all created equal. Screen time can be helpful time or empty time, depending on what's happening. The key, according to the research, is interactivity. Young children's brains learn best when new information is encountered in connection with adults who respond readily to their actions and utterances and build from there. The key takeaway is to focus your screen time with young children in ways that allow you to have authentic conversations and to respond clearly and directly to what the children are saying and doing. Beeps and flashes may get a child's attention, but they do not do as much to build lasting learning as that back-and-forth talk and play you can have with children of all ages.

The American Academy of Pediatrics has suggested no screen time for children under 18 months, but this recommendation has softened as doctors began to see that there are times when screens can be used in active ways such as showing a baby their family pictures when they are in childcare, or having a family member read them a story over Facetime. This is an evolving discussion in the education field as more and more research becomes available that might shift thinking over time (American Academy of Pediatrics, 2016; Zero to Three, 2018).

Preparing to Greet Each Child

Greeting each child by name is an important beginning to each relationship. Pronouncing their names correctly is a sign of respect and acceptance. This issue is part of a national effort to raise awareness among educators and the community about the value of addressing every person by their name. For more information, visit www.mynamemyidentity.org. No child should have to feel that their name is not valuable or that their name is too difficult to pronounce. Ask the family what you should call their child and work with them to say it the correct way.

Every school has a way to collect information about children before they start. The kinds of information requested can vary widely from place to place. School districts in the United States often send home a "home language survey" to identify students who may need some type of English language development support. These forms ask questions about the languages spoken by the child and those around the child. They may also ask about language and literacy practices at home. There are several reasons why these surveys might yield inaccurate information. Not all districts or programs provide these forms in languages spoken by registering families. Some families are hesitant to reveal language information they feel might lead to discrimination, harassment, or placing their child in an undesirable learning group. For these reasons, it is always best to learn more about families and languages through personal contact as you and other school staff begin to build relationships with the new families. Learn in advance about the legal and ethical limits on what you can or cannot ask. For example, you might ask a family about the languages spoken in their home, but not about their immigration status or country of origin.

While school districts do require a home language survey, this is not required in infant/toddler or preschool programs. However, the information is important to teach and care for children of all ages, in all settings. The importance of supporting every child's home language is discussed in detail in Chapter 2. Even if a child does not yet speak or if they seem to speak English very well, teachers need to know about those home language experiences to enhance teaching and learning. Here are some strategies to support your work:

1. Infant/toddler teachers: Ask about the language(s) used to play with and comfort babies. In addition to official languages, ask about words and phrases the family might use for familiar objects, people, and loved ones. For example, the correct Spanish word for grandfather might be "abuelo" but the family might use a personal term such as "papito Luis." Ask families to describe or send video clips of the child's attempts at saying words such as, "When he says 'bobo,' we noticed he's not asking for a bottle, but he says that when he sees his brother."

2   Preschool teachers: Ask about the language(s) used to play, converse with, and comfort the child. Ask about the songs or chants the child knows how to sing in English or other languages. Ask about their favorite books, stories, or videos. Ask about their interests so you can add materials that bring out the child's language skills in school by supporting their interests.
3   Kindergarten / reception teachers: In addition to asking about the language(s) used to play, converse with, and comfort the child, ask about the child's learning experiences. Did they attend preschool or family childcare? Did they join a local story hour or music class? Did they attend Sunday school or a day camp experience? What languages were used in those experiences? As children enter kindergarten in the U.S. or reception in the U.K., teachers find a surprising variation in the learning experiences children may have had. Knowing about each child's history with language learning in different contexts can significantly enhance your ability to personalize learning experiences for success (NCECDTL, 2020).
4   Primary grade teachers: Screening for languages and language proficiency will likely have already been completed and placement decisions made for multilingual children before they are assigned to your class. In this case, your focus will be on making sure you receive all available information on each child in your class and that you connect with any specialists assigned to that child. In addition to the child's official file, there is still much to learn about their experiences with learning in English and other languages, as well as their cultural backgrounds and activities that can enhance the work you do with them in school.

Child Screening

Formal screening procedures will likely be in place for all programs associated with school districts or national funding like Head Start. Screening is the method used by educators to get an initial impression about whether a child needs further evaluation for learning or language supports or referral for early intervention or special education services. These screenings are generally conducted in prescribed ways with published screening tools. You will need specific training to administer the screeners used by your program or school. Be prepared to inquire how to adapt this process for children who speak languages other than English (NCECDTL, 2017).

When determining the services a child might need, the U.S. Department of Education and many professional organizations recommend using multiple measures. This is an important term for early childhood educators because it means that big decisions about a child's early education will not be made with just one test score. Multiple measures can include direct observations of the child's behavior and interactions, notes from family members, and samples of a child's work that can be combined to develop a more complete picture of what a child knows and can do, how they are progressing along a range of skills, and what additional supports might be needed.

One of the most controversial issues faced by early childhood educators is the question of labeling a child versus identifying strengths and needs. Of course, the more information you have about a child, the more accurately you can tailor your learning environments, lesson plans, expectations, and interactions with each child. Many teachers, leaders, and families have concerns about how that identifying information is gathered and used. They worry that a child might be labeled in a way that would hold them back or influence how they are taught and treated in negative ways. Consider how you can strengthen your professionalism in dealing with these questions and concerns. You might work with your coach or mentor to get feedback that can help you reflect on the role of identifying information might be helping you be a better teacher or whether this information really is creating biases that make it hard to be objective about a child.

It may take some time and practice to know how to accept information from previous teachers without letting this influence your own first impressions. Many people think that hearing from a previous teacher can bias the new teacher and set the student off on the wrong foot. But one year is surprisingly little time to really get to know a child who is one of a crowd, so you really do need as much as possible information about the child and be aware of potential professional obligation to reduce personal biases.

Teachers are vital advocates for their young students. You may not be the one who makes all the decisions about screening, evaluation, services, and placements for each child, but you certainly should have a role in providing information and receiving information involved in these processes. You can also play an important role in upholding equity in your school community by speaking up about what you know of a child's skills, abilities, and knowledge. We are still finding that young Black boys are expelled more often than other children (Gilliam et al., 2016). Teacher evaluations of children's learning and behavior can be influenced by assumptions based on dialects or speech patterns some children use. This possibility can be counteracted with ongoing reflection and coaching to help teachers become more aware of their prejudices and the implicit biases that become part of the school culture.

As you prepare to be a wonderful early childhood educator of today, you will start on a path of continuing learning, self-reflection, and growth. Your openness to these processes will strengthen your progress throughout your career. The relationships you develop will support you and lean on you for support. The more you know, the more you will grow.

Choose Your Own Path Check-In

1. What have you learned in this chapter about gathering information about the children in your group?
2. If you were starting a job in one of these positions, what questions would you ask colleagues in any of the other positions to help you prepare for the students in your group?

Infant/Toddler teacher	Preschool/Nursery teacher	Kindergarten/Reception teacher	Primary teacher
ESL/EAL teacher	Special educational needs teacher	Speech therapist	Physical therapist
Occupational therapist	Early childhood coach	Education manager/supervisor	Director/headmaster/principal

Social Media Messages and Discussion Starters

- Ask a teacher: What is something you wish an experienced teacher told you when you were getting started?
- What is the most useful teacher tool in your classroom?
- What is the most useful design feature of your classroom that makes teaching easier?

References

American Academy of Pediatrics (2016) *Policy Addresses How to Help Parents Manage Young Children's Media Use*, Washington, DC: AAP Publications.

Colker, L.J., & Koralek, D. (2018) *High Quality Early Childhood Programs: The What, Why, and How*, St Paul, MN: Redleaf Press.

Franco, B. (2015) Five Questions Asked at Every Teaching Interview, retrieved from www.naeyc.org/resources/pubs/tyc/apr2015/five-questions-asked-every-teaching-interview.

Gilliam, W.S., Maupin, A.N., Reyes, C.R., Accavitti, M., & Shic, F. (2016) *Do Early Educators Implicit Biases Regarding Sex and Race Relate to Behavior Expectations and Recommendations of Preschool Expulsions and Suspensions?*, New Haven, CT: Yale University Child Study Center.

Lugo-Neris, M.J., Jackson, C.W., & Goldstein, H. (2010) Facilitating Vocabulary Acquisition in Young English Language Learners, *Language, Speech, and Hearing Services in Schools*, 41, 314–327.

NAEYC (2020a) *Developmentally Appropriate Practice Position Paper*, Washington, DC: NAEYC.

NAEYC (2020b) *Professional Standards and Competencies for Early Childhood Educators*, Washington, DC: NAEYC.

NCECDTL (2017) *Screening Dual Language Learners in Early Head Start and Head Start: A Guide for Program Leaders*, Washington, DC: Early Childhood Learning and Knowledge Center.

NCECDTL (2020) *Transitions to Kindergarten: Supporting Children who are Dual Language Learners (DLLs)*, Washington, DC: Early Childhood Learning and Knowledge Center.

Nemeth, K. (2015) Tips for Videochatting with Young Children: Staying Together While Far Apart, retrieved from www.naeyc.org/our-work/families/tips-video-chatting-young-children.

Rosproy, T. (2020) Turn & Talk: Tabatha Rosproy on the Needs of Young Children Today, *Educational Leadership*, 78 (3), 12–13.

Vesely, C.K., Brown, E.L., & Mehta, S. (2017) How home visits transform early childhood pre-service educators' attitudes for engaging families, Journal of Early Childhood Teacher Education, 38(3), 242–258.

Zero to Three (2018) *Screen Sense: What Research Says about the Impact of Media on Children Under 3 Years Old*, Washington, DC: Zero to Three.

4 Curriculum

Follow the Chapter 4 Roadmap with These Headings

Introduction	Addressing Government Standards and Benchmarks
Components of a Curriculum	Lesson Plans and Activities
The Role of Language and Culture in Curricula	Developmental Theories Influence Lesson Plans
Elements of a High-Quality Curriculum	Measuring Curriculum Fidelity
Curriculum Options	Anti-bias Curriculum
Is it a Curriculum or an Approach?	Engaging Families in Extending Curriculum
Curriculum for Learning Domains	Curriculum Trends for the Future

Chapter 4 introduces all of the many facets of early childhood curriculum planning and implementation. You will learn about the components that make up a true curriculum. You will read about the role of language and culture in curriculum and how to recognize the elements of a high-quality curriculum. The discussion then follows the different types of curriculum models and approaches and how they address the learning domains. You will learn about writing lesson plans and planning activities. The government standards and benchmarks that impact curriculum implementation will be considered. There is a section that connects major early childhood theorists with curriculum elements and the next section addresses curriculum fidelity. Forward-looking sections include a discussion of anti-bias curriculum and hidden curriculum, engaging families in extending the curriculum, assessing outcomes for children and curriculum trends.

> **Top Tips for Curriculum**
> - Early childhood curricula may be general or subject-specific, they may be established or emergent, but they should always be written down and include goals, objectives, methods, materials, and benchmarks to measure success.
> - Culture and language go together, and early childhood curricula need to address them in combination as well as to address separately the important roles of culture and language in early learning.
> - A high-quality early childhood curriculum is flexible enough to follow children's interests because a child's interests often reveal areas of prior knowledge.
> - In early childhood education, developmentally appropriate curricula are more child-centered than teacher-directed.
> - What makes early childhood curricula different from curricula for older students is the focus on early cognitive needs to learn actively, to learn the meanings of words, and to experience lots of repetition.

DOI: 10.4324/9781003089216-4

- Standards and benchmarks inform how we use curricula, but they are not the curriculum. Standards and benchmarks are like ingredients, and the curriculum is like the recipe for how to mix the ingredients and prepare them for the particular dinner guests.
- Equitable access to learning should be addressed in every curriculum. Anti-bias approaches can be added as a supplemental curriculum.
- Early childhood theorists inform the basis of early childhood education and provide context that must be filled in with readings of current research.
- Even for the youngest children, curriculum should address all learning domains.

Introduction

Curriculum is the central focus of your work as a teacher. It guides what and how you teach, as well as what you expect children to learn. Beyond that, curriculum models can take many forms. A curriculum for infants will look completely different than a curriculum for a primary classroom. Some curriculum models come with a collection of books and hours of training and practice. Others start with a few tips and a lot of on-the-spot creativity. Some are highly scripted, including exactly what should be taught and when, what teachers and students should say, along with specific ways to document children's progress. Others seek to support the role of teacher and caregiver, giving them a lot of background information to strengthen their ability to respond in the moment and take advantage of teachable moments as they arise.

There are models for schools, childcare, family childcare, and home visitors who support parents' work with their own children. A class may have one comprehensive curriculum or a collection of curricula that address particular areas of learning. In a review of the literature, John Hattie (Bullard, 2020) found that the curriculum experienced by a child has a significant effect on their achievement along with the impact of teacher practices. Successful teachers depend on effective curriculum choice and implementation. Teachers need to know how to evaluate, select, and implement a variety of curricula. Additionally, the National Association for the Education of Young Children emphasizes the importance of having a written curriculum based on research showing that "children learn more in programs where there is a knowledge-rich, well-rounded curriculum that is well planned and implemented" (NAEYC, 2020).

Now let's take a look at what you will need to know in this part of your role as an early childhood educator.

Components of a Curriculum

Whether you use a purchased curriculum or you make your own, there is a complex combination of components to consider. Some curriculum models include all of the items listed below, while others have just a few of them. The definition of what makes a curriculum is so broad, there is room for many interpretations to fit.

- *Objectives* – Measurable, actionable statements of specific expected outcomes. Learning objectives often start with a phrase like "the student [or child] will be able to …". The objective should describe the context of the learning, the skill or knowledge they will be able to show, and how you will determine they have actually learned it. Example: "After a lesson activity on comparing absorbent materials to waterproof materials, the student will be able to select the best material to mop up spilled milk from a selection of materials."

- *Scope and sequence* – The range of topics to be covered and the order in which they are covered in the curriculum. The scope may include a list of specific topics along with the learning standards they address and a description of the depth and/or breadth of the coverage. This is a critical element of the information needed when choosing a purchased curriculum.
- *Goals* – The broader ambitions for how children will learn and grow based on meeting your curriculum objectives.
- *Methods* – Actual strategies, scripts, and teaching practices to be used when implementing the particular curriculum. Curricula for younger children may include a lot of play and exploration that encourages the child's active learning, imagination, expression, and creativity. Methods are not always about presenting information or telling children things. Methods can also involve setting up the environment with engaging and meaningful materials that encourage independent play and peer-to-peer interaction as children develop skills and knowledge through problem-solving and role play.
- *Benchmarks* – The steps along the child's path to meeting an objective and/or learning standard.
- *Materials* – Many purchased curriculum models specify the books, manipulatives, equipment, supplies, and learning materials needed to follow the scope and sequence of the curriculum.
- *Assessments* – These measure the learning that takes place as a result of implementing a curriculum. They may be formal or informal, event-based, or portfolio-based. There should be some type of formative assessments designed to check on learning along the way so you can adjust your lesson plans, either for the whole group, small groups, or for individual children. Informally, this might happen when you show a toddler some materials you used in a previous activity, and they immediately remember how to use them correctly. Or it might happen more formally when you give the weekly spelling quiz to first grade students and notice that some children need more time to learn some of the words. Summative assessments are generally more formal checks at the end of a specified period such as a unit test, or an assessment of preschoolers' alphabet knowledge at the end of the school year.

Backward Design of Curriculum

Backward Design (Bullard, 2020) is a way of preparing a curriculum by starting with what you want children to learn at the end, and then working backward to determine how you will help them learn it. This approach can be adapted to make sure that you have made appropriate adaptations and plans to ensure the equitable access to learning of children who are multilingual learners.

The Role of Language and Culture in Curricula

Across the range of different types of curricula, language always plays an important role. When you teach content and skills to children, you use your language to explain and demonstrate. When there is a language mismatch, the teacher can be presenting a great lesson, but a child might not learn the skill or concept if they don't understand the language. Both methods and materials must be chosen with the language of the presenter and the receiver in mind. As you progress through your curriculum, you will also encounter language concerns related to assessments. Children need to be able to show what they know and can do, even if the child and teacher don't speak the same language.

In addition, it is important for children to see their own language as central to the curriculum that guides their learning. It should be more than translating some English words into Spanish or Korean. The curriculum should actually teach about language in general and about the languages of the children in your group. And each child should receive some support to learn curricular content in their home language.

> In my work with early childhood teachers, I have found it critical that they learn to be adaptive in their teaching practice to reflect and meet the diverse language learning needs of their students. To achieve so, they will need to constantly engage in assessment of their students' needs, before, during, and after instruction. Such practice will enable early childhood teachers to provide targeted and tailored instruction to yield better educational outcomes for each individual child.
>
> Jennifer Chen, Ed.D.
> Associate Professor
> Early Childhood and Family Studies
> School of Curriculum and Teaching
> College of Education
> Kean University

A curriculum can respond to and incorporate each child's cultural background through choices of materials, stories, songs, examples, and demonstrations. If you use a purchased curriculum, you may have to replace some of the recommended materials and lessons with items you know will be relatable for the children in your class or group.

To be truly responsive, cultural items should be included in authentic ways – not just added as an afterthought (Souto-Manning, 2013; Reid, Kagan, & Scott-Little, 2019). Look for ways to learn more about activities, materials, traditions, and stories the children encounter at home and add them to your lesson plans. For example, instead of reading a generic story that has been translated into Vietnamese, look for a story that was written by a Vietnamese author or that reflects experiences of a Vietnamese child or family. Kagan, Reid, and Scott-Little (2019) reviewed a wide array of research about the role of culture in standards and curriculum. They found that government standards often do not allow for cultural responsiveness. They recommend that teachers should go beyond the traditional and superficial approach to culture that only includes food, music, costumes, holidays and language. They found strong research evidence that "the cultural nature of early learning has shown that cultural variation affects not only social norms but also how children learn across multiple developmental domains" (Kagan, Reid, & Scott-Little, 2019).

Elements of a High-Quality Curriculum

The National Association for the Education of Young Children coordinated a major revision of its traditional Developmentally Appropriate Practice position statement in 2020. It contains a key section on curriculum. This gives us an important reminder that play is central to developmentally appropriate curricula for young children. The balance of play with teacher led instruction changes as children get older. Infant/toddler programs are almost entirely play-based. Lessons may be added with increasing time as children go into primary school. At any age, children learn best when presented with opportunities, tasks, and materials that match their age and readiness.

High-quality curriculum models are research-based, developmentally appropriate, responsive to the individual languages, cultures, and experiences of the children, and they encourage independent exploration and expression. When they are responsive and adaptable to the needs of individual children, they can also be effective tools for achieving equitable access to learning (Hartl & Riley, 2021).

> Good to know: When a curriculum is "evidence-based," there has been objective research proving the effectiveness of this particular curriculum. When a curriculum is "research-based" the authors have read some research and used some of that information to write the new curriculum.

With all these features in mind, it is also important to evaluate a curriculum for the setting and for the purpose you need. For example, a preschool classroom curriculum may not be as effective in a family childcare home. A first-grade curriculum will not be effective in a toddler class. What makes a curriculum successful is the impact it has on children's learning. Let's take a look at the "why" behind the elements of curriculum quality.

> A quality curriculum acknowledges how young children learn:
>
> 1. Repetition
> 2. Active, hands-on experiences
> 3. Active construction of new knowledge
> 4. Using new words multiple times in multiple contexts
> 5. Learning in the context of nurturing relationships
> 6. Building on prior knowledge.

Choosing a curriculum requires a lot of attention to details. There are several resources that can give you specifics about different curriculum models for different ages. You can also learn about specific birth–5 curricula used in classrooms, family childcare homes, and home-based programs, and the factors that go into evaluating early childhood curriculum using the Head Start Curriculum Consumer Report available on the Early Childhood Learning and Knowledge Center website.

In your work, you may not always have the opportunity to choose a curriculum. In some state-funded preschool systems, programs are required to use curriculum models that are approved by the state. School districts often purchase a curriculum for every classroom in a particular grade level. Even in these circumstances, knowing the features of a high-quality curriculum will help you make the best use of the curriculum you receive. You will understand what aspects of the curriculum should be emphasized and what might need to be adapted to fit your students.

Curriculum Options

Teacher-Created and Emergent Curriculum

An emergent curriculum incorporates early learning standards and high-quality practices, but leaves the planning up to the teacher or family childcare provider. Plans change from year to year, even month to month as the educator observes the children in their current group. Sometimes a curricular topic arises from a special event or question that some or all children encounter. When something significant happens, young children need help to comprehend, process, and create their own understanding. This might happen if there is a new baby in a classmate's family, a local flood, a construction project near the school, a teacher with a serious illness, or a sudden need to close the school and learn from home. You may have math, literacy, science, or other goals in mind for the current week, and you can still meet those goals by including them in studies of the emergent topic that has captured children's attention.

The key to effective use of emergent curriculum is to truly listen to children – not to assume you know what they are wondering about. This approach allows you to respond to the unique, observable, and changing needs and interests of young children (Wein, 2014). When the children in your group speak multiple languages, multiple means of gathering information to inform your emergent curriculum. In addition to asking children, you might also observe their concerns or interests, or ask family members if their child has mentioned any worries about recent events in the news or changes in the program. Pay attention to children's artwork and give them extra time to express themselves with various media during times of stress or change. These are all ways that you can tune in to what diverse children need and plan your response. You need to be willing to recognize when something is not working well or when children need more or different support. This level of responsiveness and effectiveness will not be served by simply downloading individual lesson or activity plans from various websites. If you are in a position to choose a curriculum, be a critical and informed consumer, ready to use your educational expertise to evaluate sales pitches and promotions and look deeper for the key components of quality early education.

What Is Curriculum and What Is Not

A real curriculum is like "a detailed blueprint for achieving outcomes, through specific activities, defined methods, and listed materials" (Bullard, 2020). It is not just a stack of lesson plans or a bunch of activities you want to do with the children. A curriculum is also not a list of state standards or benchmarks. Your school or program may have all teachers use a purchased assessment tool that comes with books or apps filled with activity examples – but these are suggested activities – *not* a curriculum. If you consider these elements to be ingredients, then the curriculum would be the recipe you use to combine the ingredients in certain ways to make the best possible meal.

Breadth vs. Depth

Teachers often struggle with finding a balance between breadth and depth of content. You may be tempted to cover as much information as possible, but that means you can't explore each topic deeply with the children. In many cases for early childhood education more is not better. For example, trying to talk to kindergartners about 15 different animals from Australia may seem valuable, but children may not be able to retain or remember so many new and unfamiliar terms. Choosing just two or three animals and studying them in depth with two-way interactions and multiple media across several days is more likely to result in lasting, accurate, and detailed knowledge. Learning a lot of concepts and vocabulary words that are not well understood and not remembered will not be as effective as learning concepts/vocabulary words with greater depth and full comprehension.

Of course, there will be times when you really do need to provide a brief exposure to more content or vocabulary. For example, you might tell an infant "yes, that's another airplane" when they point to the sky, then get back to your planned activity. The important thing is to make these choices with an understanding about when depth is preferrable and when breadth is more on target.

Teacher-Directed vs. Child-Centered Approach

Curriculum models usually address a balance between teaching that is directed by the teacher and teaching that focuses on following the lead of the child. The question of how to achieve a balance between teacher-directed learning and child-centered experiences is of critical importance in the early years. This has particular ramifications for language development. We know that children need to practice language – they need to talk and sign in order to learn words, speech sounds, grammar, syntax, and phonemes – both in their home language and in a new language. When children spend too much time listening passively to a teacher talk, they may not have enough time to process what the teacher is saying and are spending less time producing language and actively learning. When we say "active learning," we are talking about physical and mental activity that supports learning. Children need to try things and see the results of their attempts, they need the experience of identifying and solving problems, and they need to spend a lot of time building and navigating relationships with adults and peers.

Yet, letting go of control of learning is one of the most difficult adjustments for early childhood educators to make. You might feel like the only time you are teaching is when you are presenting information to the children. Research shows, however, that when a teacher acts as a partner to the children as they explore, investigate, discover, and express what they learn, more lasting learning can occur (Kaput, 2018).

> Traditional sayings illustrate these roles:
> "Be a guide on the side, not a sage on the stage."
> "The one who is talking is the one who is learning."

Traditionally, in the U.S. and U.K., many high-quality early years programs focus on child-centered curriculum, but you will see more teacher-directed learning as children get into primary grades. Many first and second grade curriculum models do not allow for play-based learning anymore. However, there are still many options for child-centered learning through projects, studies, and collaborative inquiry.

Child-centered learning involves including the specific interests of the children in your group. Teacher-directed learning might include topics the teacher thinks will be interesting to the children, but teachers using a child-centered approach actually ask the children and families about their interests and experiences and observe children's play to determine how to follow their unique and valuable interests to engage them fully in active learning.

Comprehensive and Supplemental Curricula

To support learning for the whole child, a comprehensive curriculum is best because it creates a unified approach to supporting learning in all learning domains. It allows teachers and specialists to collaborate on creating lessons, activities, and environments that build on each other and lead children on connected pathways to learning.

> Mrs. Singh teaches kindergarten using a comprehensive curriculum. She meets regularly with the ESL teacher, the physical therapist, and the music teacher who spend time with her students. She updates them on topics she will cover in the coming weeks and the materials she plans to use. Next week she plans a study of butterfly growth cycles because the class has butterfly chrysalis samples ready to open. She has storybooks and nonfiction in the languages of her class, observation kits for outdoor explorations, and new journal books for writing about the butterflies. She has worked related content into math, social studies, and approaches to learning lesson plans. Now she shares her plans with the ESL teacher, physical therapist, and music teacher so they can incorporate butterfly motions in physical therapy, butterfly songs in music class, and some additional books and videos in the school library for children to discover in their home languages when they work with the ESL teacher. The children benefit from the connections they can make to strengthen their learning in their general education class and during their special times. Instead of jumping from one unrelated topic to another, these children experience a nearly seamless learning day that allows them to maintain focus, reinforce what they've already learned, and form a stronger foundation for new learning because of the connections across domains.

When a child is participating in a program that uses a comprehensive curriculum, this kind of cross-discipline collaboration and information sharing can make learning smoother and more effective for children.

There are also many supplemental curriculum resources to cover specific skills or knowledge domains, such as a handwriting curriculum or a social-emotional learning curriculum. When these are added to your existing curriculum, you will need to make choices about how to fit in the supplemental activities during the day, as well as how to help the children transition from one curriculum to the other. Supplemental curriculum models may provide specialized focus on an area of identified need for the children. You might also find that you can use your assessment data to make enhancements to your comprehensive curriculum to achieve the same results in a more cohesive way.

Sometimes you might need to add a lesson or unit to focus on a culturally or locally relevant topic or a current event. For example, if you live in an area where there is water but no snow in winter, you might replace the study of snow and ice in your curriculum with a more relevant one about different modes of fishing. Or you might need to add a unit to help students understand a pandemic and vaccines. It is important to consider what you are replacing in your standard curriculum. Most high-quality curriculum models use a carefully thought-out progression of learning content, so you would want to find a way to address the same learning objectives with the supplemental content you are adding. This will ensure that the order of skills, vocabulary, and concept knowledge can progress in line with the planned curriculum.

Is it a Curriculum or an Approach?

As we have described, there are lots of ways to define curricula. Some are more structured, and others act more like a foundation to prepare teachers to develop their own activities. Examples of curricula that are more child-centered curriculum models include HighScope and The Creative Curriculum. There are other well-known frameworks for early learning that provide information about ways to approach teaching and learning without providing the same level of structure as a fully designed curriculum. These are often called early childhood approaches rather than curricula, such as Project Approach, Reggio Emilia, Bank Street, Montessori, and Waldorf.

Another example of an approach that can be added to an early childhood curriculum is the Pyramid Model. This model provides teacher training, teaching strategies, and materials for children to enhance social/emotional development and to prevent or address challenging behaviors. It is meant to be used in addition to and woven into the existing curriculum.

Universal design for learning (UDL) is an approach that developed out of the universal design movement for preparing environments that take away barriers to access. We talked about universal design ideas in Chapter 3 such as posting picture communication boards so that all children can communicate, whether they are confident speakers, or DLLs, or children who are shy. UDL was created specifically to adapt the learning environment in proactive ways based on brain science. It can be used with other curriculum models, and it provides strategies for engaging the interest of all learners, representing information that is accessible to all learners, and using action/expression in ways that allow every learner to show what they know and can do (Brillante & Nemeth, 2018, and forthcoming in 2022).

There are several approaches to learning that involve extended projects. There is some evidence showing that this deeper, long-term, hands-on type of learning has many advantages for preschool and primary learning. Some teachers assign projects as part of their curriculum, but these often have an expected outcome and are controlled by the teacher. Project-based learning (PBL) is an approach that puts the students in control of developing a question, then designing a project to find answers that have meaning in school and in the world beyond the school walls. Within this approach, many different learning objectives can be addressed.

The Project Approach is also a way to add project work to an existing curriculum. It was developed by well-known early childhood experts, Lillian Katz and Sylvia Chard, who wanted to support more active, inquiry-based learning that supports deeper investigations by young children. The Project Approach has recommended steps for planning, implementing, and creating a culminating event to celebrate what the students learned.

> I visited a school in another country. I was invited to be part of a panel of experts to speak to educators about supporting language connections in learning. The hosts asked the speakers to suggest inquiry questions that could be used for student projects for 6 months leading up to our visit. When we arrived, we were brought to visit preschool and primary school classes. Some of the preschool students wanted to explore how animals communicate. The teacher stepped back and invited the children to take me around the room and tell me about the artwork they had posted to represent what they learned about animal language. In a second-grade classroom, students showed me 3D depictions of their investigation into how plants react to human language. Again, their teacher stepped back and invited me to engage in a discussion with students about how their work might help us understand human communication. These examples were then woven into our panel presentations for teachers the next day.

Many early childhood curriculum models organize learning into periods of time or themes. This approach has been met with varying levels of success and may or may not comply with developmentally appropriate practice. It does seem that choosing a subject of study for a week or more can provide an anchor to help lesson plans stay connected to a cohesive learning experience. But overly broad or frivolous themes may do more harm than good. Look for themes that are easy to understand for the children in your group. Remember that a theme based on a broad category or impractical topic is going to be very difficult for children who are dual language learners (DLLs) to understand. For example, a theme like "friends" is too vague to provide support for learning and planning. In explaining what a friend is in your majority language, you will likely lose the connection with children who are DLLs. If you want to examine a theme like "ways we help each other," you may be able to demonstrate what it means to help each other and investigate different ways of helping or being helped. Holidays are often considered developmentally inappropriate as themes or topics but a theme like "what is new in springtime?" gives children a chance to explore changes in the temperature, their clothing, the ways they play, and the plants and animals in their community. This provides a wealth of branches for exploration that tap into children's prior knowledge and help children who are DLLs to build learning connections (NCECDTL, 2019).

Play-based curriculum focuses almost entirely on providing high-quality materials and environments, then allowing children to learn and grow through spending most of the day playing independently. This kind of sophisticated play has been shown to result in lasting learning as well as creativity, initiative, and problem-solving experiences. Another interesting approach is found in Nature Schools, or Forest Schools in the U.K. Serving primarily preschool or kindergarten/reception, these programs conduct most or all learning outdoors in natural settings, encouraging children to investigate all learning domains via their natural explorations. Professional organizations like Forest School Association describe a deeply commited approach rather than simply holding some activities outdoors.

Curriculum for Learning Domains

Learning domains are the topic areas to be covered by early childhood curriculum. These domains are identified by state or national government agencies, curriculum publishers, or other organizations and agencies. The lists are quite similar, but not always identical, and they are subject to change as new trends and thinkers enter the picture. You will need to know how to address the learning domains that apply to your position. Generally, the learning domains are set up with benchmarks that apply to different age ranges. The benchmarks often recommend a particular sequence that should be followed when early skills are needed to properly develop the later knowledge and skills. In the U.S., thousands of programs work with the Head Start Early Learning Outcomes Framework (Head Start, 2015). In England, programs serving children aged from birth to age 5 follow the Early Years Foundation Stage Standards (U.K. Department of Education, 2021).

Curriculum for Literacy

There is a great deal of concern and controversy about how to teach reading to young children. This debate is fueled by worries about the high number of children in the U.S. and the U.K who are struggling to read even as they get to be 8 and 9 years old. Research shows that a child who is not reading by age 9 is unlikely to fully master reading. Government agencies get involved to recommend or dictate reading instruction methods and standards, yet these recommendations do not generally result in big improvements in the overall literacy rates. Most experts agree that teachers can benefit from a stronger knowledge of early language and literacy development – the "why" that informs their work. Understanding the "how" and what works best for which children is still a matter of disagreement in the field (Roberts, 2017; Paradis, Genesee, & Crago, 2021).

Here is what we do know about getting children ready to learn to read. There is no evidence that starting earlier leads to greater success. If a child is interested, they might learn the alphabet at age 3, while others don't learn the alphabet until they turn 5. We have no data to prove one will do better or worse than the other. Children can learn the alphabet or character system of their home language first, and they will still learn the English alphabet when needed.

There are five components of early literacy and language: Alphabet knowledge and early writing, background knowledge, book knowledge and concepts of print, oral language and vocabulary, and phonological awareness, that every child must be exposed to, but we do not actually have research to show how much time should be spent on each one. We also know that children may begin by learning the five in their home language or English or some balance of both. Researchers find that starting with some support or connection to the home language works best to build a foundation of knowledge that fuels later learning of English (NASEM, 2017).

Children need to be active participants in the process of learning to read. Research shows they need to use words and sentences, act out and discuss stories (Shanahan & Lonigan, 2015; Dickinson & Porche, 2011), and do their own writing to really learn – children cannot learn to read by passively listening to stories, instructions, and lessons – and they cannot learn to read with comprehension if they are taught by rote memorization, drills, worksheets, and flashcards.

Curriculum for Math(s)

Math is one of the cognitive domains. Blending skills with content is better than isolated skills. Compare the learning experience of a child who is asked to practice sorting red and green buttons to that of a child who is asked to sort the folders and give the green ones to classmates who are ready to move on to the next activity. Most skills can be taught with meaningful content and materials that have intrinsic meaning. Math learning depends on an orderly progression of skill learning, so finding content to embed those skills is important to keep students engaged and relating to their learning and moving along on the continuum. In general, children will have to learn the words for numbers and math concepts, plus learning counting, operations, measurement, and spatial sense. Researchers acknowledge that more study is needed to clarify best strategies for teaching math to linguistically diverse groups, but the research is clear that language is an important component of math learning (Lewis, King, & Schiess, 2020).

Curriculum for Science

Science is another example of a cognitive domain. It involves learning about scientific thinking and science concepts such as biological science and physical science. In early education, most science exploration involves interesting hands-on activities that support the learning of concepts and vocabulary.

Curriculum for Technology and Engineering

Young children benefit greatly from being allowed to explore simple and digital technology and basic engineering. These topics teach them how things work, how to make them work, and the words needed to talk about them. Computers and tablets help with technology learning, and makerspaces are great for engineering development.

Curriculum for the Arts

In addition to learning about the esthetics and beauty of art and the media and techniques used to produce art in its many forms, art has elements of technology tools, science (e.g., combining colors or mixing textures), and math (counting and comparing). Art can be a valuable means of expression as well as a source of much conversation.

Curriculum for Social Studies

Social studies may include learning about the roles of community helpers, geography, current events, history, and the basics about how your system of government works. When these topics are presented with cultural and linguistic responsiveness, they can be great sources of language learning.

Curriculum for Health and Wellness

This domain may include learning about physical development and our bodies, nutrition, gross and fine motor work, and self-care supports such as yoga or simple meditation for young children. It also addresses mental health, which may also be part of social emotional learning/development.

Curriculum for Social Emotional Learning/Development

These two domains are often put together in learning domains. We refer to them by the acronyms SEL or SED. We want young children to learn how to express and control their feelings and how to develop strong, mutual relationships with other children, family members, and educators. This also encompasses the sense of belonging.

Helping children get along and develop a level of comfort with diversity may be one of the most important responsibilities of early childhood education programs. Research has shown that children as young as 4 years may treat each other differently when languages are not upheld in the classroom. English speaking children may tease and bully their non-English speaking classmates and underprepared teachers may add to these problems (Chang et al., 2007). It seems that teaching children some of each other's languages, providing communication assistance like picture boards, can help. Research also showed that children as young as 4 years can learn specific strategies to help them communicate effectively with peers who speak different languages. According to Hirschler (1994), you can teach children to avoid conflict by speaking slowly and clearly, by pointing and demonstrating to show their friend what they mean, and by waiting patiently for the other child to answer. In addition, teacher modelling through self-talk and parallel-talk can help children build the talking skills they need to resolve conflicts with peers.

Language Curricula

There is a strong body of research about helping young children learn and grow in programs where they are going to learn the community's majority language as a new language (NASEM, 2017). Based on this research, several authors have created ESL/EAL curriculum models. Many other organizations provide resources to support existing curriculum such as The British Council and Colorin Colorado. There is far less information available about how to choose effective curriculum models for programs that are teaching a new language to children who are English-speakers or majority language speakers. Keep in mind that a curriculum that provides some materials in another language, such as Spanish, is not a true bilingual curriculum. To be effective, the curriculum needs specific, intentional teaching methods that engage emergent bilingual children and that support metalinguistic awareness. Simply taking content that was written in English and translating to another language may result in working that is not fully accurate in the new language.

Some approaches focus more on providing a strong platform of teacher training rather than offering a fully formed curriculum for school adoption. They identify key skills and knowledge that make teachers more effective in working with linguistically diverse groups and puts that into professional development programs and kits. A different kind of approach is designed as an intervention to help schools improve the way they serve children who are DLLs. One such approach is the Sheltered Instruction Observation Protocol (SIOP), which involves intensive teacher training on specific strategies for use in general education classes for students who are new to English. SIOP has been used most extensively with older primary students and above, but is being added to earlier grades as schools are noting its success (Echevarria, Short, & Peterson, 2012).

Addressing Government Standards and Benchmarks

All teachers and their school leaders must be familiar with state standards that apply to their program. These standards come from a variety of sources. Find out what you need to know from national or state government, and which departments apply to your work. For example, schools in England have to comply with Early Years Foundation Stage standards. In the U.S, a first-grade teacher might have to address federal benchmarks, state standards, and English language development "can do descriptors" when WIDA standards have been adopted by their state. These standards are generally meant to make sure children at each age receive the content that's expected – but they do not dictate teaching methods or lessons. You will need to use your chosen curriculum while making sure each standard is addressed. In the U.K., there is a national curriculum from the Department of Education for ages 6 and up (years 1, 2, and 3 included).

Most lesson plan templates and assessment tools will provide space for you to indicate which benchmarks or standards are being covered within your curriculum. Remember that the standards are like ingredients, but you still need a recipe to turn your ingredients into a meal. Likewise, you will need to plan how to teach and what to teach so that the standards are included but not the drivers of children's everyday experiences.

Lesson Plans and Activities

When you teach in a school or work with most sophisticated curriculum models, you will be asked to write lesson plans to describe what you have arranged for each child and all the children every day. Some schools provide required templates. Some curriculum models also offer templates. You will need to know what is required of you. Without these requirements, you should still consider writing lesson plans to document how you plan to implement your own chosen curriculum.

A highly detailed lesson plan will cover the whole day, with activities planned during each portion of the day. It will indicate the objectives to be covered and the materials needed. Expected actions/scripts for teacher, assistant teacher, volunteers, and children will be indicated. Some type of benchmark or assessment will allow you to show what was accomplished by the written lesson. And, you should have space to add adaptations to personalize learning for individual children with additional languages, cultural references, connections to a child's Individualized Education Program (IEP) or Individualized Family Service Plan (IFSP) and personalizations related to what you've noted about children's interests.

Other lesson plans might just describe a small or large group activity with a learning objective, the materials needed to do it, and a question about how you'll know if the children met the objective. Whether long or short forms, lesson plans do not need to look like a plan for what teacher will say and do. Developmentally appropriate practice would support lesson plans that describe how the teacher plans to prepare the environment to guide child-centered learning activities. In these cases, teachers might describe how they will introduce an activity in English and other languages, or how they will use a video to show children options for participating, then link the learning objectives to outcomes that will occur during a period of play and exploration. A well-planned environment can act as an engaging and meaningful guide for valuable play-based learning at any age.

Developmental Theories Influence Lesson Plans

Many child development theorists influence the way curriculum models are written and implemented. These theories provide context for understanding the reasoning behind various curriculum models. You will also need to read about recent research to determine what works for the children in your class or group and to support curriculum implementation. Now let's take a look at how some key theories might inform your development of lesson plans and activities.

Some developmental theorists viewed child development as a series of stages that are marked by distinct changes in how children think and learn. Jean Piaget and Erik Erikson described their own stages of child development, but their theories hold a broader view of development.

Piaget and focused on cognitive development and Erikson focused on psychosocial development. Over the years, researchers have called into question some of these early claims, but there are components of these theories that are still very influential in the field. Erikson identified 8 stages across the lifespan, each characterized by a crisis that must be resolved in a positive way for the person to progress toward a healthy and productive adulthood. At ages 3–6, Erikson believed children faced a crisis where they needed to begin making decisions and taking initiative in their own learning. If they were met with negative responses to their efforts, their prevailing experience would be to feel guilt – thus the stage name "initiative vs. guilt." He was describing development as an interplay between the child's internal cognitive development and effects of the responses the child receives to each new category of behavior (Gullo & Graue, 2020). This helped us to understand the balance between the effects of nature and nurturing in the developing child. Erikson's 8 stages of development are:

- Birth–18 months: trust vs. mistrust.
- 18 months–3 years: autonomy vs. shame and doubt.
- 3–6 years: initiative vs. guilt.
- 6–12 years: industry vs. inferiority.
- 12–18 years: identity vs. role confusion.
- 18–40 years: intimacy vs. isolation.
- 40–65 years: generativity vs. stagnation.
- 65 years–death: ego integrity vs. despair.

Piaget's work focused on describing cognitive development. Stages were just a part of his theory. As with Erikson's theory, there have been researchers who found exceptions to the claims made about the ages or outcomes of the stages, but the stage theories continue to inform understanding that a 2-year-old child does not think like a 5-year-old or an 8-year-old. This understanding will tie into your use of the principles of Developmentally Appropriate Practice (NAEYC, 2020).

The most important components of Piaget's work are based on his research with young children to learn how they take in and store new knowledge. He found that children do not simply absorb vocabulary or concepts as they are presented. Instead, children use their own ways of thinking and what they know from prior experience to construct new ways of understanding information they encounter. Viewing children as active learners, Piaget found that there was an inseparable connection between the information from the environment and the individual brains' way of processing that information (Gullo & Graue, 2020; Pinter, 2017). This awareness has helped early childhood educators understand a critical truth: what you present is not exactly the same as what children learn. Each child interprets, questions, and mentally acts upon your information so what they remember may have varying degrees of similarity to what you taught. When preparing lesson plans, this is important to keep in mind. It explains why lesson plans must include more than just what the teacher will say or provide. To ensure learning, lesson plans also have to address connections with child's prior knowledge, intentional opportunities to act on new words and concepts in home and new language, and frequent checks for understanding.

> Example of preoperational construction of knowledge: A 4-year-old girl and her mother watched a segment about power blackouts on a well-known educational TV show for young children. The next day, during a storm, the power in their own house went out. The mother asked her daughter if she remembered the TV story from the day before. "Do you understand what happened to our lights today?" The girl said "Oh yes! The black came out and walked up the steps and turned off our lights just like on TV!"

Piaget's stages of cognitive development:

- Sensorimotor stage: birth–2 years.
- Preoperational stage: 2–7 years.
- Concrete operational stage: 7–11 years.
- Formal operations: 12 years and up.

In addition to their explanation of stages, Erikson and Piaget also shared the "constructivist" view that knowledge is constructed rather than simply absorbed. Another influential constructivist was Lev Vygotsky. He also highlighted the connection between the social aspects of adult–child interactions and the cognitive processing of new information. He believed that children learn new words and concepts through this connection between the actions of the teacher and the child's own mental actions. Vygotsky described "the zone of proximal development" as the range of information between what the child already knows and what is too much for them to learn at a given time. Within that zone, the role of the adult is to facilitate the child's exposure to new words and information that is manageable yet not too repetitive for the child. To do this, you must be very aware of what each child knows and is ready for (Pinter, 2017). The supports you provide are now known as "scaffolding" to gradually help the child progress from the familiar to increasingly advanced levels of new knowledge (Gullo & Graue, 2020). This means adapting your scaffolding supports to be culturally and linguistically appropriate to work for each child.

Howard Gardner contributed to our understanding of how to meet children's learning needs by describing what he called "multiple intelligences." These multiple areas where a child might have an elevated area of interest or talent that can help them learn in all the other areas (Pinter, 2017). While the notion that different people have different areas of specialized intellectual capacity, the existing of these intelligences has not been clearly proven in research (Gullo & Graue, 2020). More recently, other writers used this work to popularize an unsupported belief that children are born with particular, set learning styles. Some people describe themselves or children as "auditory learners" or "visual learners" but this not supported by research. Studies have shown that some people prefer certain types of information over others, but they change under changing circumstances. We also know that each person might learn some things better by listening and other things better by reading or watching (Nancekivell, Shah, & Gelman, 2019). Experts advise early childhood educators to use Gardner's theory of multiple intelligences to enhance the variety of experiences provided to each child and all children without labeling any child one way or another.

Gardner's Multiple Intelligences (Gullo & Graue, 2020):

- linguistic
- logical-mathematical
- spatial
- musical
- kinesthetic
- interpersonal
- intrapersonal
- naturalistic.

Behaviorists like B.F. Skinner took a different view of learning. Rather than describing different types or stages, Skinner believed that all behavior occurred and was repeated as a result of response to stimulus and the application of reinforcements or consequences. Skinner, along with other behavior theorists, expanded the understanding of how learning can happen due to outside influences (Gullo & Graue, 2020). Now we know that these positive and negative reinforcements can be used to enhance learning, but they are not the only factors that make learning happen. In your work with young children, you will encounter some times when a reward or consequence will change a child's behavior in desirable ways. But, you will face many more times when a reward or consequence seems to have no effect or the opposite of the intended effect. There are many factors at play in determining children's learning and behavior, and the consequences and reinforcements you provide will only be part of this picture. Your work will involve a balance of behavioral techniques and scaffolding children's active learning experiences.

A particular focus on infant development by John Bowlby led to "attachment theory." He found that infants depend on establishing a secure, safe relationship with their parent or caregiver to feel confident enough to explore what they find around them (Gullo & Graue, 2020). This theory has led to the modern practice in infant care to assign a primary caregiver to each infant so they form a bond that builds that valuable sense of confidence while away from their families. Other writers added to this understanding of infant development, including Magda Gerber and T. Berry Brazelton.

Measuring Curriculum Fidelity

When a curriculum is written and designed, research is done to ensure that using the curriculum will result in children's learning. Following a chosen curriculum faithfully and consistently is important to ensure desired outcomes for children. This is called "curriculum fidelity." Some curriculum publishers provide a curriculum fidelity checklist for individual educators or a whole grade or program to evaluate how well the curriculum is being used. You can do this yourself if you don't have a published curriculum fidelity measure. Either through self-reflection or partnering with others, make some observations about how closely you are following the scope and sequence and using the recommended strategies and materials.

Data gathered from child assessments can be compared to the curriculum implementation report to look for connections. For example, in a school where most teachers report not having time to do the math activities recommended in their curriculum, they also notice that the children's math scores are lower than expected. This is a strong indicator that additional attention is needed to shore up the math portion of the curriculum and that there may be a need for updated professional development (Bullard, 2020). This can be complicated because there is also a need to personalize lessons to meet the needs of individual children or to address an emergent curriculum event (Wein, 2014). Achieving the best balance between curriculum fidelity and responsiveness to individual needs should be established with colleagues and supervisors at your school.

Anti-bias Curriculum

This chapter has provided a lot of information about curriculum models, tools, and implementation – all things you can see and track. There is another component of the learning experience that is not as obvious. "Hidden curriculum" is a term we use to describe unwritten traditions, expectations, and biases in any learning environment. Many times, these are unintended messages that can be addressed when staff become aware. For example, a school may provide excellent supports for including all languages, abilities, and cultures, but their website might only have pictures of typically developing White children. Or a school might state a commitment to supporting children who are DLLs, but they have made no significant effort to recruit or hire bilingual teachers. A family childcare provider might have wonderful, engaging plans for the toddlers in their care, but might not realize that keeping the TV on in the background all day is interfering with children's attention and interaction. These are all things that require feedback and reflection, and a willingness to respond with appropriate changes.

One way to start is to take personal responsibility for looking carefully at what is visible in the environment. From the moment someone approaches the school or home, what will they see? What is on display? What words are used? What forms are provided? Are the races, languages, cultures, and abilities of the children and families represented throughout? Are there rules that may exclude some children and families? When the school gives an award to one student, what is the unspoken impact on all the other students? We can communicate almost as much by what we don't say as we do by what we do say. Do you ask children about their fathers when not all of them have a father currently in their household? Do you assume all families have exposed their children to Christmas or that all families are comfortable with the celebration of Halloween? Uncovering any hidden curriculum is a valuable exercise in working toward social justice. It is not an effort that should be done by an educator in isolation. Feedback from visiting colleagues, an anonymous suggestion box for families, or a friendly conversation with a neighbor may help you develop a greater sensitivity to the messages in your environment that should be changed to be more inclusive and effective. Can you think of a time when you first became aware of an example of a hidden curriculum?

While anti-bias actions and reflections are important to the growth and success of any educator, teachers must also see themselves as part of a community or system. You may encounter bias or discrimination happening around you in the workplace. Silent acceptance of inappropriate language or actions can be as harmful as committing these acts yourself. You will want to work with school leaders to develop a personal and shared understanding of how to handle examples of bias and what supports can be provided to enable change. According to Louise Derman-Sparks, Julie Olsen Edwards, and Catherine M. Goins in the second edition of their *Anti-bias Education* book, there are four goals that need to be part of anti-bias work in early childhood education (Derman-Sparks et al., 2020). Educators need to work toward supporting and respecting the identity of each adult and child, to celebrate the rich diversity in the class, school, and community, to uphold justice and fairness in play, learning, and work, and to adopt an active approach to making needed changes.

Engaging Families in Extending Curriculum

Throughout the early years, partnerships between families and educators ensure successful early learning experiences. Many curriculum publishers include specific guidance about engaging families in curricular extensions and provide handouts that can be sent home. Whether or not these are provided to you, consider how your own choices about working with family members can enhance the effectiveness of your curriculum. Newsletters about past lessons might not foster much engagement from families. Assignments and requirements for their time may also be overwhelming for some families. Always provide a choice of activities to be responsive to the needs of different families. Be sure to include information at the reading levels and in the languages needed by the families. Communicate with the children about what their families are receiving so they are able to make the connection between what they do at home and at school.

For infants, a curriculum extension might be sending families a song that you've been singing with the children, or texting them a picture you talked about with the children that day. For older children, you might send home copies of specific wordless books or stories that families can use in their home languages to support topics that are also being learned at your program. Some families of older children might be looking for home activities that seem like lessons. Other families will not enjoy that, or not have time for that. Another option would be to just send home a topic for conversation or an open-ended question the family could ask the child to bring a bit of the curriculum home.

You might also ask families to send things to school to enhance the cultural and linguistic responsiveness of the lessons and activities you plan. This two-way relationship engages both you and the families in a partnership with both sides contributing to learning within the guidelines of the curriculum. You will find lots of ideas in Chapter 7 to enhance your family engagement plan.

Curriculum Trends for the Future

Before the pandemic of 2020 caused so many school closings, curriculum writers did not have a reason to consider how their products would be used in remote learning formats. As schools began to open up, educators are having to adjust to a variety of formats. There will be all in-person classes, all online classes, and hybrid situations. The question becomes more than how you will handle teaching in those different formats, but also how will you implement your written curriculum in so many options. This also means that there will be a lot more technology hardware and software tools appearing on the scene. Children, families, and educators will all need training to use them and support to keep them working. It remains to be seen whether developers are ready to create learning technology that will provide equitable access to learning for all children.

Other trends to watch will include attention to equity and social justice to ensure that the zip code or postal code of a child's residence does not limit their early education options. As the diversity of languages continues to grow in young children, you are likely to see more resources and attention devoted to meeting the needs of multilingual learners and their families. Changes in funding may change the balance of private programs to school district or government funded programs for birth to age 5. Changes in funding often bring about changes in requirements, expectations, and accountability for outcomes. With these future trends in mind, being fully prepared to evaluate, choose, and implement new and changing curricula will be important for all early childhood educators.

Choose Your Own Path Check-In

Age/setting	Note examples of developmentally appropriate, linguistically responsive curricular activities for each of these settings
Infant care center	
Toddler play room	
Outdoor learning environment	
Family childcare home	
Open preschool/nursery classroom	
Kindergarten/reception classroom	
Academic primary classroom	
Space for individual or small group therapies	
Family education space	
Virtual learning	
Remote learning home environment	

Social Media Messages and Discussion Starters

- Nearly all early childhood curriculum models report having little or no supports for languages other than English and Spanish. What would you like developers to change?
- The universal design approach to early childhood curriculum involves proactively ensuring that every child has equitable access to learning. What's one strategy you use to make sure no child is left out of learning?
- All early childhood educators learn about the theorists that form the foundation of knowledge in our work, but can you think of an example of when you actually refer to a theorist during your lesson planning?

References

Brillante, P., & Nemeth, K. (2018) *Universal Design for Learning in the Early Childhood Classroom*, New York: Routledge.

Bullard, J. (2020) *Creating Curriculum in Early Childhood*, New York: Routledge.

Chang, F., Crawford, G., Early, D., Bryant, D., Howes, C., Burchinal, M., Barbarin, O., Clifford, R., & Pianta, R. (2007) Spanish-Speaking Children's Social and Language Development in Pre-Kindergarten Classrooms, *Early Education and Development*, 18 (2), 243–269.

Derman-Sparks, L., Edwards, J.O., & Goins, C.M. (2020) *Anti-bias Education for Young Children and Ourselves*, 2nd ed., Washington, DC: NAEYC.

Dickinson, D.K., & Porche, M.V. (2011). Relation between Language Experiences in Preschool Classrooms and Children's Kindergarten and Fourth-Grade Language and Reading Abilities, *Child Development*, 82 (3), 870–886.

Echevarria, J., Short, D.J., & Peterson, C. (2012), *Using the SIOP Model with Pre-K and Kindergarten English Learners*, Boston, MA: Pearson.

Gullo, D.F., & Graue, M.E., Eds. (2020) *Scientific Influences on Early Childhood Education*, New York: Routledge.

Hartl, S., & Riley, C. (2021) High-Quality Curriculum is a Transformation Tool for Equity, retrieved from www.ascd.org/el/articles/high-quality-curriculum-is-a-transformation-tool-for-equity.

Head Start (2015) Head Start Early Learning Outcomes Framework, retrieved from https://eclkc.ohs.acf.hhs.gov/interactive-head-start-early-learning-outcomes-framework-ages-birth-five.

Hirschler, J. (1994) Preschool Children's Help to Second Language Learners, *Journal of Educational Issues of Language Minority Students*, 14, 227–240.

Kagan, S.L., Reid, J.L., & Scott-Little, C. (2019) Diverse Children, Uniform Standards: Using Early Learning and Development Standards in Multicultural Classrooms, *Young Children*, 74 (5), 46–54.

Kaput, K. (2018). Evidence For Student-Centered Learning, St. Paul, MN: About Education Evolving.

Lewis, B., King, M.S., & Schiess, J.O. (2020) *Language Counts: Supporting Early Math Development for Dual Language Learners*, Sudbury, MA: Bellwether Education Partners.

NAEYC (2020) *Developmentally Appropriate Practice Position Paper*, Washington, DC: NAEYC.

Nancekivell, S.E., Shah, P., & Gelman, S.A. (2019) Maybe They're Born With It, or Maybe It's Experience: Toward a Deeper Understanding of the Learning Style Myth, *Journal of Educational Psychology*, 112 (2), 221–235.

NASEM (2017) *Promoting the Educational Success of Children and Youth Learning English: Promising Futures*. Washington, DC: The National Academies Press.

NCECDTL (2019) Organizing Learning Experiences, retrieved from https://eclkc.ohs.acf.hhs.gov/sites/default/files/pdf/dll-planning-organizing-thematic-instruction.pdf.

Paradis, J., Genesee, F., & Crago, M.B. (2021) *Dual Language Development and Disorders: A Handbook on Bilingualism and Second Language Learning*, 3rd ed., Baltimore, MD: Paul H. Brookes.

Pinter, A. (2017) *Teaching Young Language Learners*, 2nd ed., Oxford: Oxford University Press.

Reid, J.L., Kagan, S.L., & Scott-Little, C. (2019) New Understandings of Cultural Diversity and the Implications for Early Childhood Policy, Pedagogy, and Practice, *Early Childhood Development and Care*, 189 (6), 976–989.

Roberts, T. (2017) *Literacy Success for Emergent Bilinguals*, New York: Teachers College Press.

Shanahan, T., & Lonigan, C. (2015) The Role of Early Oral Language in Literacy Development, *Language Magazine*, retrieved from www.languagemagazine.com/5100-2.

Souto-Manning, M. (2013) *Multicultural Teaching in the Early Childhood Classroom: Approaches, Strategies, and Tools Preschool–2nd Grade*, New York: Teachers College Press.

U.K. Department of Education (2021) Statutory Framework for the Early Years Foundation Stage (Standards for Birth–Age 5 Being Revised for 2021), retrieved from https://assets.publishing.service.gov.uk/government/uploads/system/uploads/attachment_data/file/596629/EYFS_STATUTORY_FRAMEWORK_2017.pdf.

Wein, C.A. (2014) *The Power of Emergent Curriculum: Stories from Early Childhood Settings*, Washington, DC: NAEYC.

5 Meeting Individual Needs

Follow the Chapter 5 Roadmap with These Headings

Introduction	Disabilities and Delays
Teaching Individual Children	Supporting Each Child Through Transitions
Conversations for All	Challenging Behaviors
Personalizing in Remote Learning	Racial Equity and Anti-Bias Practices
Getting to Know Individual Children	Experiences of Stress and Trauma
Screening, Evaluation, and Assessment	Conclusion
How Schools Ensure Individual Needs Are Met	

Chapter 5 introduces approaches to meeting the individual needs of each learner. We use terms like "personalized learning," "differentiated instruction," or "individualized" planning. To build your understanding of the "why" and "how" of these efforts, this chapter describes key factors for consideration in teaching individual children. Strategies such as conversations for all and personalizing in remote learning are provided. The chapter then offers guidance for getting to know children as individuals, including the use of screening, evaluation, and assessment. School systems are discussed. The rest of the chapter covers specific circumstances that require your attention, such as children with disabilities and delays, supporting children through transitions, challenging behaviors, racial equity and anti-bias practices, and experiences of stress and trauma. These features are united by a common theme of preparing all early childhood educators to be ready for children from different experiences, cultures, abilities, and languages (DECAL).

> **Top Tips for Meeting Individual Needs**
>
> - Two-way, sustained conversations with each child are necessary to ensure they understand, to respond to their thoughts and questions, to encourage their critical thinking, and to give them opportunities to use new language and knowledge.
> - Informal and formal screening, assessment, observations, and information from families are all used to inform you about the individual interests and learning needs of each child so you can plan to differentiate.
> - When working via remote learning, meeting the individual needs of children is just as important as during in-person school, but may look different.
> - Multilingual children who have a genuine speech/language delay or disability will show it almost equally across both or all of their languages. If a child shows different levels of proficiency in their languages, this is likely due to different levels of exposure or practice.

DOI: 10.4324/9781003089216-5

> - Experiences of stress and trauma may have significant impact on language, learning, and classroom behavior. A strength-based approach emphasizes strengths and assets while supporting children's adjustment and learning progress.
> - When working with infants and toddlers, a primary caregiver should be assigned to each baby to provide a strong, responsive bonding relationship that is tuned in to the child's language development and prior experiences.
> - A screening or assessment that is only in English does not measure a child's "language development." It only measures their English development. No child assessment is accurate for multilingual children unless it addresses all of their languages.
> - All interventions, services, and education plans for young learners should include specific guidance about addressing their languages and cultures.

Introduction

Learning begins with the child. Each child is unique, so the experiences and materials that will help them grow and learn must be tailored for their particular needs. Working in early childhood in the 21st century places the responsibility for each child firmly in your capable hands. Teachers don't plan to only be effective with some children. In this case, the educator can transition from the traditional phrase "I'll do my best" and shift the focus to each of the children by saying "I'll be the best educator or caregiver or therapist for this child that I can be." With this focus in mind, you need to be well-informed and well-prepared to understand each child's needs and to meet each child's need to grow and learn.

Language is central to the work of meeting the individual needs. You will need language to communicate with families and children to identify the child's needs and interests. You will need language to develop relationships with families that keep you informed about the child's changing needs. You will need language to communicate your thoughts and feelings to the child and you need language to understand the child's expressions of thoughts and feelings. Two-way communication is necessary to have an ongoing, effective teaching and learning relationship with each child.

Focusing on each child as an individual is the most powerful way to ensure equity in early education. It targets your attention away from thinking about categories and groups, and keeps you thinking about each child as a person in their own right. This enables you to foster equitable access to learning in four critical ways:

- Getting to know an individual child's learning and language needs helps teachers ensure the child has *equitable access through comprehension and content.*
- Developing the ability to engage in a nurturing relationship with each child across differences in language and culture helps teachers ensure *equitable access through relationships.*
- Knowing a child well enough to encourage their independence and provide them with developmentally appropriate activities in any setting helps teachers ensure *equitable access through agency.*
- Respecting and responding to a child as an important individual who has a meaningful place among peers and adults in any setting helps teachers ensure *equitable access through belonging.*

> Equitable outcomes start with taking genuine interest in learning each child and family's story and getting to know them individually. (Use an interpreter if you need to!) Take on the role of learner with each relationship – learn the children's and families' backgrounds, community, interests, strengths, and goals. Reflect on how you can incorporate their unique qualities throughout the year, so they feel valued. This will serve as the foundation for a trusting and supportive relationship, and lead to the child's success.
>
> Dr. Deborah Mazzeo
> Early Childhood Teacher, Researcher, and Leader

We discussed the Universal Design approach in Chapter 3 as a way to set up an accessible and welcoming environment for all children and families. An open approach that anticipates children's needs can facilitate meeting the needs of each child. It is more effective to have a welcoming and prepared environment ready for every child than it is to have a less responsive setting that requires you to keep adding adaptations for particular children. To summarize the range of needs that Universal Design can help you to meet, we use the term "DECAL," meaning that all early educators should be prepared to work with children from different experiences, cultures, abilities, and languages.

> **What is DECAL?** Personalizing the learning experience involves addressing these categories:
>
> - **D**ifferences that make each child unique.
> - **E**xperiences and background that might include trauma, stress, and instability, as well as home literacy practices, prior group care or school experience, and the levels of support available at home.
> - **C**ultural factors influencing behavior, mood, interacting, learning, and responding to questions.
> - **A**bilities and differences such as advanced language ability or physical disability that would affect how the child learns, participates, and relates.
> - **L**anguages understood and spoken, and match between the educator's language and the child's language.

DECAL was created to acknowledge that early childhood educators are expected to be generalists, ready to teach any child that comes your way. You won't always have all the information you need about each child because they are so young, so you need to prepare to work with the child you see before you (Brillante & Nemeth, 2017).

Now let's examine how this could look in practice.

Teaching Individual Children

Infants and Toddlers

Working with infants and toddlers in group care settings or early intervention clearly demands careful attention to the characteristics and needs of each child. Even though they don't talk, you need to fill their environment with interesting, nurturing, and relatable language. You can ask families for the words and phrases they use to refer to the child's body parts and care routines so you can use words with each child that mirror what they hear at home. You may learn a familiar song for each child while also singing some songs with all the children together. You will find that you engage in more boisterous play with some children and take a quieter approach with others as you get to know them. And you will adjust your interactions as each child develops over time. Instead of upholding your "style" of infant or toddler interaction, you will focus more on the child's style and temperament and match to that. You will attend to what captures each child's interest both outdoors and inside. For example, when outside, some children might be fascinated by the birds and planes overhead. Others might be crouching to touch stones and insects. It is important to keep notes on all these choices and changes as they will inform your efforts to create personalized plans for each child. In turn, these plans can support your interactions with families and inform a substitute if you will be absent.

Another way to personalize interactions with infants and toddlers is to consider their experiences, recent as well as long-term. Since babies can't tell you how their morning went or how they are feeling, it is important to make time to connect with their family every time the child comes to you. Many programs have a "drop-off" procedure that invites the family member to come in with the child, take off their coats or outer clothes, and then change their child's diaper, if needed. This creates a gradual transition for the child from family member to teacher and gives the adults a few minutes to talk about what happened the previous evening or weekend, how the child slept, or whether the child will be picked up early for a doctor appointment. While this calming and communicative transition is very important for the child's adjustment, there will be times when it is just not possible. Create an alternative for those times such as a phone or text message check-in with a family member so you can be more aware of what the child needs that day.

> Good to know: Document everything you've learned about each child and what you do to support their individual learning – at any age. This will be a needed resource in case there is a substitute while you are absent or to share with families. Without documentation, all your information about each child goes with you if you are out or if you leave the position.

Considering a child's experiences also means celebrating their immediate and long-term milestones and positive experiences. For example, you might witness the infant's first steps, or learn from the family that their toddler is really good at climbing, opening doors, or imitating animal sounds. These positive experiences can be just as informative to your planning as challenging experiences.

Experts make a very important recommendation for those working with infants and toddlers. Since so much of their learning and development depends on a secure attachment with one or more adults, the practice of assigning a primary caregiver to each child is recommended. This means that the baby should have the opportunity to develop a stable, dependable relationship with one person while in childcare. This person will maintain regular communication with the family and get to know the child nearly as well as a family member in order to be responsive and supportive as the child learns and grows (Sosinsky et al., 2016). While it is also useful for the child to have positive interactions with a variety of staff members to get to know the adults in their daily environment, the focus should be on strengthening that special bond that respects the individuality of each child.

Ideally, the primary caregiver would speak the same language as the child's family to provide continuing support in the home language. If that is not possible, the primary caregiver should work closely with the family to learn songs, rhymes, and familiar terms to use with the child to build those language and cultural connections. This helps to support the baby's social-emotional development as well as their cognitive-language development (Nemeth, 2020). Strategies include talking to the baby and narrating what they are experiencing, speaking in a calm and positive tone, responding when the child vocalizes by echoing their sounds and expanding on their speech attempts, and playing with words, sounds, songs, rhymes, and stories. It is important to also leave plenty of space for the child to respond with vocalizations and actions. Be prepared to spend most of the time on the floor with the infant, following their lead as they explore toys and learning materials, and occasionally introducing new actions or materials. Use photo books or digital tools to show the child photos from home and talk about things that help the child feel connected to home while they are in your care (Nemeth, 2012).

Caregiving routines such as feeding and changing are excellent opportunities to focus on building that relationship. Always show the child respect by letting them know what is about to happen. You might say "I think your diaper is wet. You must feel a bit chilly. I will take you over to the changing table now" before interrupting the child's play to take care of this task. Caregiving routines also give you and the infant or toddler plenty of face-to-face interaction time where they can pay special attention to what you are saying as you perform the necessary actions.

Always keep in mind that infants and toddlers develop at their own pace. It is not the goal of infant/toddler care to try to accelerate that pace. There is no evidence that walking or talking early leads to learning advantages later on. Meeting each child's individual needs includes the practice of providing each infant and toddler with ways to practice existing skills and try out new ones without pressure from adults.

Preschool/Nursery

Working with children ages 3–5 years in preschool or nursery involves just as much responsibility for gathering information, organizing it, and finding ways to use it as working with infants and toddlers. However, as children grow and develop, their interests, abilities, language skills, experiences, and cultural awareness become more complex. So you need to pay attention to and address the complexities that influence what and how 3–5-year-old children learn.

Nurture a special relationship with each child by spending one-on-one time with them. This can happen in unexpected and authentic ways such as walking with them on a neighborhood trip, inviting them to help you clean up a spill, or grabbing a piece of paper and sitting by their side to draw pictures together. Being in proximity helps you and the child bond with each other and is as useful for learning each other's nonverbal language as it is for learning spoken language.

In quiet times – not in front of the group – ask the child to teach you something or tell you how to say words in their home language. Revisit a topic of conversation you've discussed with them previously. These are times when you can have deeper, multi-turn conversations that reveal more about the child that you can use to plan learning experiences going forward. And be sure to document these informal interactions as well.

When you are planning to present information to children to introduce a theme, project, or activity, be ready to personalize. Not all children will understand what you say. But keep in mind that your goal is not to present information. Your goal is to make sure each child understands the information. For example, you might show a video or learn some of the key words in the home languages of the children. Most of the time, you can accomplish your goal of reaching each child more effectively by using small groups rather than large groups such as circle time. Use assistants and well-trained volunteers during small group times to facilitate planned small group activities, especially if they speak the children's languages (Nemeth, 2009).

When children have delays or disabilities, they shouldn't be treated as if they are younger than they are. This is part of the individualizing experience. For example, some experts recommend arranging the bookshelf according to topics (e.g., bears), with different levels of books on the same topic. Instead of putting all the board books in one location, the bilingual books in another location, and the word-heavy books on a different shelf, put all the books about bears together so everyone can find the level they need (Brillante & Nemeth, 2017). Arrange the furnishings in the classroom so children can reach things for themselves and make choices of activities, snacks, materials using picture choices or sounds.

Staying in touch with each child's experiences is also important in the preschool years. Most programs have a sign-in procedure that invites arriving children to choose their name or write their name each day and put their belongings in a cubby. Your challenge will be finding ways to use that time to have a meaningful check-in. Having a child tap a picture of a face to indicate how they're feeling that day is not very useful. In the scurry of signing in and starting the day, we can't expect young children to reflect accurately and identify one name for one emotion that represents all of what they are feeling.

Aim, instead, for a brief conversation with a specific question. If you ask a young child how they are feeling, you may just get a random quick answer. But, if you ask them how they got to school this morning or what they saw when they first woke up, that may start a conversation that reveals how they are feeling. This approach is also helpful for those who may greet a child at other times of day for a therapy session or other individual meeting. Some children may arrive in groups or busloads. You might have a few calming activities ready for them to start on their own as they check in. You may not be able to talk to each child before they put belongings in their cubby, but plan to stop and chat with anyone you missed during that first morning activity. If the child is not able to tell you with words, you can make that morning connection by taking a moment to pause and observe their activity, using their body language to get an impression of how they are doing, and using your nonverbal skills to communicate that you see them and are there to help if needed.

It is also important to understand a child's broader experience. Children can be profoundly affected by continuing stress or sudden stressful events. There are some stress factors that seem obvious, but other events may cause stress in ways you may not expect. For example, a child who experiences unstable housing may be under constant stress that can affect their learning and behavior. Knowing this about the family can help you understand how to support and nurture the child with a clearly predictable routine. But a child who is used to taking the bus to school may become distraught if the bus is not available one day. This may not seem like an important event to an adult, but your goal is to understand how this might affect the child. Children may be affected by factors such as a change in sleep pattern, hunger, tooth pain, or family conflict in their morning. Continuing patterns of stress may also be a factor that shows up in unexpected ways. For example, a child with a family member experiencing mental illness or addiction may not report an event each day or may not be aware of their daily experience of anxiety or sadness, but these things may show up in lack of attention or challenges with self-control.

> A televised profile of children living in a high-poverty city featured a bright and cheerful 4-year-old who experienced homelessness with his mom. On his first day of kindergarten, he was asked a few screening questions to see if he knew numbers and counting. When asked: How many meals do we have a day?, he just blinked. He had no experience with set mealtimes called breakfast, lunch, and dinner. But he knew lots of other things that were not addressed in the checklist. How might you have handled your first encounter with that child?

Families and children need you to ask about and honor positive experiences as well. Finding out that a family with limited resources makes time to visit the library with the child every week or that a child who is new to English is spending afternoons playing in the garden of a neighbor who chats with them in English will give you great insights into how to reach this child and be open to observing what they know and can do.

Kindergarten/Reception

There is a lot of emphasis in our field on getting children ready for school, but the individualized view of education calls for schools to be ready for the whole range of children who will enroll. We do want to help 4-year-olds be prepared for the step up to greater academic and behavioral demands of kindergarten/reception, but we want to do this in ways that are developmentally, linguistically, and culturally appropriate (Pepper, 2017). This means appropriate for 4-year-olds in general as well as for each child's unique circumstances. All professionals who have contact with young children entering kindergarten/reception should have a deep enough understanding of child development to work effectively with children at any level of maturity, ability, language, and preparedness.

Some children may seem easier to be with than others. You may feel more comfortable with some children than others. Some educators may enjoy spirited children and others may feel they're at their best with multilingual children. We all have our own unique talents and interests just as the children do. But every child deserves the best that education and educators can offer them. When a child enters school, a ready program and ready educators can and will provide that. No child should be blamed or denied services when they are the right age for kindergarten/reception, even if they don't fit with some standard view of what a 5-year-old "should" be able to do.

When children enter kindergarten in the United States and reception in Great Britain, they may experience more screening and assessment than they did in the preschool years. They may be assigned to additional services such as speech therapy, classes for special educational needs, English language development assistance. If they attend class within a primary school, they will be subject to the expectations and resources that are provided by the government. Personalizing learning for these children will now include plans for helping them participate in government-funded services and follow government guidelines, while still supporting each child personally. Ideally, you will exchange information with all who work with each child and build collaborative teams that work together with a child's particular and complex needs in mind.

When a child qualifies for English language development services, all the professionals who work with that child should extend the value of those services by learning to include similar supports in their own work. Similarly, if a child is participating in occupational therapy to learn skills for getting dressed, other professionals can use those skills in games and dramatic play supplies to extend opportunities to practice.

On the other hand, there will be children who do not qualify for specialized instruction, but may still have different language or slight delay that requires adjustment in the general classroom. When you personalize instruction for children, don't think of them in separate, siloed categories like ESL/EAL vs. not ESL/EAL or special education vs. general education. Instead, recognize that individuals appear along a continuum in any area of categorization. The more you can learn about a child's daily and long-term experiences, the more you can fill in the gaps of your understanding about what that child needs. While they may not have a diagnosed disability, they may have experiences that interfere with their ability to participate in learning or social interactions.

In addition, the screening tools we use to identify services needed by young children are not perfect and they are rarely available in languages other than English. This can result in decisions that under- or over-identify children for needed services. So, all professionals that work with a child must know how to support all aspects of that child's learning and development regardless of placement decisions. This is not to deny the value of specialists in the field. Their expertise is vital to our work. Every educator is not meant to be an "expert" in everything. But all early childhood professionals share a deep understanding of early learning and development, and they can prepare to facilitate or extend the specialists' work and benefit from consulting with them.

In kindergarten and reception, any child learning in two or more languages continues to need encouraging opportunities to use and develop both/all their languages. Children with adverse experiences need understanding and patience. Children with positive experiences and special interests need to be recognized and allowed to express these strengths. Children with identified or potential disabilities need to feel included with their peers. All these statements link to one particular responsibility of early education: to help all children encourage each other, to be patient and understanding with each other, to recognize each other's strengths, and to help all their peers feel accepted and included. When you focus on meeting each child's individual needs, you also model what it means for each child to be a valued member of the school, community each of their peers is a valued member of the school community.

Primary Grades

What is the role of individualized instruction in primary grades and levels? When you work in first, second, or third grade, or in years 1, 2, and 3 in England, you will usually be expected to follow one or more established curricula that have been assigned by the school and that are aligned with state or national standards for primary learning. Yet the science tells you that you should find ways to meet the individual needs of each child to help them reach their potential (Pinter, 2017; Chumak-Horbatsch, 2012). Certainly, the primary grades are also populated by children who have a broad range of abilities, experiences, and behaviors that affect their learning. Here are some strategies based on the DECAL model.

Use the classroom furniture to encourage collaboration and helpfulness among the children so a child who is bilingual can help their friend who is newer to English (Honigsfeld, 2019). A child who is confident in math can help their friend who is struggling. Provide some settings that reduce excess stimulation for children who need to focus and areas to get away to recover from a stressful moment. Meet the children's physical needs in ways that support those who may not have those needs met at home, such as providing ample bathroom breaks, healthy snacks, and access to water.

Build in a way to check in with each child as an individual when the day begins. This goes beyond a quick greeting. Even at these ages, asking a child to say how they feel in one word or pointing to one image can be seen as superficial or inaccurate. We all have multiple layers of feelings and experiences. When you check in with a child, you need to be ready to follow up with celebration, acknowledgement, or help as needed. This may also help you notice something in the child's experience that may affect how they do that day. As children get older, their awareness of peer reactions grows. They don't want to be singled out for attention if they are having a difficult morning. Find subtle and respectful ways to offer support. For example, a child who did not get much sleep might have trouble staying on task, so you might ask them to help you erase a board or stack papers to give them a break from sitting and working.

Unlike earlier years, teachers may not have direct contact with families when the child arrives at school. Email and text messaging can be time-friendly ways to check in and get to know families and their experiences and invite their input. Make it clear that you are just as interested in the child's strengths and achievements as you are in knowing what might be challenging them.

In Chapter 2, we talked about Cummins's research (Cummins, 2000) showing that it takes most children seven or more years to fully develop academic fluency in a new language, and that is influenced by many additional factors in each child's life. This means that a child who is a dual language learner (DLL) will still need some support for learning and communicating in their home language (Chumak-Horbatsch, 2012). Providing a digital or picture dictionary for the child that connects their two languages can help. Adding sticky notes to a child's textbook with some key words translated can also help (Nemeth, 2009).

One strategy that helps children gain access to academic vocabulary needed for upcoming lessons is pre-teaching key vocabulary. Even if children are not yet fluent in the language of instruction or they experience delays in reading or comprehension, they still need to understand the words in the lesson to complete the lesson (Honigsfeld, 2019). Pre-teaching may include individual or small group discussion, visual prompts, or showing a peer how to help introduce key vocabulary and make sure everyone has an idea about what they mean (Skibbins, 2020). While peer language buddies can be an effective addition to the classroom format, make sure you provide some training or guidance beyond just saying "please help your friend understand what's in that paragraph" (Chumak-Horbatsch, 2012).

Even though you may have a very full curriculum in the primary grades, it is still a good idea to identify ways your curriculum honors the diversity in your school and community, and find ways to add diversity and cultural responsiveness. For example, you might set up displays and individual exploration areas for children to investigate during free times. Swapping out some purchased hands-on materials with natural materials or culturally relevant items from home will also add that element of connection for all the children.

Sign Language

Sign language is an active and visual support for language that can enhance communication for all young children. Additionally, you will see sign language used along with individual services to young children which might mean speech therapy, reading help, and occupational or physical therapy. These specialties require a lot of preparation and learning the science behind methods, and the details of the methods but that preparation may not prepare you for linguistic or cultural diversity. Yet, your intensive work with individual children will make that knowledge even more valuable. Again, you will be in the position of needing to introduce or explain an activity with the child, who may or may not understand what you say. Be prepared to enhance the ways you communicate. Even if you are working on a skill that seems to have little to do with language, still language will be the medium that makes it possible for you to do your work. Sign language, as discussed in other chapters, is an example of an adaptation that can help you communicate with children who are nonverbal or who speak a different language (Chumak-Horbatsch, 2012). Signs can be used in conjunction with spoken words to facilitate communication, enhance your ability to get the child to work on needed areas (Daniels, 1994).

Small Groups

For infants to age 5, you may have more flexibility in the group sizes you organize. This is important because researchers are clear in stating that whole group lessons, read alouds, and activities are generally less effective than smaller groups with young children, especially infants and toddlers. In large groups, children don't get as much time to talk, to fully express their thoughts, or to get responses that help them with their individual learning needs. Sometimes a large group activity was a success, but when educators watch a video, they realize it was a success for just some of the children while others were looking away, squirming, or otherwise not paying attention. As children move to the primary grades, they may have to spend more time in whole group listening and participation activities. When that happens, use scaffolds such as giving individual children the English and/or home language vocabulary they'll need to practice for the activity. Other ideas include preteaching some of the content, and assigning children to pair with a child who can help (López & Páez, 2021).

Another value of choosing small groups over large group instruction is that you can tailor the examples you use to engage children in learning new skills and content to fit their needs. For example, you might use zoo animals to illustrate sorting when doing a whole group activity, but not all of the children have been to the zoo. In small groups, you can use zoo animal examples for those who are interested, have a second group talking about the zoo animals in another language, and a third small group that is learning about sorting in the block area because block play has captured their interest.

Presenting Information

Adjusting how you present information to children is not always easy. We still see many instructors and writers giving teachers strategies and scripts that are not inclusive of children with different experiences, cultures, languages, or abilities (Pinter, 2017). Watch for red flag terms in articles, courses, and books. For example, when a curriculum guide or lesson plan tells you to "explain" or "describe" something to the children, you should ask, "How"? You need to know how to provide explanations and descriptions that are accessible to all children. You may need to simplify wording without simplifying the message. That means reducing the number of words used and relying on repeated sentence frames without making the message seem babyish in content. You may also need photos, videos, or demonstrations to show as well as tell (Chen, 2016). Some children, especially infants and toddlers, need to actively explore objects and materials with all their senses to fully understand.

Another kind of red flag guidance comes in the form of brief scripts that advise you to "tell the child this" or "ask the child that." These should not be taken literally. Consider these scripts as guides you would adjust to meet the language and ability needs of individual children. So instead of "tell the child ...," you might interpret this as "convey to the child using spoken words, sign language, visuals, or demonstrations." Is it possible to ask questions of a child who doesn't speak your language or who does not talk yet or talk much? Yes, it is.

Try learning to ask short questions in the home languages of the children, or in the target language and record responses for later translation. Practice signs for words like what, where, how, and why to introduce questions so all children are aware.

Conversations for All

Conversations are critical to early learning and language development. From birth, babies benefit when we play turn-taking games using our voices. As language develops, two-way conversations provide a needed platform for children to learn new words, practice using them in context, and build social relationships, as well (Shanahan & Lonigan, undated).

Conversations must be happening to get a high score on classroom observation tools such as the Classroom Language Assessment Scoring System, or CLASS. This tool collects observations of high-quality instructional interactions that arise from warm, nurturing relationships and encourages children to be curious explorers and learners. This is tied to research we discussed in Chapter 2 about the importance of oral language and the importance of receiving feedback from a responsive partner (Shanahan & Lonigan, undated). And in the context of our discussion here, a conversation is an ideal way to interact with an individual child. It allows you to provide information at the child's level in language they understand. It allows you to check for the child's understanding. It also allows the child to show you what they know and can do.

Think about the conversations you have with other adults. If someone just peppers you with questions that require one-word answers, you will soon lose interest or feel the questioner is not really interested in what you think. A true conversation involves both parties being engaged in topics of shared interest, where both express their thoughts and feelings, consider, analyze, and respond to the information being shared. We want nothing less for conversations with children. In addition to upholding these valuable features of conversations, educators also try to embed content and vocabulary that are part of their lesson plans and support activities.

Educators often wonder how to have conversations with children who are not speaking or who speak a different language. The key is to be truly present with the child. Get down on their level, block out distractions, and focus intentionally on the child so you can pick up any and all ways they use to interact with you. If they are engaged in an activity like playing with clay, doing a puzzle, or practicing writing their name, you can go along and do the same activity with them or beside them, exchanging looks and gestures to invite the child to show you what they are doing. Learn a few open-ended questions in the home languages of the children or sign language, then be prepared with a voice translation app or a recording device so you can record to find out later what was discussed. Provide scaffolding to help the child respond in English when possible.

You can also support children to have more effective conversations with each other when they don't have the same language or language skills. Researchers have identified three behaviors that facilitate peer conversations with diverse participants; young children can learn them easily. Help your students:

- speak slowly so their peer can understand them;
- be patient and give their peer a chance to understand their question and think how to answer; and
- use pointing and gestures to show their peer what they want the peer to know.

Conversations are so important for language and learning that some educators actually count them. Consider making a list of the children in your care or caseload and marking each time you have a sustained conversation with a child. Teachers report noticing they had more conversations with some children than others, and no conversations with some children during an entire week. Tracking these events helps you to identify trends and changes you want to make.

Personalizing in Remote Learning

We have discussed many ways to personalize learning for young children. Remote learning can provide several advantages for getting to know each student and responding to their individual needs. Since families generally have to provide all or some support for young children to participate in online classes, educators get a chance to observe more of those family interactions. You might learn about some things the child can do at home that you might not see in school. And you can build your relationship with the child while they are in the comfortable setting of their own home. Without the pressure of managing the behavior of a whole group of children, you can really concentrate on working directly with each child alone or in small groups online.

For infants and toddlers, remote learning generally means that the teacher or early interventionist will reach out to the family members to support their interactions with their child. You can demonstrate how to tell family stories to engage infants in any language or show families how to narrate play when toddlers are playing with their toys. Older toddlers are more likely to be able to interact across screens and recognize you after several visits. They may even remember you and ask for you when the screen is turned off. These are signs that you are building a valuable relationship with the child remotely.

Children who are 3 and 4 years old begin to use the features of the computer or handheld device with more confidence, but still need adult support. Their need for active, hands-on learning is the same as when they are in person. Many, if not most, so-called learning games have not been evaluated by independent researchers to uphold the claim that they result in actual learning. Just because a game has numbers in it doesn't mean it actually results in sustained math learning. Choosing apps and computer games for preschoolers takes a critical eye. Look for apps that support developmentally appropriate learning activities such as creative, open-ended drawing or storytelling. If they claim to teach content, look for a minimum of glitz and noise, and look for activities that promote active thinking and problem solving with meaningful content. Avoid random, unrelated bits and pieces that look like math problems or memorizing. A better focus is to interact directly with children, engaging them in story reading and story acting, or exploring and experimenting with authentic items. Use the screen as a window to relationship building and problem solving. When children do not speak the same language as the teacher or specialist, they may benefit from a greater balance of supported work directly with their family members so they can develop the strong foundation of knowledge and skills in the home language before transitioning to English (Pinter, 2017).

Children who are 5–8 years old may be able to handle working independently for some screen time, or working directly with the teacher or specialist without family help. Even though they may benefit from more time with peers learning and discussing together, it is also important for you to have those all-important conversations with each child or in small groups so you can make sure they are learning and find out what they understand and can use. It may seem more efficient for you to conduct whole group lessons, but shorter times with smaller groups may ensure stronger learning foundations and greater individualization.

As with in-person learning, prepare to present information with a variety of demonstrations, videos, and home language supports. You might pre-teach needed vocabulary by sending the words home to families who can explain their meanings to children before the lessons start. Lessons and projects using similar materials and content help children at a variety of levels to have the extended time they need to work with new words and concepts and build both their home language and English development.

As you can see, this section on personalizing remote learning weaves the role of family members throughout the recommendations. This serves as a reminder of how helpful families can be as their child's first teacher and greatest cheerleader. On the other hand, when considering each child's experiences, you should be aware that some home environments are not conducive to remote learning. Families sometimes resist having their home visible during online learning. Adults may be juggling their own work and supporting learning for multiple children on limited devices and wi-fi signal. A personal conversation with each family to find out what they are comfortable with is warranted before remote learning starts.

Getting to Know Individual Children

Information about children forms the foundation for all individualized teaching and learning. There are five main avenues for you to gather that information: formal records, observing children, interviewing or surveying families, tests and screeners, and asking the children about themselves.

Child records might come from their previous care or school setting as well as early intervention or special education services. You will also want to see each child in person to understand their choices, interests, motivations, abilities, temperament, and more. Child observations should be detailed, objective, and specific (Chen, 2016). This not the time to make generalizations. These are not observations: "This child is always in a bad mood." Or "This child hates to go outdoors." Or "I think the parents always baby that child and now he's spoiled." Objective observations simply describe exactly what you see and hear, marking day, time, and context. First, capture several objective observations at different times and in different contexts, then you might begin to interpret the information you have. Try to avoid stereotypes like "All American Indian girls act like that." Keep an open mind in case there is another explanation for what you see. For example, a child who is not speaking in the class of 4-year-olds might have hearing impairment, or they might not speak the language of the class, or they may be experiencing serious stress, or they may have a developmental delay. Combine careful observation notes about exactly what you see, when, and under what circumstances with interviews with family members. Work as a team with family members to decide on a few focused strategies, then try them, take more observation notes, and adjust your strategy.

Asking families for information about their child begins at the moment of enrollment. Some basic information can be found on the school's enrollment forms. More in-depth information is acquired over time within the context of the growing relationship between educator and family. Ask families manageable questions in simple, clear language or translated into their own language. Always keep a positive tone that demonstrates respectful interest in the child without invading the family's privacy (Chen, 2016). Finding out information about the child when the family comes in for a family–teacher conference at the end of the first child assessment, grading period, or half-term is much too late in the process. There should be ongoing phone contact, in-person contact at school or at a public meeting place, or video chatting to build the relationship while also getting information that can help you teach each child.

Screening, Evaluation, and Assessment

Screening and Evaluation

Developmental screening is usually standard procedure whenever children are enrolled in early childhood care, education, or services. In Head Start programs and other government funded programs, screening is required within the first six weeks of school. Used in addition to information from families and observations of the children, purchased screening tools are meant to provide a brief report of a child's language and development at that moment to determine if further evaluation is needed. To be as accurate as possible, purchased screening tools should be administered exactly as directed. They should also be culturally and linguistically appropriate for the children (Chen, 2016). But since very few screening tools are available in languages other than English, programs often have to make adaptations such as hiring and training interpreters, engaging and training bilingual volunteers, asking adult family members for help, or changing some of the items in the screener to be more recognizable. Each of these steps might reduce the accuracy of the screener as it was originally written but will give a more informal and relevant picture of the child's status.

If the screening results indicate a child's language is not at the level expected for their age, further evaluation will be needed to determine if this is due to a language difference or a true disability. With a family's written permission, the child will be referred for more intensive evaluation, placement decisions, and, if needed, an Individual Family Service plan (IFSP) (for children up to 3 years old) or an Individualized Education Program (IEP) for children ages 3 years and up in the United States. In England, children who are identified as having Special Educational Needs and Disabilities (SEND) when they are aged 5 and under received some services as described on the UK Schools and Education website (Gov.uk, 2021). From age 5 through 15, children with disabilities will be covered by an Education, Health, and Care Plan (EHC plan). Supports and EHC plans are developed based on observations and an assessment of each child. This process is more than just one test – it relies heavily on multiple measures including family input and teacher observations.

WIDA Assessments for Language

WIDA is the organization that has developed language development standards for preschool through grade 12 in the U.S. Most states have now adopted the WIDA standards in their official policies for teaching children who are English learners. WIDA has also developed widely used language screening tools and assessments, including the WIDA MODEL for kindergarten and the ACCESS test for grades 1–12. These assessments include reading, writing, listening, and speaking, but they are not designed for use during remote learning.

Language differences result in widely varying practices regarding decisions for young children. Some programs tend to under-identify children with developmental delays or disabilities because they are not sure if they are seeing a language difference or a true disorder (Bevan, 2018; Paradis, Genesee, & Crago, 2021). But delaying evaluation until the child is more fluent in English may make the child wait for many months before getting needed services. When special services or therapies are needed, it is always better to start early.

If the school is concerned that the early intervention program or special educational services are not appropriate for a child with additional language who may be struggling, those programs should be examined and improved to create a better fit for diverse children. If a young child is identified for special services, and they begin to catch up to their peers, it may have been true that the child really didn't qualify for those services, but they can be provided in such a way as to help the child progress until a better understanding can be reached. Many times, children who receive IFSP services or preschool special education are given the boost they need to exit from the program altogether.

Some schools over-identify children for special services (Bevan, 2018; Paradis, Genesee, & Crago, 2021). This may indicate they don't have confidence in the general education teachers to support children who are DLLs, or it may be a sign that some staff view understanding and speaking an additional language as a weakness. To further complicate things, there are times when stress and trauma experiences can affect a child's development in ways that might be temporary or permanent. So, in addition to language differences, knowns and unknowns about a child's home life might also be at play. The work of making important placement decisions about young children must be collaborative and inclusive of families across disciplines to get the full scope of what is known about the child's needs.

Assessment

> As teachers assess young DLL children's skills and capabilities, they need to understand what children can demonstrate with and without the use of language.
> (López & Páez, 2021, p. 126)

Ongoing assessment, or formative assessment, measures how and what the child is learning within the curriculum. This can be formal or informal. For infants and toddlers, it may be a question of carers making notes about children's behaviors that demonstrate milestones or benchmarks such pointing to objects, responding to requests, or saying a word. In preschool, assessment generally takes the form of recording anecdotes and samples of the child's language and work for their portfolio. Older children begin to experience quizzes, assignments, and other forms of more formal grading of their progress. These are all ways of learning more about how far each child has progressed, where they might have gaps, and what they need next.

This is important information to document and plan for a personalized approach to each child's learning. It should include information about what a child knows and can do in both of their languages.

How Schools Ensure Individual Needs Are Met

IEP/IFSP

Children identified to have significant delays or disabilities will receive services described in one of these plans. According to the Council for Exceptional Children Division for Early Childhood, these plans must be culturally and linguistically responsive to meet each child's needs.

ESL/EAL/ELD

When children are identified below the school's or government's level of English proficiency, they may be placed in a bilingual education class or English as a Second or Additional Language class that focuses on teaching English by providing general language supports and may have multiple languages. They may also receive English as a Second or Additional Language services where a specialist teacher sees the child briefly once a week, or comes in to co-teach with the general education teacher, or provides consultation to the general education teacher instead of direct services to the child. These are all options for classroom formats, but we must keep in mind that research clearly shows the importance of supporting each child's culture. So, whether the child is placed in a fully bilingual class or a class that focuses on teaching English, and regardless of their age or ability, children should experience an environment that respects and uses their home language and culture in meaningful and continuing ways.

Positive Behavior Supports

Positive Behavior Supports (PBS) and other systems for addressing challenging behaviors emphasize a personalized approach for each child that takes into account cultural and linguistic impacts on behavior.

Response to Intervention

Response to Intervention (RTI) is a system used in many primary schools and some preschools in the U.S. to address behavioral issues before they cause the child to experience gaps in progress that might lead to placement in special education. The value of PBS and RTI approaches is that they both work intensively with the individual child and support the teacher while paying close attention to what situational experiences might be contributing to the child's challenges so that supports can also be offered to the families.

Before- and After-School Programs and Clubs

In some places, these out-of-school-time experiences go beyond mere supervision. They may flexibility outside of required curricula to allow children to pursue their interests, build social skills, practice language, and get homework help.

> A London primary school offered after school care in the form of special interest clubs so children could join a cooking club, an outdoor game club, or a puzzle club. Bilingual staff were recruited to meet the language needs of the groups, and one-on-one aides were hired when needed to assist a child with disabilities to be included in the group.

A significant amount of research has demonstrated that children who are learning in two languages often use both of their languages within one sentence. This is code-switching and it is considered a sign of linguistic and cognitive competence. It means that multilingual children are able to pull words from any of their language systems to create meaningful communication – and it happens in an instant. Researchers recommend that adults should not model code-switching as children need to hear language models that demonstrate fully correct sentences in each language. Recent research has paid more attention to code-switching and is now using the term "Translanguaging" to describe this process in the context of learning. These researchers are finding evidence that this process is a natural way for the brain to develop fluency in both languages and it should be built into the school day with intention and documentation (López & Páez, 2021; Garcia & Wei, 2016). In the future, we may see translanguaging classrooms as a formal category of English language development services.

Disabilities and Delays

Whether growing up with one language or more, children who also experience delays and disabilities depend on the supports educators provide for their language development. They also depend on educators to plan ways to use language that will help them learn and grow in all areas and domains (Bevan, 2018; Brillante, 2018; Paradis, Genesee, & Crago, 2021). Here are some strategies and approaches to try.

Speech and Language Delays and Disabilities

When children have true speech or language disability, it will appear equally in both of their languages. If you find that a child seems behind in one language but on target in the other, it is likely that they are just working on learning both languages at difference speeds. When it has been determined after screening and evaluation that a multilingual child has a speech/language delay or disability, be sure to provide strong, intentional, and comprehensible input in both languages. Watch for the child's responses to determine which of your strategies seems to work the best. Classroom teacher, ESL/EAL teacher, special education teacher, and speech therapist should all work together to create a cohesive plan for the child.

Autism Spectrum Disorders

When a child is on the autism spectrum and has two or more languages, it may seem overwhelming to support both or all languages, especially if the child is not verbal. Keep in mind they have had plenty of language exposure in their environment. If the child is not yet verbal, you won't know which language or what topics are retained by and familiar to the child, so it will be important to continue providing stimuli in both or all languages. It may help to do this on a very clear schedule rather than randomly trying words here and there. For example, let the child know that you will use Spanish during free play and English when reading stories. All language input should be carefully planned, repeated, and enhanced by additional supports.

Intellectual Disabilities, Attention Deficit Disorders, and Learning Disabilities

Recalling that research shows children at all ability levels benefit from ongoing support of both of their languages, along with culturally relatable content, plan ahead for materials, books, and activities that match the languages and experiences of each child to help them stay focused and to progress.

Vision, Hearing, and Physical Disabilities

Language supports are also very important for children with vision, hearing, and physical disabilities. You will need to consider how to use enhancements such as assistive technology, braille, and sign language in ways that make sense to each child. These strategies need to be linguistically and culturally appropriate to help children make strong learning and communication connections.

Supporting Each Child Through Transitions

Young children experience so many transitions, and yet transitions are some of the most difficult things for young children to cope with. There are transitions in the daily schedule, transitions from home to school or care, transitions from one class or program to the next, and transitions from preschool to kindergarten (or nursery to reception in the U.K.). Supporting children through transitions is an important component of personalized learning. Upsetting transitions cause a great deal of stress and can set a child's progress back. This stress and interference with learning can be prevented with careful attention to transitions, both large and small.

The first step in supporting any child through transitions is to look at the situation through the child's eyes. For example, you may look at the clock and realize it's lunch time, but the child may be in the middle of the best block tower they ever built. You may think moving from the infant room to the toddler room next door in the same building is not such a big deal, but a child may be experiencing outside stress that makes coping with this additional change very upsetting. With the personalized focus on what's happening with each child, your approaches to transitions can improve a great deal.

Try to keep a predictable schedule so all children have a comforting sense of what's happening next. When it is time to move from one room to another or out to the playground, consider how you can minimize empty wait time that leads to boredom and acting out. Turn waiting times into game and conversation times, and plan ahead so there is less time to wait. Be sure to give children advance notice that a transition is about to happen. Use words and nonverbal signals to let children know what is happening. For example, play or sing the same tune every day at clean up time or at bathroom time. To reduce confusion and stress, learn some transition time words in children's home languages.

Be aware that a child entering your program or class may be away from their family for the first time, or they may be switching from a familiar school or beloved caregiver. As an adult, you may know that everything will work out fine, but the young child has no idea if they will be safe, welcomed, or competent in the new place. Now imagine if that child is not able to communicate in the new setting. It can take weeks or months before shared language and mutual understanding are established. Imagine what it would be like to be a young child who is away from home for the first time in a place that doesn't understand you and you don't understand the adults or the children. Young children need to be fully supported from the very first day of any transition because their first experiences of terror or comfort set the stage for how they will do in the new environment.

One strategy is to learn a few key words in the home language to make the child feel safe and comfortable on the first day. Not only does this help the child understand and be understood, but it also communicates that you are interested in the child's comfort and care enough to try using those words and learning more. Ask family members to teach you how to say the words the way they say them to the child. Also ask the family and the prior teacher or carer to share some of the child's interests with you.

> A child with cerebral palsy and some cognitive delay was assigned to a new year 2 class in a new building where nobody knew him. Fortunately, the new teacher reached out to the previous teacher and asked what they could suggest to help the boy feel more comfortable on his first day. They learned that trains were the boy's favorite topic of conversation and that he felt knowledgeable, competent, and calm when talking about them. So, the new teacher made sure there were several books about trains waiting at his assigned desk when he wheeled into his new class the first day. The teacher did not demand the boy follow the full schedule, but allowed him some quiet reading time until he felt comfortable talking to the teacher and some seatmates about interesting train facts. The other children were impressed and asked him several questions.

Challenging Behaviors

At major professional conferences, the sessions on changing challenging behavior often have the biggest audiences. Clearly, early childhood educators are puzzled by a lot of children's behaviors that challenge them. As with many of the other topics we've covered, a child's challenging behavior is more likely a sign that something in the teaching environment or practices needs to change than something in the child that needs to be "fixed." For example, when routines and rules in a child's home don't match what's expected in care or school, this can result in a variety of acting out behaviors. A child who is never put down for a nap at home may not know how to handle nap time in school when everyone is told to lay down and be quiet. This kind of mismatch may result from cultural norms or individual family habits.

One thing we do know is that young children use behavior to communicate (Brillante, 2018). They may not always be conscious of it, but their behavior carries a message. An infant who keeps crying even after being fed and changed is clearly trying to get another need met. A child who runs away from circle time in preschool/ nursery may be expressing frustration because he doesn't understand the teacher's language and he's bored sitting there gaining nothing.

The two most effective steps to take are to prepare in advance to meet the linguistic, cultural, and developmental needs of the child before their behavior gets out of control, and carefully observe and interact with the child to try to determine what their behavior is trying to tell you. Listen first, consider the cultural and experiential factors that might be included, then support the child in ways that would calm the behavior and prevent it from happening again (Kaiser & Sklar, 2019). For example, if a child is acting out because they don't understand what is being said, you can do more to help them understand in future so there will be less need to act out. If the child seems to act out around nap time, ask the family about routines they use to help the child get ready for sleep so you can mirror their practices.

Finally, remember that comparing children to each other or singling a child out for an award or demerit are ways that might have more negative effects than positive. Preventing challenging behaviors by anticipating and responding to each child's needs will bring the best results.

Racial Equity and Anti-bias Practices

We addressed the issue of racial equity and anti-bias practices in Chapter 1. We include this topic here as well because racial equity depends on being able to view each child as an individual. For example, in the past few years, much attention has been given to important research showing that African American boys were most likely to be suspended or excluded (Gilliam et al., 2016) from early care and education. It was important to understand this was happening so that early educators and programs could change their perspectives, behaviors, practices, and policies to better meet the needs of young boys of color. The downside was that in developing responses and resources to improve the situation, African American boys were lumped together as a homogeneous group. Many young boys of color are highly active during the day, but not all of them are. So, in your efforts to prevent inequity, be careful not to lean the other way and show preference to an entire group or category of children. Developing habits of cultural humility, openness to learning, and respecting each individual child and family will also help you prevent bias in your own teaching.

Experiences of Stress and Trauma

Many young children experience stress and trauma in their lives. Factors like poverty, food insecurity, and fear of institutions may impact immigrant families at a higher rate than native born families (NASEM, 2017). These factors also affect African American families, American Indian and Alaskan Native families. This information is important to know but does not replace the need to get to know each family and child. We call this a "trauma-informed approach" to teaching: "Stress and adversity expressed by children undermine learning and impair physical development" (Institute of Medicine and National Research Council, 2015, p. 4).

In their book, *Beyond Crisis: Overcoming Linguistic and Cultural Inequities in Communities, Schools, and Classrooms* (Zacarian, Calderón, & Gottlieb, 2021), the authors highlight the recent newsworthy issues of inequity such as uneven responses to natural disasters and the pandemic. They gathered voices from the field to report on strength-based approaches to helping children cope with stress and trauma. This "strength-based approach" has been developed to step away from devaluing people by focusing on adversity. While children do suffer from adversity, the conversation should always begin by honoring the strengths they do bring to care and school. Language and culture play important roles in all of the supports we provide to children and families. The first step in helping is always to listen. Start by "identifying strengths, and needs" (Zacarian, Calderón, & Gottlieb, 2021, p. 20). Solutions should only be developed with input from all involved. Seeking and supporting this input requires a culturally and linguistically responsive approach to reciprocal communication (Zacarian, Alvarez-Ortiz, & Haynes, 2017).

Conclusion

This chapter on personalizing learning to meet children's individual needs covers many complex issues. However, they can be summarized by recognizing your commitment to DECAL as you identify and implement strategies for teaching children from birth to 8 years, with different experiences, cultures, abilities, and languages. You will succeed at meeting these complex needs by being open to understanding each child and family, and by being prepared with a strong background of knowledge and skill to inform your work.

Choose your Own Path Check-In

Age/setting	*What information would you want to receive from or provide to each of these early childhood professionals to ensure that a particular child will have the best possible personalized learning experience?*
Infant care center	
Toddler play room	
Outdoor learning environment	
Family childcare home	
Open preschool/nursery classroom	
Kindergarten/reception classroom	
Academic primary classroom	

Age/setting	What information would you want to receive from or provide to each of these early childhood professionals to ensure that a particular child will have the best possible personalized learning experience?
Space for individual or small group therapies	
Family education space	.
Virtual learning	
Remote learning home environment	

Social Media Messages and Discussion Starters

- What is a strategy you use that helps young children who are DLLs communicate with you and each other?
- Did you know? To distinguish between a language delay and a language difference, assess a child's progress in both of their languages. If their progress is similar in both or all languages, then the delay is probably due to an underlying cause.
- Did you know? You need to perform screening and assessment for young children in each or any of their languages to determine if they have a language delay or language difference … But there are no available tools in languages other than English and Spanish?

References

Bevan, A. (2018) *English as an Additional Language (EAL) in Practice: Supporting the Language and Communication of EAL Learners in the Early Years*, London: Practical Preschool Books.

Brillante, P. (2018) *The Essentials: Supporting Young Children with Disabilities in the Classroom*, Washington, DC: NAEYC.

Brillante, P., & Nemeth, K. (2017) Teaching Emergent Bilingual Learners with Disabilities and Challenging Behaviors in Preschool, *Journal of Multilingual Education Research*, 7, article 5, 41–58.

Chen, J. (2016) *Connecting Right from the Start: Fostering Effective Communication with Dual Language Learners*, Lewisville, NC: Gryphon House.

Chumak-Horbatsch, R. (2012), *Linguistically Appropriate Practice: A Guide for Working with Young Immigrant Children*, Toronto: Toronto University Press.

Cummins, J. (2000) *Language, Power, and Pedagogy: Bilingual Children in the Crossfire*, Clevedon, U.K.: Multilingual Matters.

Daniels, M. (1994) The Effect of Sign Language on Hearing Children's Language Development, *Communication Education*, 43 (4), 291–298.

Garcia, O., & Wei, L. (2016) *Translanguaging: Language, Bilingualism and Education*, New York: Springer.

Gilliam, W., Maupin, A.N., Reyes, C.R., Accavitti, M., & Shic, F. (2016) *Do Early Educators' Implicit Biases Regarding Sex and Race Relate to Behavior Expectations and Recommendations of Preschool Expulsions and Suspensions?* New Haven, CT: Yale University Child Study Center.

Gov.uk. (2021) Children with Special Educational Needs and Disabilities (SEND), retrieved from www.gov.uk/children-with-special-educational-needs/special-educational-needs-support.

Honigsfeld, A. (2019) *Growing Language and Literacy: Strategies for English Learners*, Portsmouth, NH: Heinemann.

Institute of Medicine and National Research Council (2015) *Transforming the Workforce for Children Birth Through Age 8: A Unifying Foundation*, Washington, DC: National Academies Press.

Kaiser, B., & Sklar, J.R. (2019) Valuing Diversity: Developing a Deeper Understanding of all Young Children's Behavior, *Teaching Young Children*, 13 (2).

López, L.M., & Páez, M.M. (2021) *Teaching Dual Language Learners: What Early Childhood Educators Need to Know*, Baltimore, MD: Paul H. Brookes.

NASEM (2017) *Promoting the Educational Success of Children and Youth Learning English: Promising Futures*, Washington, DC: The National Academies Press.

Nemeth, K. (2009) *Many Languages, One Classroom: Teaching Dual and English Language Learners*, Lewisville, NC: Gryphon House.

Nemeth, K. (2012) *Many Languages, Building Connections: Supporting Infants and Toddlers who are Dual Language Learners*, Lewisville, NC: Gryphon House.

Nemeth, K. (2020) Rocking and Rolling: Nurturing Infants and Toddlers with Diverse Language Experiences, *Young Children*, 75 (2).

Paradis, J., Genesee, F., & Crago, M.B. (2021) *Dual Language Development and Disorders: A Handbook on Bilingualism and Second Language Learning*, 3rd ed., Baltimore, MD: Paul H. Brookes.

Pepper, A. (2017) *Kick-Start Kindergarten Readiness*, Lewisville, NC: Gryphon House.

Pinter, A. (2017) *Teaching Young Language Learners*, 2nd ed., Oxford: Oxford University Press.

Shanahan, T., & Lonigan, C. (undated) The Role of Early Oral Language in Literacy Development, retrieved from www.languagemagazine.com/5100-2.

Skibbins, H. (2020) *6 Key Considerations for Supporting English Learners with Distance Learning*, Sobrato Early Academic Language (SEAL).

Sosinsky, L., Ruprecht, K., Horm, D., Kriener-Althen, K., Vogel, C., & Halle, T. (2016). *Including Relationship Based Care Practices in Infant-Toddler Care: Implications for Practice and Policy*, brief prepared for the Office of Planning, Research and Evaluation, Administration for Children and Families, Washington, DC: U.S. Department of Health and Human Services.

Zacarian, D., Alvarez-Ortiz, L., & Haynes, J. (2017) *Teaching to Strengths: Supporting Students Living with Trauma, Violence, and Chronic Stress*, Washington, DC: ASCD.

Zacarian, D., Calderón, M.E., & Gottlieb, M. (2021) *Beyond Crises: Overcoming Linguistic and Cultural Inequities in Communities, Schools, and Classrooms*, Thousand Oaks, CA: Corwin Press.

6 Environment and Materials

Follow the Chapter 6 Roadmap with These Headings

Introduction	Learning Connections with Technology
Designing Learning Environments	A Welcoming Entrance
Health and Safety	Furnishings and Learning Centers
Universal Design	Learning Outside the Classroom
Culturally Responsive Environments	Strategies and Practices to Enhance the Learning Environment
Following Children's Interests	Conclusion

The environment and materials create the setting for early learning. Chapter 6 explores the many aspects of planning and using culturally and linguistically diverse classroom materials. The chapter covers designing learning environments with health and safety in mind, using a proactive universal design approach. Important components of learning environments will be covered in sections on culturally responsive choices and following children's interests. Setting up the furnishing and designs are addressed with respect to learning connections and technology, a welcoming entrance, and the furnishings and set-up of learning centers. Outdoor learning and special practices are discussed at the end of the chapter.

> **Top Tips for Planning Environment and Materials**
> - The placement of furniture can make a significant difference in young children's learning experiences. Loud areas should not be next to quiet areas. Art areas should be near a sink, and there should be plenty of space for multiple children to use each area.
> - Choose items that represent the authentic experiences of the children in each group to infuse their culture into the environment.
> - Plan proactively to use furnishings and learning materials that provide access to learning for all children, such as picture communication boards, rather than treating differences as problems that have to be solved later. This is *universal design for learning*.
> - Classroom labels do not add to environmental print if no one mentions them. Swap out traditional labels for new ones with words and phrases that can be conversation starters in the languages of the classroom.
> - Avoid stereotypes in early learning environments. Ask families what is meaningful for them and their children.

DOI: 10.4324/9781003089216-6

- Avoid language tokenism in early learning environments. Just teaching "hello", or the colors and numbers in another language does not facilitate true communication. Aim for words and phrases that you and the children will use in learning and play.
- Cultural items that are not used for meaningful learning do not really add to the diverse experiences in early childhood education. Be sure to talk about, demonstrate, or in some way put culturally relevant items to use.
- Culturally and linguistically appropriate items can be brought from home or found in the community at libraries, or from community contributors.
- When it's not possible to bring culturally and linguistically relevant items physically into the classroom, they can still be part of learning via photos or videos.
- The early learning environment should be dynamic and should grow with the children. Puzzles they found challenging in September will get boring after a few months, so replace them with more challenging examples. Always keep some familiar items available but others should be changed regularly to maintain interest.

Introduction

The environment provides a general context for teaching and learning. It also includes tools, materials, and displays that will be used in planned and spontaneous activities. In this chapter we will talk about overall approaches to classroom design along with specific choices of objects and equipment. Some basic principles guide environment planning across ages and settings. Other guidance will address particular ages of children or types of early care and education formats. Ideally, you will begin planning each learning environment with language in mind. How will the elements of the surroundings communicate with, educate, and inspire the children and adults that participate? How do the sounds, sights, materials, equipment, and even the smells and textures comfort and stimulate children? Does every child and adult feel welcomed and sustained over time? Let's answer these questions and more.

Think about the classrooms you remember from your early years. What role did language play in those experiences? There may have been important words on rules, notices, and warnings ("do not touch!"). You might remember whimsical words on posters and books. There may have been useful words associated with toys, games, technology, and other learning materials. And, there may have been language in the form of music, fingerplays, or images that contained no visible words at all. Adults and children may be aware of some language and oblivious to other examples. The learning environment is so much more than furniture. Language and culture are woven throughout. Your job is to make the use of language both inclusive and intentional.

Designing Learning Environments

In your work as an educator, you are likely to design a variety of classroom environments. A classroom is just one example of the types of spaces you might need to address. Teachers need to consider the physical space, the furnishings available to you, the surfaces for displays, storage, and work, and access to needed amenities. They make many choices about purchasing and making things for the environment, and for displaying things the children choose or make. They also think about the ages, abilities, interests, cultures, and needs of the children who will be in that environment. No two groups will be alike, no two years will be alike. Every member of the class or group has a right to access the things they need to see

The Meaning in the Environment

As you plan to fill your environment with things – supplies, displays, books, toys, manipulatives, learning tools, technology, and more – you will have to make a surprisingly large number of decisions. These are important decisions because the right materials make a lot of learning happen in your setting. Depending on your school policies and the curriculum you'll be using, you may be able to fill the environment with things that support independent exploration, progressive learning, and peer interactions. For infants, this means low shelving with items that babies can crawl to and use to make things happen, such as simple plastic blocks, bowls with scoops, mirrors, and rattles. An adult might interact while the baby is playing with the toys, but independent discovery with these items is also valuable for the child's development.

When you work with 3- and 4-year-olds, your environment will look like it is filled with toys, but each will be chosen for its learning value and support of independent play and interaction. For children in primary years, you will often find that the established curricular activities take up more time, leaving less time for independent investigations or free choice. This is even greater motivation to make careful decisions to include the most meaningful items available for independent work.

In linguistically diverse classrooms, one of the most important factors in choosing materials is the intrinsic meaning that material holds. When children are not able to understand the teacher's words as they explain how to use a learning material, the item itself should have an observable function or purpose. Interacting with items that have intrinsic meaning will likely result in learning and skill building. For example, sorting strips of paper into piles by color simply results in a few piles of paper strips. The teacher might use their language to talk about the skill of sorting, but children who don't understand those words will not benefit from this activity. If you asked children to sort something with intrinsic meaning, such as socks or cutlery, they would be able to see the meaning of using their sorting skills whether or not they understood the teacher's words. It really doesn't matter if a plastic bear goes in the red pile or the blue pile. But if you sort the cutlery and give your classmates forks on a soup day, that has meaning. If you sort the socks and some friends get mismatched pairs, that has meaning. When children count, sort, estimate, stack, assemble, insert, remove, wear, or pretend with any items in the classroom, there should always be an intrinsic meaning built into the items so the skill brings results and makes sense for the child. Maria Montessori was a pioneer of this approach to planning environments. According to the American Montessori Society website, Montessori designed materials that were "self-correcting" so that children could work on one skill at a time with objects that helped children learn on their own. For example, if a child chooses to play with a frame that houses pegs in size order, a peg placed in the wrong order will not fit, prompting the child to keep trying until all the pegs fit and the proper order is revealed.

What does it mean to call the classroom environment "the third teacher" as we often see in writings about the Reggio Emilia approach to early education? Practitioners in this approach list the child's teachers as: the family, the educator, and the environment. A high-quality environment is filled with materials and displays that provoke thought, exploration, and communication.

(Strong-Wilson & Ellis, 2007)

Many different factors contribute to planning such widely divergent surroundings, but there are some considerations that should always be part of the planning. These fall into three main categories: health/safety, universal design, and cultural/linguistic responsiveness. Let's take a closer look.

Health and Safety

Ensuring the health and safety of all children is always a priority. When working with young children, you may have state childcare licensing standards, education regulations, as well as local health department rules to keep in mind. Depending on who owns and operates the school or program, rules and guidelines can be very different from place to place. Look for recommendations about the number of children allowed per square foot and per adult according to the ages of the children. In addition, if the school or program is involved in any quality rating or accreditation programs, added requirements will need to be addressed. There will be rules about bathrooms, cleaning supplies, changing facilities, and running water. Light and ventilation are key considerations. You will need to be sure your set-up gives you the ability to observe and supervise every child at all times.

Health and safety regulations also refer to nutrition, safe handling of food, and attention to food allergies. For example, for infants, propping bottles is not recommended, so adults need to be available to hold and feed each baby. Introducing solid foods should be done in partnership with the families and current health guidance. At the same time, some curriculum approaches recommend ways of serving food that may or may not fit with the standards and regulations at your school. This might happen if you work with preschool or nursery children in an elementary school building. Many early childhood experts promote family style meals that encourage young children to pour, pass, and serve themselves to develop independent eating habits and motor coordination. This is not always possible in some settings.

It is important to understand and support cultural traditions around food and eating, while remaining within the boundaries of health and safety requirements. No child should be made to feel embarrassed about their food or the way they eat. In some cultures, it is considered necessary for parents to hand feed their child well into their fourth year. We do not actually have research to show this is bad for the child, nor do we have research showing that it is better for the child to feed himself. These are cultural preferences that have been written into early childhood guidance and standards in some places. This is a good reminder that some of the practices or skills we think are so important for young children to learn and do may actually just be culturally influenced preferences rather than actual needs (Reid, Kagan, & Scott-Little, 2017). Can you think of other practices you are learning in your early childhood coursework that might be derived from cultural traditions?

Another area of controversy has to do with the hard and soft surfaces used in the learning space. Studies show that too much background noise can make it harder for children who are dual language learners (DLLs) to recognize speech sounds in their new language (Language Magazine, 2016; Society for Research in Child Development, 2016; Guerra et al., 2021). One of the best ways to reduce background noise in early childhood settings is to have soft materials that absorb excess noise such as carpeting, cushioned furniture, drapes, and soft wall coverings. Unfortunately, some states and localities ban all soft materials in early childhood programs because they may harbor allergens that can be harmful to children. These are both serious concerns, so there is no easy solution. Alternative ways to reduce background noise and create comfort in multilingual classrooms are to have soft surfaces that are not made of fibers – such as rubbery tiles on floors and wall hangings that are not woven.

Universal Design

Many experts and some state standards/guidelines recommend the use of a universal design approach to preparing learning environments for children of all ages. Universal design means setting up environments proactively with space, displays, and materials that are open-ended and adaptable so any child can use them to learn in their own way. Rather than approaching adaptations as a remedy for a problem, universal design anticipates a variety of needs and finds the most universal options to meet those needs. The approach provides equitable access to learning without labeling children or making any individual or group of children feel inadequate or excluded (Brillante & Nemeth, 2018).

For example, picture communication boards were first designed to help non verbal people communicate by pointing to pictures that express their thoughts or feelings. It was soon learned that young children can benefit from this adaptation regardless of their language or ability, so offering picture communication boards has become a universal design element to facilitate communication in early childhood programs. Using simple sign language, also called "baby sign language," is another way to help any child communicate and understand.

Universal design began as a way to rethink public spaces and make them more accessible to people with disabilities. You can see how this approach became part of our everyday life in places that have doors that automatically open and close when you approach, or on sidewalks that have curb cuts. People who can't push heavy doors need those automatic openers to enter buildings – but having them is useful to every person. Curb cuts originally were designed to make it possible for people in wheelchairs to move around town, but they also proved useful for people with baby strollers or wheeled luggage, and we now realize that a curb cut includes everyone, excluding no one. So, we no longer consider universal design as a method for addressing special needs. It is a way of thinking and planning that opens opportunities for all (University of Washington, 2021).

In early childhood settings, consider the range of physical, communication, and comfort needs of the children in your care. Arrange open spaces that can accommodate children walking, crawling, and/or using wheelchairs or walkers. Have safe play and learning materials on shelves at heights accessible to children who are standing or sitting. Create quiet play and workspaces for children who need some time with less distraction. Identify some open spaces for children who need to use up some energy and move around. Offer a variety of seating options. Place self-care equipment such as coat hooks and hand washing stations so all children can confidently take care of their own needs. And, of course, pay close attention to making all entries and exits completely accessible.

Consider a variety of options to help children express themselves, communicate with adults and peers, and to comprehend information for play, learning, and self-care. One tool is baby sign language which many hearing infants have already started to learn, but will also be helpful for children with speech and/or hearing disorders or different languages so all can communicate on equal footing. For example, picture communication boards can be available from the first day of school, and they should be easily changeable to meet a variety of needs. Pay special attention to the messages on those boards to be sure they are neither too general and simple, nor too complicated. Remember, they are meant to meet the communication needs of the users. What do the children need to say and understand when using these boards? You could make picture communication boards with poster board, clear pockets, and printed pictures with written labels. You can also create printable picture communication boards with software designed for this purpose, or you can use digital boards that are available as apps on mobile devices so they can be wherever they are needed. Use pictures as well as words in multiple languages on labels and supplies. Offer picture menus for choices children need to make. Create a hook and loop board or felt board with pictures that children can post themselves to identify their projects, accomplishments, or plans. Have a translation app with voice translation capacity ready to support adult-child or peer-to-peer interactions.

Another way to support equitable access to learning is to provide supplies children might need whether or not their families are able to contribute. Keep spare clothing and underwear so children can continue to participate after something happens to what they are wearing. Provide extra mittens, hats, and jackets so all children can go outdoors together. Provide a secure storage container for each child to safely keep their own items like pencils, water bottles, snacks, combs, or anything that they might want to keep at school. Not all children have privacy or stability in their home environment, so it can help them feel secure to know they have a place to store things that belong to them at school (Brillante & Nemeth, 2018).

Consider how you will make lessons, explanations, and descriptions understandable for all children, even if they don't speak your language. In addition to talking things through, be prepared to show objects, video, or photos, or to do demonstrations. You also need to give linguistically diverse children many different kinds of opportunities to show you what they know and can do. At times, you might have to record what they say and find a staff member or family member to help you translate for your records and to help you respond to the child.

Culturally Responsive Environments

Effective space design across all ages and settings focuses on welcoming the cultures, languages, and characteristics of all children and families. Regardless of where or whom you teach, you can be sure that every child and family has a right to equitable access to information and learning. Every child and family should see themselves represented in the displays, materials, and practices of the learning setting. A sense of belonging is important to ensure that each child feels seen, nurtured, and respected, and it is also important for each family to feel recognized, honored and to feel they play an important part in the shared responsibility for their child's learning. From the time they are babies, children learn best and feel most accepted when they see themselves represented and they feel that learning activities are relatable to them. Be sure to include posters, toys, puzzles, books, music, dress-up clothes, kitchen and housekeeping items, furnishings, outdoor play materials, and all other types of materials that show a full range of diversity. Look for different skin colors, ages, styles of dress, living arrangements, genders, languages, occupations and activities, abilities, and family members. Keep in mind that these items have value when they are authentically relatable to the particular children in the group. Many times, plastic items or imitation costumes purchased from catalogs are unrecognizable to the children. Asking for items from home, or finding things in local shops, thrift stores, and flea markets may help make better connections (Table 6.1).

Table 6.1 Items to request from homes

Item	Uses
Clean, empty food containers	Remove any safety hazard, use clear adhesive paper to laminate and reassemble containers
Clean, old clothes	Ask for clothes with a purpose like items that represent parents' jobs, or the hobby of a family member, and use other items as material to remake into familiar doll clothes, seat cushions, or costumes
Music	Simple instruments, a visiting family member who can do a sing along, or recorded familiar songs
Safe tools	Safe, age-appropriate tools for traditional cooking, building, gardening, or other kinds of work
Containers	A bag of bottle caps is one step, but a variety of containers with different lids make a great culturally relevant matching game
Photos	Photos of family members, pets, activities, culturally relevant items that can't be brought to class – use them to create changeable posters, class-made books, puzzles, felt boards, blocks, and game pieces
Print materials	Magazines, newspapers, and catalogs from other countries or in different languages for pretend play, collages, or projects
Recyclables	Large cardboard boxes to make forts, shops, and airplanes; empty milk jugs to make bowling pins or building blocks; old shoe boxes and margarine and oatmeal tubs to create musical instruments
Seeds and plant sprouts, along with growing containers	Enhance class planting projects by using the types of plants usually grown in the children's homes or allotment gardens
What would you add?	How would you use it?

Cultural responsiveness starts with the images and materials that are immediately observable in your learning environment. Then, it must become embedded in the physical environment as well as in the content and practices you will undertake. There are several steps you can take to strengthen your cultural responsiveness:

- Practice cultural humility by being open to learning about the cultural beliefs, practices, and traditions of the children, families, and colleagues with whom you work. Be willing to recognize when you have made a mistake or an assumption.
- A cultural humility approach – that openness to learning about the cultures of others – will help you avoid using stereotypes or exhibiting biases. Invite others to discuss your learning environment choices with you to gain diverse perspectives.
- Base cultural responsiveness on the real experiences of the people in your work environment. This is more authentic than looking up a certain language or group on the internet or in an article.
- Remember that items and images that are meaningful to young children may not be the same as the things that represent culture to adults. For young children, their culture is experienced in their own homes and communities. They may not be aware of flags, or special costumes from their family's home country (Souto-Manning, 2013). Your partnership with the family is the best source of information and things that represent each child's culture.
- Avoid a superficial or token approach to cultural representation. For example, posting an image with the word "hello" in multiple languages can be seen as a welcoming message. However, if that's the only place these languages appear in the environment, it may become clear to the visitor that there is no effort to really get to know or understand them – and that sign becomes just a token piece of diversity with little value to the ongoing relationships you need to build with families and children.

- Include meaningful representations of cultures in displays, materials, food, music, and activities. Resist the temptation to use holidays to represent cultures. Holidays are generally celebrated on certain days, so they do not support the deeper inclusion of everyone's culture as an ongoing part of all you do. Holiday celebrations may seem cute but may not fully be understood as personally meaningful to each child and family. This is a good topic to invite input from families to see what would make them comfortable. Another approach would be celebrating friendships or seasons in less disruptive, more low-key ways while emphasizing a more stable, developmentally appropriate routine (Colker & Koralek, 2018).

As you weave cultural connections throughout the environment, supports for the languages of the children, families and colleagues will also be connected. Now, let's take a closer look at how cultural elements influence early learning across ages and settings.

Culture Connections to Support Learning

Familiar items from home may help children connect their existing knowledge to new learning of skills, concepts, and vocabulary. In addition to helping children and families feel comfortable and respected, they also create a strong foundation for learning. Partner with family members to learn more about the items each child uses, enjoys, and understands at home. These are items that might make great additions to the learning environment. For example, there are many ways to practice counting. When a child counts new or unfamiliar items in school, they may not understand what the items are for or what they are called or why they are counted. This experience is even more difficult for children who are learning in a new language. But, when you start with items they know about and have used, they already know what they are called and why they are counted, so they can focus more on the actual practice of counting. As they develop the knowledge and skills you are looking for with items from home, then they can be ready to build layers of new learning, branching out to unfamiliar materials.

The U.S. Office of Planning, Research, and Evaluation devised a Cultural Items and Language Use Checklist and wrote a report about how these items were used (Bumgarner et al., 2020). The study examined observation records for group settings for infants, toddlers, and preschoolers. They found that many cultural items were present in these settings, but they were rarely used. For example, they found that 65% of preschool classrooms had cultural displays, but only 12% were seen being used. This highlights a shocking and useful point: Simply displaying something that seems culturally relevant is not enough to ensure it will be used in play, learning, or conversation.

Connections are made when items are not only relatable, but usable for learning. Setting up a cultural corner with a few items on a shelf or one poster in the room is not likely to facilitate conversations between children or between adults and children. Look for culturally relevant items with intentional plans to bring them into play and learning activities.

> One of my favorite cultural connection examples came from a New York preschool teacher. She asked each family to email or text in a photo of what their child had for a meal – just a photo of their plate or serving. With these digital photos, the teacher was able to create a book to help her multilingual class talk about colors, quantities, foods, and other elements in the photos. She also printed out the images, cut them to shape, and laminated them to make authentic cultural pretend food items for pretend play. Can you think of more ways to use these photos?

Following Children's Interests

A respected tradition of NAEYC's Developmentally Appropriate Practice has been a focus on following a child's interests to facilitate learning at any age. This is another way to incorporate children's cultures into early education (NAEYC, 2020). It is a good idea to ask families about their children's interests before they start in your class or program so you can prepare a few things in advance to welcome children and make them feel at home. Here are questions you can ask in English and other languages.

- What are your child's favorite toys?
- What are your child's favorite lullabies/songs, books, or stories right now?
- How does your child like to help family members at home?
- What outdoor activities does your child enjoy?
- What are some of your child's favorite locations in your neighborhood?
- What is something that usually gets your child to communicate through facial expressions, vocalizations (e.g., cooing, babbling), body movements, gestures (e.g., pointing), trying to say words, or talking (one word, two- or three-word phrases, simple sentences, complex sentences)?

Even before children begin to talk, they are recognizing and cataloging sounds and words from the language they hear around them. They look to the adults in their lives to talk to them about the things they find amazing or puzzling or irresistible. By the time children begin to say words, they already understand many words for the things they have explored. When children use a language at home that is not used at childcare or school, they many know many more words for the things that are important to them in their home language. If you want to know more about what a child knows and can do at times when they may not be ready to tell you, just look for clues in the objects and experiences they find interesting. The questions here help you get that information from families. While they are in school/program, try spending time with each child, watching what they reach for and examine. Certainly, it is a good idea to ask a child about their interests when you are able to communicate with language. Even before children can talk or if they are using a language you don't know, you can learn so much by being present with the child and playing alongside them.

> The most important childhood story is the one that children tell about themselves. In my work, I see that when teachers cherish a child's language, they enable children to freely share about themselves, their families, culture, and customs. These rich stories become the building blocks that shape a child's personality in adulthood. Teachers are the most important architects in this process.
>
> Vasanthi Rao
> Dual Language Learner Project
> CDRC
> University of South Carolina

Cultural Supports from the Community

Many community organizations, government agencies, and businesses make great partners to bring culturally and linguistically responsive materials to early childhood programs.

Reach out to cultural organizations and embassies to ask them for posters, artifacts, books, and games that represent the countries and cultures of your children and families. These could be part of your local community, or they might be located in a distant city – but you can still reach out via phone or email.

Build a relationship with your local children's librarian. Libraries can access children's books in many languages, and about diverse cultures. But they can also provide so much more. They may be able to find music, videos, mobile apps, computer software, travel books with photos of different countries and locations, culturally diverse cookbooks, music books, and more. Even if they don't have the materials you need right away, they have interlibrary loans and catalog options along with the capacity to research and find resources you may not know exist. These can all be great temporary additions to the learning environments for all ages.

Visit flea markets, cultural fairs, and festivals in the community. This gives you a glimpse into the local colors, flavors, and sounds that represent the families that are participating in your program. It can also be a great way to purchase items you can use for projects, pretend play, and lesson plan supports. All these suggestions can help you enrich the learning environment you plan by replacing many of the primary color plastic items with real items that help children of all language and cultural backgrounds to learn and use (Table 6.2; Nemeth, 2009).

Table 6.2 Culturally responsive learning materials by age

Age/setting	Examples of cultural items
Infant care center	Photos of the child's family members that can be laminated and made into baby-safe books and blocks
Toddler playroom	Items from home to be used for pretend cooking, e.g., empty food packages, scoops, presses, or pots
Outdoor learning environment	Garden with plants suggested by family members, outdoor play equipment used in culturally relevant games
Family childcare home	Used clothing from families for a dress-up area
Open preschool/nursery classroom	Songs and chants from home that can be done in the home language and English
Kindergarten/reception classroom	Journals with writing prompts in the child's home language, provided by their family
Academic primary classroom	Pictures of family pets or familiar animals from the child's community or home country for extended studies
Space for individual or small group therapies	Small toys from home as conversation prompts and motivators
Family education space	Lending library of children's books, cookbooks, and other areas of interest representing languages and cultures of participating families
Virtual learning	Game pieces or art supplies sent to the children's homes so they and the teacher can have the same materials to create something meaningful to them while participating in remote learning
Remote learning home environment	Suggestions for families to use items from home to discuss comparisons such as heavy/light, sink/float with their children

Learning Connections with Technology

The number of digital options for early learning is growing rapidly. Many programs faced a sudden shift to remote learning or hybrid models of teaching in 2020, and some of these trends continue. As early childhood educators are learning more about ways to use technology to engage families and support children's learning, we are discovering more about how it can work to support or impede learning for children who are DLLs and their families. A lot has changed since NAEYC partnered with the Fred Rogers Center in 2012 to create their joint position statement, "Technology and Interactive Media as Tools in Early Childhood Education Programs Serving Children Birth – Age 8" (NAEYC & FRC, 2012). In 2015, the U.S. Department of Health and Human Services posted a report from the Office of Planning, Research and Evaluation called "Uses of Technology to Support Early Childhood Practice" Building on that report, the U.S. Department of Education created "Guiding Principles for Use of Technology with Early Learners" (U.S. Department of Education, 2016). Both reports relied on an extensive review of research at the time. We continue to see a lot more research on these topics, but the basic principles have not changed:

- Digital technology can effectively support learning when used properly.
- Digital technology makes it possible to provide equitable access to early learning for all children.
- Digital technology with the capacity to support interactions between families, children, and educators can enhance outcomes for children.
- Digital technology has the biggest impact on early learning when adults participate with children.

Technology can facilitate two-way communication with families using text messaging programs, email, translation software or apps, printers, social media, video and photo exchanges, and even phone calls. There are many software packages and online platforms designed to make it easy for schools and programs to send and receive information with families. They can be used to let families see what their child is doing during a particular day, to stay informed about school news, and to see assessment reports. Many of these programs as well as text messaging apps allow the teacher to send one message in English while all recipients can receive that message in the language of their choice. These programs also invite family members to send messages, comments, and questions – all ways to build powerful partnerships. These efforts follow Principle #4 above to use technology to strengthen relationships among children, parents, families, and early educators.

Adaptive and assistive technology may be needed by children who have disabilities (Brillante, 2018). These items may include devices that make it easier for them to stand, move, or control switches. Some children may need technology to help them hear, communicate, or participate in assessments. Voice to text programs allow children to compose words, messages, and stories when typing and writing are difficult. This is one area of technology that requires attention to linguistic and cultural appropriateness. Many children who have disabilities are also growing up with two or more languages. When that is the case, we know that research supports continued learning in both, or all their languages. There is no reason to believe that learning in two or more languages will be confusing to a child – read more about this in Chapter 5. On the other hand, helping children with disabilities or special educational needs to develop their home language and new language can be beneficial, enabling them to build linguistic assets that help them communicate in school and with their families. So, as technology resources are being planned for each child, you can participate by advocating for resources that reflect the languages and cultures of each child.

Teachers have more choices for apps, software, and websites to use in their work than ever before. This can be empowering but it can also be overwhelming. You will want to know which programs are being used by your school and families and find out which come with the most help. As recently as 2020, there were very few mobile apps in the U.K. or the U.S. designed specifically to teach concepts and skills to children who speak languages other than English. Some good alternatives are open-ended apps that use no language or that allow users to record their own language. Keep in mind Principle #1 of the U.S Department of Education guidance that says technology can be an effective tool for learning … when used appropriately. Just because an app or computer game seems cute doesn't mean it will provide a meaningful learning experience for children. Always keep the ages, abilities, and languages of the children in mind as you review apps, software, and websites. They should have the same developmentally appropriate characteristics as other materials you use for teaching. Do they engage children in active participation rather than rote memorizing? Do they use examples that are meaningful across languages and cultures? Do they invite children's creativity, problem-solving, or critical thinking? And are they inclusive of all children, regardless of language and ability?

There are two categories to consider as you plan to use technology to present information and lessons to students: using technology when you are together in-person and using technology to teach because you cannot be together in-person. In many ways, these categories overlap, especially since many teachers are trying to duplicate the in-person experience even when students are not able to come to school. For preschool/nursery and up through primary grades, many teachers use document cameras to display papers or book pages up on a larger screen – or they share their screens when conducing classes remotely via video chat programs such as Zoom. You may use digital whiteboards in school that allow you to display information in large format and allow you and the children to interact with the screen. You might also simulate this experience by using the whiteboard features, Jam Board app, the Padlet website, or other options that let the teacher display information to students learning remotely and gives them ways to interact with or respond to the information. These are ways to ensure all children have access to learning through technology, as recommended by the U.S. Department of Education in Principle #2.

Children over 18 months benefit more from these strategies, but infants get very little from technology. There are some cute apps to introduce them to using tablets or to keep them occupied when they might otherwise be bored. But there is little evidence that these devices provide any lasting learning for infants and toddlers. In fact, the American Academy of Pediatrics advises against the use of technology for any child under the age of 18 months. I suggest a couple of exceptions to this admonition: live video chats with family members (especially in support of the child's home language) and using them to show and discuss with the child photos and videos of their loved ones.

U.S. Department of Education Guiding Principle #4 reminds us that technology is more engaging and results in more learning when it is used in the context of responsive interactions and shared viewing with children and adults. One interesting line of research has revealed that, while young children learn very little from passively viewing information on screens, they do learn quite a bit of language when interacting with a responsive adult over video chat programs. This is important because digital platforms can open the door to family participation in young children's learning, especially when supports for the home language are needed (Nemeth, 2015).

Digital media open many doors for young children to explore and create independently. Planning for an in-person classroom may include ideas for the placement of and safe access to desktop computers or tablets that children can use to do research, view video examples that support lessons, practice skills, or to type, write, draw, and create. When children are learning remotely, they should be taught how to use digital media appropriately. Equitable access to learning requires schools to find ways to make sure every child has access to the internet and the devices needed. With remote learning for young children, there is an added component of dependence on an adult in the home ready to help the child use the technology, so remote learning must take into account how you will also teach the family members.

> Storytelling apps such as Draw and Tell or My Story give children and adults ways to work alone or to collaborate to create and record their own digital stories. These apps allow users to upload photos, draw on the screen, insert digital stickers, type, or fingerspell. For children who are DLLs, the most valuable feature is they enable voice recording. For example, you might take some photos on a walk to the duck pond. Engage the children in choosing photos, adding drawings, and typing or dictating words to the story over multiple pages. The app can be sent home to invite family members to narrate the same story each in their own language. The story is then saved as a video with a link that can be sent anywhere in the world to share the personalized story.

Finally, there are many ways in which technology can be helpful to teachers. You may use computers, tablets, and smartphones to record observations of children's learning. You will often need digital translation apps to help you understand and talk with the children. You may also find a wealth of professional learning opportunities that range from micro learning such as bits of information you obtain via Twitter or Facebook live, or online articles, podcasts, videos, recorded webinars, asynchronous courses, and live synchronous broadcasts. All these options can add to your growth as a professional and help you identify exactly the learning content you wish to pursue in the language you prefer. You can also step into providing professional development for your colleagues by discussing your own strategies or disseminating links to resources you've found valuable. Digital access allows you to follow conferences when you can't attend in person or to view talks by famous speakers from the comfort of your home. And they give you plenty to think about and bring to your work as an educator.

A Welcoming Entrance

First impressions make a difference. This starts with the entrance of your classroom or home. For infant/toddler rooms, there should be space for family members to sit down or put their baby down to take off coats and update you about the child's morning. Preschool/nursery programs generally provide space for the child to sign in and put away their jackets and lunchboxes. Family members may come in with their children, so there should be enough space for families to come and go and say goodbye to their child. In primary school, children generally enter the classroom all at once, without family members, so there needs to be clear space for all to rush in and put away their belongings. Many successful schools and programs set up a welcome area with water, coffee, and maybe some pastries or fruit to give family members a place to relax and socialize with other members of the school community or family childcare home.

Your plan for the entry should be engaging and relatable to young children and their families. As the days go by, many teachers use the space on or next to the door to post examples of the children's work. In the past, we may have seen a row of identical pictures that children made under direct control of the teacher. Now we understand the importance of allowing children to express themselves and we look for displays the represent the children's individuality. The décor can also be made relatable by posting welcoming words in all the families' languages. There should also be a clear, organized plan for how the children will enter and exactly what they can do when they arrive. This kind of structure is comforting for children and makes for a smoother morning. For children who may have experienced a stressful morning, it is a good idea to have a quiet corner where they can go to calm themselves before entering the buzzing, bustling world of the classroom.

Furnishings and Learning Centers

As you plan to arrange furniture in your classroom, you will need to consider safety, flexibility, and durability. Most infant/toddler classrooms have an open floor plan that emphasizes free exploration for babies. But, furniture should be strategically placed so children who can run will not find an open runway that would be unsafe for crawling infants. Preschool/nursery classrooms are arranged with some open space, and some of the space arranged to form learning or topic centers. Reception/kindergarten classrooms are sometimes more like preschool or nursery rooms and other times more like primary classrooms. Primary classrooms generally have more children in the space and more of an academic orientation that focuses on sitting in desks and listening to the teacher. But much depends on the requirements of the school or program where you will work.

For ideas about how to plan your space, look to other teachers in the same building who are subject to the same rules and traditions as you will be. For additional guidance, classroom observation tools offer some important insights. These classroom assessments tie their scoring systems to research demonstrating what brings best results with children. Find out if you might be evaluated using CLASS (Classroom Assessment Scoring System), ECERS (Early Childhood Education Rating Scale), FCCERS (Family Childcare Environmental Rating School), ITERS (Infant Toddler Environmental Rating Scale), ELLCO (Early Language and Literacy Classroom Observation designed for preK–grade 3) or similar tools.

For example, the ECERS-3 has ratings for preschool indoor space arrangements that are linked to improved learning outcomes for children, organized in the following categories (points are assigned in each category to indicate how well the environment is designed to support optimal learning):

- Furnishings for care, play, and learning.
- Room arrangement for play and learning.
- Space for privacy.
- Child-related display.
- Space for gross motor play.
- Gross motor equipment.

The ITERS-3 (Infant Toddler Environmental Rating Scale – version 3) has the following categories related to the environment to serve as a guide (see ERS, undated):

1 Indoor space.
2 Furnishings for care, play, and learning.
3 Room arrangement.
4 Display for children. (FPG, 2021)

The CLASS has three subcategories for rating high-quality interactions in preschool classrooms and it relies on scores for teacher-child interactions that provide instructional support, practices that provide emotional support, and classroom organization. The third category addresses features of classroom set-up that support effective teaching and learning (Piant, LoParo, Hamre & LoCasale-Crouch, 2007).

All the classroom assessments we mention include a rating of how the learning environment is organized. It is important to note that many state- or federally funded preschool programs have some requirement of minimum classroom observation scores to maintain or increase funding for the school or program. Now let's take a look at the key elements of high-quality early childhood environments.

Play areas – Spaces set aside with a collection of toys or play materials for children to enjoy as they wish.

Interest areas – Areas set apart with furnishings and supplies designed to guide a particular focus of exploration and interaction, centered around an area of interest that is labeled accordingly.

Cozy space – An area for calm, comfort, and quiet play or reading.

Block space – Usually in a corner so children moving from area to area won't knock over someone's building, and the noise of block play doesn't disturb children in other areas. There are shelves or containers for various types of blocks and related materials. (Block play is generally assumed for infant, toddler, and preschool environments. It is gaining popularity in kindergarten and reception classrooms after being left out for a number of years when academic lessons were more in favor.) There are many kinds of blocks, some designed specifically for infants that may be made of foam stuffed fabric or washable plastic, and some for large play structures for preschool, and some for primary grades that aid counting and measuring. You can find blocks designed to represent the architecture of different countries or you might work with the children to make your own culturally relevant blocks by gluing pictures of people and structures onto existing blocks or milk cartons. In any case, blocks are so open-ended that they make it possible for almost any child to play almost anything. This encourages the use of imagination, problem-solving, language, and spatial reasoning, in addition to fine and gross motor skills. When children play with blocks, they reveal so much to you about what they enjoy and what they know and can do (Hansel, 2016).

Book area or class library – A setting with comfortable furnishings and shelves or containers of books. High-quality classrooms display at least five books per child that exemplify:

- Diverse languages, cultures, and races.
- Fiction stories, poetry, and non-fiction.
- Variety of vocabulary and reading levels.
- Varied formats including paperback, hardcover, big books, board books, and class made books.
- Different topics that change with focus and interest. For example, when children are pursuing a particular topic or study, there should be books to support it.

Literacy supports – There are many ways to fill the environment with supports for early language and literacy for children of all ages. In the early years, we want children to be immersed in a literacy-rich environment filled with environmental print. How does this look in practice? Your planning should clearly focus on what works for the ages of the children in your group, as well as the languages spoken by children and their families. You will also ensure that images and content are culturally relevant, and literacy examples are intentionally chosen for active learning.

Environment and Materials 97

One factor unites all these factors: Letters and words in the environment only facilitate literacy and learning if they are noticed and used. A cluttered visual environment can be overwhelming and confusing, so children are more likely to block out the materials all around them. The most effective choices are planned for learning in the here and now, and they are changed to meet children's evolving needs and interests and the purposes of your lesson plans. If you put something on display in the environment and notice, after a week or two, that it is not being talked about or used for learning ... take it down. This includes unused word walls, extra chairs, posters that are never discussed, or old environmental labels that get no attention. Table 6.3 shows are some examples of literacy supports you might plan for different environments.

Table 6.3 Actionable literacy supports in different settings

Age/setting	*Literacy supports on display*
Infant care center	Cards posted at the changing station with home language words and phrases used during diapering
Toddler playroom	Posters with words to a favorite song in the home languages of the children, spelled phonetically, and English to help adults lead the songs for all children to learn each other's languages
Outdoor learning environment	Safety rules shown as pictures with simple messages in all the languages that adults and children use to remind each other to stay safe
Family childcare home	Simple menu of snacks and meals planned for each day with pictures and words in all the languages of the children
Open preschool/nursery classroom	Use of classroom labels as conversation starters. Instead of a label on a shelf that says shelf in three languages, place a label in the three languages with an open-ended question about what is *on* the shelf along with a few phrases that adults and children could use to talk about the materials there
Kindergarten/reception classroom	Writing table with paper, envelopes, journals, pens, pencils, and markers with sample letters and characters children can use to spell out words they want to try to write
Academic primary classroom	Two word walls with similar words posted – one wall for English only, the other wall with columns of color coded words in children's languages
Space for individual or small group therapies	Speech prompts in the child's home language and English along with matching props based on the child's interests
Family education space	Posters with inspiring and motivational quotes suggested by family members, in the families' languages
Virtual learning	Self-created video chat background with a few key words you will use in a lesson – invite children to call out when they hear you use the pictured words
Remote learning home environment	Home literacy bags with books in children's home languages along with wordless books and puppets and a note with link to a video demonstrating fun ways to share and discuss stories with children

Dramatic play center – Depending on the age of children and the curriculum being used, the dramatic play center may have a set array of materials children can use to pretend household activities with dress-up clothes, dolls, kitchen equipment, and play foods. Other items might include old phones, briefcases, woodworking tools, and items reflecting the work of children's families. Some teachers change the focus of the dramatic play area to go along with topics children are exploring such as creating a pretend pet shop after visiting a local pet store. Dramatic play centers appear in infant/toddler and preschool and nursery programs, and, less frequently, in kindergarten and reception spaces.

Art area – In addition to containing art supplies and surfaces such as easels or tables, the art area should be near running water for cleanup and there should be space for papers and objects to dry and be displayed. Art activities give children an outlet for their creativity while also building fine motor skills. By providing different media such as paints and clay, you also encourage learning about textures, comparisons, and other important content knowledge. You should know the difference between art (creating something new) and crafts (following instructions to make something specific) and provide examples of both. Don't hesitate to expose children to high-quality art through prints, visits to a museum, or video examples.

Music space – Some classrooms make music exploration available to children as part of free-play and work times. Others provide musical instruments and recordings at the direction of the teacher or a music specialist. This can be an area where many languages and cultural traditions can be experienced.

Science, Technology, Engineering, and Math (STEM) area – These subjects may be covered in one area or separated into areas for math manipulatives, science and nature objects, and makerspaces that encourage technology and engineering thinking. These spaces must be organized to support real learning. In addition to supplies, you will need to show children how to use the materials and identify learning goals for participating. You might include a series of photos to guide children's interactions with the materials or show a video. Also include writing materials or child-proof cameras so children can document their explorations and findings. This part of the environment might also contain living things such as class pets, live plants, or containers of caterpillars and butterflies. Infants and toddlers are natural born scientists, so be sure to include items that are developmentally appropriate, such as metal pots and plastic bowls along with wooden spoons and plastic blocks so the babies can experiment with the sounds made by different materials – after you give them a brief demonstration.

What is a makerspace? Children from toddlers to primary grades and beyond show amazing creativity, planning, and critical thinking when they encounter engaging spaces with open-ended materials they can use to capture their imagination. Some schools and libraries have makerspaces outdoors in pleasant weather. This provides a lot more space for children to create structures out of big pieces of cardboard, different kinds of fasteners, plastic table cloths, and plastic plumbing pipes, for example. Remember that makerspaces are meant to be open-ended. You might start the children with an essential question or a problem to be solved, such as "how can we move water to the garden?" They do not impose expected products. You will be amazed at how young children can turn what seems like trash into amazing treasures and practical solutions.

(Heroman, 2017)

Learning Outside the Classroom

Outdoor Play Space

Planning an outdoor space for play and learning may be as simple as building time into your schedule for a few minutes on a playground, or it may be as complex as setting up a fully designed outdoor classroom where children may spend hours exploring and learning with interest centers similar to the ones you planned for inside. Of course, safety is a priority with outside space. As long as there is adequate fencing, shade, and surfaces, you can do art, music, literacy, math, and pretend play. Paintings can be clipped to the fence. A pretend outdoor kitchen can encourage lots of dramatic play. Signs in several languages can be posted on the play equipment. Story times can happen on a blanket under a shade tree. These ideas can be adapted for any age and any setting.

Science and nature learning can be enhanced with outdoor space as well. A school garden is a wonderful place to bring together children, teachers, family members, and volunteers. You can ask a committee of family members to plan the garden including flowers as well as edible plants. Preparing and eating fruits and vegetables they have grown is a great way to get children aware and interested in eating healthy. Learning in many domains can be accomplished in planning, tending, and harvesting a garden.

Teacher assignments can play a role in how you think of your time with children in outdoor play spaces. In schools where random adults are assigned to "playground duty" there is not much incentive to combine play with learning. But, for teachers who are assigned to take their own groups outdoors, they can plan formal or informal opportunities to extend and deepen learning in line with curricular objectives. Actions can range from simple interactions like "How many jumps will it take you to reach the grass?" to more complex calculations like "We want to have a picnic lunch outdoors. What do we need to plan for that?" to academically relevant lesson enhancements like "We read a story about a spider weaving a web this week. Now I see some spiders on the fence. Here are your journals. Let's write or draw our observations and talk about them when we go back inside."

Developmentally Appropriate Field Trips and Neighborhood Explorations

Venturing outside of your classroom or program can expose children to the world around them and give them plenty to talk about. A field trip can be a short walk around the block or over to a new playground. Or it can be a pre-arranged visit to the post office or a local bakery or pizza shop. These are developmentally appropriate options that are meaningful and relevant to children. The best trips for young children are short in duration and supportive of learning objectives you have planned for them. Children in primary grades may be able to handle longer trips away from school to view art, nature, or musical performances, for example. All field trips work best when they are woven into learning activities that happen before and after the trip. For infants and toddlers, every walk outside is like a field trip. There is always something to notice, comment, question, and remember. Take photos to show them as soon as you return to the building to give them more opportunities to practice their expressive and receptive language

The same types of strategies can be used on virtual field trips. Many services, shops, museums, and organizations offer formally organized virtual field trips or informal video chat visits that give children a wonderful opportunity to explore local locations and special places. In addition, you can invite children's authors, illustrators, museum educators, and other experts to visit your class via video chat and interact directly with the children.

Strategies and Practices to Enhance the Learning Environment

Finally, it's time to pull together the key idea-generators that early childhood educators need to think about when planning a learning environment. Make plenty of space to display children's artwork, writing, and creations – both on paper and in 3 dimensional formats.

There should be space to display ongoing projects so children who worked on something one day can see it kept safely for when they return the next day. Children's art should be displayed at their eye level. In fact, most things that children need to see and use should be posted at their eye level. It is OK if the upper walls seem a bit bare. Remember that visual clutter is not good for early learning, but opportunities to see their productions on display gives children a sense of agency and accomplishment. Young children, even toddlers, can participate in small group planning for their physical environment. Hold group meetings to invite children's input about what art or materials should be on display in their own environment.

Find a balance between predictable and new. To some extent, young children benefit from the comforting experience of seeing some of the same things in the same places every day. But too many things in the environment for too long may mean they no longer get noticed or used. Find a few key items to change and rotate, making the environment dynamic and attention-getting. Young children, especially those who are new to school or new to your language, really thrive when they know what to expect. Post picture schedules to help them stay focused as activities change. Use the environment to help children feel supported and in control. Use light switches and songs to spark clean-up time. Give children the items they need to help with cleaning surfaces or clearing tables after meals. Have the room and materials set up so children know what to do as soon as they come in and can get started on a meaningful and engaging activity. Incorporate some traditions you've learned from the families and create your own traditions with the group you have.

Aim to focus on active learning and interactions in all of your planning. Be prepared for change. Don't cling to a certain way you have always done things. Each child, group, and set of families will have different needs and different funds of knowledge (cultural traditions and personal experiences) to contribute.

Dynamic and Meaningful Environments

As children grow and progress, their environment should change with them. As children gain experience with your puzzles, put some away and bring out more difficult ones. Start a felt board with just a few pieces, and add more as children develop more sophisticated stories. Keep out some favorite books and add new ones on a regular basis to keep children looking for more. Post questions for conversation in different languages in the primary classroom based on what's new in the world or the neighborhood. If you have posters or pictures of the children and their families, make sure to change them regularly to maintain interest.

Conclusion

Establishing a highly effective learning environment is very important for children. It is also an important way for teachers to unleash their own creativity. You may have a budget to buy materials and furnishings, or you may borrow some from libraries or other teachers. One way to keep the environment interesting is for a group of teachers or family childcare providers to exchange items every so often. You may spend a little time or a lot on making and preparing materials for your classroom or setting. There are many websites and apps available to give you ideas but be a critical consumer and choose carefully. Don't forget this time-honored saying in early childhood education, "Cute is the enemy of quality." Your goal is to introduce quality with every decision rather than be influenced by things that look cute but do little to support learning. Always be ready to evaluate the displays, materials, and furniture arrangements in case changes need to be made. For example, an alphabet poster near the ceiling is unlikely to help young children learn the alphabet. A poster with finger spelling signs for the letters of the alphabet in a room of children who don't know the alphabet will have little effect. However, a poster made of photos of each child with a family member can be discussed over and over again. Always look for items that ensure equitable access to learning and build a sense of belonging and agency for all children across all languages, cultures, and abilities.

Choose Your Own Path Check-In

Age/setting	What specific materials are truly necessary for each of these settings?
Infant care center	
Toddler play room	
Outdoor learning environment	
Family childcare home	
Open preschool/nursery classroom	
Kindergarten/reception classroom	
Academic primary classroom	
Space for individual or small group therapies	
Family education space	
Virtual learning	
Remote learning home environment	

Social Media Messages and Discussion Starters

- Name five things in your classroom that you and the children actually use. Now, name five things you never touch or talk about ... And consider removing them!
- Did you know? Background noise is like auditory clutter and it makes it hard for multilingual children to hear and learn speech sounds in their new language.
- Learning materials with intrinsic meaning allow the child to learn in any language. What are some examples of objects and manipulatives with intrinsic meaning?

References

Brillante, P. (2018) *The Essentials: Supporting Young Children with Disabilities in the Classroom*, Washington, DC: NAEYC.

Brillante, P., & Nemeth, K. (2018) *Universal Design for Learning in the Early Childhood Classroom*, New York: Routledge.

Bumgarner, E., Caswell, L., Layzer, C., Wolf, A., & Barrueco, S. (2020) *Select Findings from the Migrant and Seasonal Head Start Study 2017: Cultural Items and Language Use Checklist*, Office of Planning, Research, and Evaluation.

Colker, L.J., & Koralek, D. (2018) *High Quality Early Childhood Programs: The What, Why, and How*, St Paul, MN: Redleaf Press.

FPG (2021). Environment Rating Scales, Chapel HIll, NC: Frank Porter Graham Child Development Center retrieved https://ers.fpg.unc.edu/environment-rating-scales.

Guerra, G., Tijms, J, Vaessen, A., Tierney, A., Dick, F., & Borste, M. (2021) Loudness and Intelligibility of Irrelevant Background Speech Differentially Hinder Children's Short Story Reading, *Mind, Brain, and Education*, 15 (1), 77–87.

Hansel, R. (2016) *Creative Block Play: A Comprehensive Guide to Learning through Building*, St Paul, MN: Redleaf Press.

Heroman, C. (2017) *Making and Tinkering with STEM: Solving Design Challenges with Young Children*, Washington, DC: NAEYC.

Language Magazine (2016) The Bane of Background Noise, *Language Magazine*, December.

NAEYC (2020) *Developmentally Appropriate Practice Position Paper*, Washington, DC: NAEYC.

NAEYC & FRC (2012) Technology and Interactive Media as Tools in Early Childhood Programs Serving Children from Birth through Age 8, retrieved from www.naeyc.org/sites/default/files/globally-shared/downloads/PDFs/resources/position-statements/ps_technology.pdf.

Nemeth, K. (2015) Tips for Videochatting with Young Children: Staying Together While Far Apart, retrieved from www.naeyc.org/our-work/families/tips-video-chatting-young-children.

Nemeth, K. (2009) *Many Languages, One Classroom: Teaching Dual and English Language Learners*, Lewisville, NC: Gryphon House.

Pianta, R, LoParo, K.Hamre, B., & LoCasale-Crouch, J. (2007) Classroom Assessment Scoring System Manual Pre-K, Baltimore, Brookes Publishing.

Reid, J.L., Kagan S.L., & Scott-Little, C. (2017) New Understandings of Cultural Diversity and the Implications for Early Childhood Policy, Pedagogy, and Practice, *Early Child Development and Care*, 189 (6), 976–989.

Society for Research in Child Development (2016) Background Noise May Hinder Toddlers' Ability to Learn Words, retrieved from https://neurosciencenews.com/noise-toddler-word-learning-4718.

Souto-Manning, M. (2013) *Multicultural Teaching in the Early Childhood Classroom: Approaches, Strategies, and Tools Preschool – 2nd Grade*, New York: Teachers College Press.

Strong-Wilson, T., & Ellis, J. (2007) Children and Place: Reggio Emilia's Environment As Third Teacher, *Theory Into Practice*, 46 (1), 40–47.

University of Washington (2021) What is Universal Design?, retrieved from www.washington.edu/doit/what-universal-design-0.

U.S. Department of Education (2016) *Guiding Principles for Use of Technology with Early Learners*, Washington, DC: U.S. Department of Education.

7 Family and Community

Follow the Chapter 7 Roadmap with These Headings

Introduction	Connecting with the Community
Communicating with Families	Communication Tools and Resources
Supports for Learning at Home	Transitions
Families Contribute to Learning Environments	Conclusion

Chapter 7 is about working with families and the community, but it is also about building a community within and around the school or program. This is important to ensure equitable access for children and families, as well as equitable treatment of staff. This chapter begins with a discussion about communicating with families and supporting learning at home. Next, the direction shifts to consider what families can contribute to enhance the learning environment at school. Topics related to building a sense of community and using appropriate tools and resources to communicate are addressed. Supporting families through transitions into, through, and out of your school will also be covered.

Top Tips for Partnering with Families and the Community

- Two-way communication with families should feel like a genuine partnership with both sides contributing information that helps the other.
- Great relationships start with first impressions. Plan culturally and linguistically responsive welcomes for families right from the start.
- Learning at home can be quite an adjustment for any child, but young children need almost constant support from adults as well. Family members need training, coaching, and praise for a job well done.
- Communicating with families should not be piecemeal or overload. Collaborate with colleagues to organize and simplify information that goes home to families.
- Adults respond better when a communication makes them feel involved and needed. Don't just send news or a shopping list. Invite families to give input and contribute materials to the classroom.
- Advocacy is an important part of a teacher's role. How will you advocate for yourself and your students? How will you participate in advocacy for the field?
- Having a young child, especially if you don't speak the language in your community, can be very isolating. For the sake of the family and the child, make an effort to foster a sense of belonging for all.

DOI: 10.4324/9781003089216-7

> - Get to know the children's librarian in your community. They take requests, do searches, and find resources you might not even know exist to meet the needs of all of your children and families.
> - Find out about the organizations and services in your community that are prepared to help families who speak languages other than English.
> - Encourage developmentally and culturally appropriate ways to support learning in Tribal or heritage languages for children who already speak English.
> - Find a variety of ways for families to participate in the classroom or program. Not everyone is comfortable reading stories to busy children.

Introduction

The work of teaching young children is strengthened by partnerships with families and support from the community. Major reports identify "working with families" as a key educator competency (National Academies of Sciences, Engineering, and Medicine, 2017). These connections flow in several directions and take many forms. Language plays an important role in all aspects of family and community engagement. It is important to build a relationship with each and every family in equitable ways that are inclusive of all languages, cultures, and experiences. We also need to consider the language used when educators, families, and community members interact with each other. The information they exchange with each other can also help to facilitate language development and learning for young children. Fortunately, there are many tools and resources to help.

Many schools establish family engagement plans. Teachers generally describe these plans as a list of activities provided for families, messages sent to families, things done for families, and requirements of families. These types of plans focus more on family involvement – what you want families to do – rather than a two-way relationship. It is as if many educators think family engagement is all about broadcasting or pushing information and experiences out to families. The most effective programs and educators, however, do as much listening and asking as they do telling and requiring (Koralek, Nemeth, & Ramsey, 2019). This is why you see a focus on relationship-building in this chapter.

There are many ethical considerations to think about when engaging with families. For example Everyone in the school community needs to understand and uphold the principles of confidentiality. Be mindful of the rules about taking and sending pictures and videos, communicating via social media, and working with informal interpreters to talk with bilingual families that are part of the written and implied rules of your workplace.

Communicating with Families

Let's take a look at the kinds of information that might be communicated, the ways that communication can happen, and the special circumstances that educators might need to address. As you become familiar with these components of family and community engagement, think about how you would implement them in different ways depending on your position.

Beginning the Relationship

Relationships start with first impressions. Know about the languages in your community to use as you plan and prepare your welcome for families. There are formal and informal ways to get to know the families of children entering your program or school. Most school districts have a "home language survey" and other written forms for families to complete. All Head Start preschool and infant/toddler programs, as well as some schools and preschool programs, send teachers or social workers out to conduct home visits and get to know the families. When families don't want a school representative to come into their home, some will meet with family members in a local coffee shop or park. More recently, educators have found ways to get to know families over online meeting platforms or phone calls, when necessary.

If you were the parent of a young child, what would you hope to discuss with a school official or home visitor during your first meeting? What would make you most comfortable as you begin this relationship?

Putting yourself in their place – considering their point of view–can go a long way in helping you understand how to communicate effectively with diverse families. You will need information to:

- Identify the best way to communicate with each family – what language and what mode of communication will work best
- Have an accurate description of the child's language background so you can plan for supporting their home language and prior knowledge (also called background knowledge in early literacy work)
- Plan activities and materials that will be familiar to the child and will respond to their interests. For example, what does the family do on weekends? What songs or stories does the child know? What toys do they play with at home?

(Koralek, Nemeth, & Ramsey, 2019)

If this type of information is not collected before the child enters the program, it can be gathered gradually over the first few weeks through brief conversations, emails, or text messages. It will be critical for planning how to meet the individual needs of each child. Be sure to set aside information that might be of a private nature. Build a file of non-confidential information that can inform all members of the school community who might work with that child and family. Who needs to know about the child's languages and interests? Family support workers, English as a Second Language (ESL) teachers, behavioral support teachers, special education teachers, speech, physical, and occupational therapists, reading specialists, even school librarians, and music, art, and physical education teachers can all work more effectively with children and families if they know more about them.

> In my experience, using just English is one way to silence many children. Remember that your heritage language is your *identity – a vital part of your culture.* Connecting with children and families starts with respect for and interest in their language(s). Using a child's language in class shows that you care and is one way to give every child a voice. Find out as much as you can about the language(s) used in the home – from the children, from personal observations, and from parent engagement activities *that get at actual versus reported home language use.* The more you know, the more you'll grow, and your children will smile and shine!
>
> Anita Pandey
> U.S. Liaison, Childhood International, 2017–2020
> NABE Board Member, 2014–2017

Also, in the beginning of the family's relationship with you and the school, they will want to know more about what their child will be learning and how they will spend their day. There will be many policies, rules, and resources to explain to them. This can be very daunting to family members of young children. Consider the added difficulty for family members who are not fluent in the language used by the school to express these important things. Some adults may have unpleasant memories of their own school experiences. You will want to build a relationship based on mutual respect and trust—but that takes time and patience on both sides (NAEYC, undated). Family engagement will never be a one-size-fits-all situation. A positive start and a focus on relationship-building lays the groundwork with families to facilitate all of the other work you will do together (Gonzalez-Mena, 2014).

As you read through this chapter, you can see that it addresses many of the changes to home-school connections that began in the 2020–2021 pandemic shutdowns. A lot was learned about tools and strategies to maintain family engagement when in-person interaction was not possible. Be sure to consider how the things we've learned in the recent past can inform the professional choices you make in your future as an educator.

Information Provided to Families about Their Child's Progress

What do you remember about the progress reports or report cards that informed your family about how you were doing in school? Many U.S. elementary schools continue the tradition of sending home report cards with grades and comments four times a year. Some schools in the U.S., England, and other countries are trying different ways to communicate with families about their child's work. Some form of report to families is prepared in most preschool and infant/toddler programs as well.

In many cases now, a purchased curriculum is associated with a child assessment tool or, website, or software that enables teachers to enter anecdotes and examples of each child's learning and behavior to form a portfolio assessment. This collection of samples and stories provides a much more detailed accounting of what the child knows and can do than a traditional report card. It can also be informative about what the child needs next. Portfolio assessments are most common in toddler and preschool classroom settings, but may be used in kindergarten and early primary grades as well. These assessment programs generally have features that allow the teacher to send regular updates to families and provide a more formal compilation for a periodic report. These sophisticated platforms also aggregate data about all children in the school so leaders can follow trends and learn more about what is working and what areas need professional development support across all staff members.

Communication with families is always part of planning and implementing child assessments in the early years. Families need clear information about how their child's progress will be assessed, what they will be told, and what are their opportunities to respond. A strong relationship with each family lays the foundation for constructive discussions about their child's progress and needs. These conversations are not always easy as there may be times when you have to talk about concerns or challenges presented by the child. Presenting objective reports without judgement and listening to the reactions of the family members will help you work together to support the child along their learning path (Koralek, Nemeth, & Ramsey, 2019).

Most schools and programs plan a family–teacher conference either in-person or via video chat at least once a year. Some programs structure these meetings as a simple explanation about what's in the written report card or progress report. Others include multiple family members, invite any therapists or specialists that may have been involved with the child, and may even invite the child to participate and show what they have learned. It will be important for you to get comprehensive guidance from your employer about what is expected of you and what kinds of variations are allowed.

Families may need supports to ensure they can each participate in the process set up by your school. They may need an in-person interpreter or a translated report. They may need to participate via video chat or they may not have the ability to do that. Some families may need to bring all their children if they don't have childcare. Some may have to come later in the evening or on weekends due to work schedules. If professional interpreters are used, they should receive information in advance about the importance of confidentiality and accuracy for these topics. If interpreters are not available, try to have written information translated and provide informal interpreters such as bilingual staff members to help. Children should not be used as interpreters for high level information such as progress reports or placement changes (Gonzalez-Mena, 2014). Think about ways to make sure each family feels welcome and confident that they will be treated with respect. Every family should expect to hear some wonderful things about their beloved child as well as an honest assessment of the child's strengths and needs. For this reason, not all family–teacher meetings will be equal, but they can be equitable when you focus on responding to the needs and preferences of each family.

True two-way relationships with families should also foster an ongoing exchange of information so that families feel welcome to send information about their child's accomplishment or concern at any time (NAEYC, undated). If a family was aware their child was struggling with a particular skill, it would be more helpful for you to know about it when it happens rather than waiting for the family to tell you when you are presenting them with the completed progress report. Further, the involvement of the family in exchanging information about their child supports their role as a partner in the process.

Fostering a Sense of Belonging

A lot of unspoken messages can be found in the environment of the school and your classroom. Do families see representations of themselves? Is there a sense of depth and authenticity to the choices of displays and materials available? Keep in mind that a simple sign with the word "hello" in several languages may be one small piece of a welcoming environment. But, "hello" is not a word that has lasting communication value throughout the day. If that's the only place where a family or child sees their home language, the positive impact of that sign will be very brief. Families need to not only see a token reference to their language and culture, but to find meaningful connections throughout their child's classroom and the entire school (Koralek, Nemeth, & Ramsey, 2019).

You can communicate as much by the things that are not said as by the things you do say. A set of forms that is available in three languages is not welcoming to the families who speak the fourth or fifth language and are left out. "I'm trying to learn more Spanish" is a very different message in a diverse community than "I don't speak Spanish." Images should represent all kinds of families. Even when families speak the same language, they may not all be from the same place or speak the same dialect. It is important to honor each and every one. Work together with colleagues and families to stop implicit bias and unintended messages. To be fully effective, this work should involve every member of the school community (Koralek, Nemeth, & Ramsey, 2019).

> As a woman of color working in the early childhood field, I believe it is imperative for ECE educators to understand the importance of language justice. Language is power! If dual language learners and their families feel their language is considered less, they are less likely to speak up or advocate for themselves. It is our jobs to embrace all the languages in our classroom.
>
> Shu-Chen "Jenny" Yen, Ph.D.
> Professor, Child and Adolescent Studies
> California State University, Fullerton

When you prepare the learning environment with contributions from families, you can ensure that seeing familiar items respected, used, and displayed can add to that sense of belonging. As Dr. Yen says above, "language is power" and culture is powerful as well.

Language Isolation

As an early childhood educator, you should be aware of not only the languages spoken by families, but of their language context as well. Some families live in a community where their non-English language is all around them. But what happens to the family who experiences language isolation? They may have moved to a new area where they don't yet speak the language in the community and their own language is so uncommon that they don't know anyone who can communicate with them in their home language. This can be a very stressful experience added to whatever challenges the family may have faced as they moved to your community (Vesely, Letiecq, & Goodman, 2017). Look for ways to identify this issue, offer reassurance, and find ways to connect with these family members. This might include exchanging happy videos of their child enjoying school, identifying an interpreting service that can help when they have questions about school or social services, or accompanying them to the public library to ask for child and adult resources to help to build that important sense of belonging.

Advocacy

Another way to build that important sense of belonging is to advocate for diverse families and to teach families to advocate for themselves and their children. We mean advocacy in the broader, social justice sense, as well as for more individual purposes. Families need help and they need to be empowered to find where they fit in the community and how to get what they need (Cooper, 2021). To effectively advocate for their children and families, people need information they can understand. Check with your school to make sure key documents and contacts really are made available to each and every family. Invite more experienced bilingual families to join a team of language ambassadors. Provide them with some training about supporting newcomer families and helping them navigate school system rules and expectations, and helping them feel connected to the school community. In their community-based research, Vesely, Letiecq, and Goodman (2017) found that many immigrant families who experienced isolation and trauma also experienced fear or distrust of institutions as well as an inability to learn about community resources. They may not come to school, or to you, looking for help and support. They may not behave in ways you expect. But the families that are hardest to reach may be the families who need you the most.

Information for Families

While it is important to keep families informed, it is important to be respectful of their time and attention. Families with young children are often juggling many work and parenting responsibilities along with a variety of other demands. Work to refine and organize the messages provided for families so the most important messages really do get noticed. Above all, remember that your goal is a two-way relationship rather than a one-way presentation. Remember that information has more impact when it invites families to take some kind of action or participation and makes them feel like valued partners in the process.

When you have something critical to tell parents, transmit it in more than one way, such as a newsletter and a text message or phone call reminder. Word all messages to families with inclusivity in mind (Gonzalez-Mena, 2014). Use plain language to ensure access for people with different levels of literacy. Double check your messages to be sure you don't use jargon–terms or acronyms that may be understood by people in some groups but not others. "Back to school night" is an American tradition, but families from other countries might not know that means a meeting where parents (and not children) come to school some weeks after children go back to school. Spell out terms instead of using initials. Use positive phrasing. "Sending the permission slip early helps us plan a successful event" is better than "If you don't send the permission slip on time, your child will be excluded from the event" (Koralek, Nemeth, & Ramsey, 2019).

Inclusive communication can address headings, titles, and special events. "Multicultural Day" may seem like diversity is only recognized on a specific day. You will honor all the cultures of your school community all the time, but you might host a "Recipe Sharing Day" or a "Family Music Night" to focus on specific traditions that everyone can learn about and enjoy. "Donuts for Dads Morning" sounds like a great way to bring fathers into the program, but imagine how children feel when they don't have a dad in their lives, or they have a dad that is deployed overseas. Consider hosting "Favorite Grownups Visit" events and letting everyone know this means moms, dads, relatives, guardians, and foster parents. Holiday celebrations may also be cause for concern. Some holidays arise from particular religions. Some families practice religions that prohibit the celebration of any holiday. Some holidays are specific to certain regions or countries and may be unfamiliar to others. And, not all people from a particular country or culture will celebrate holidays in the same way. While it may be hard to give up favorite holiday traditions, many experts recommend against such events because they may not be inclusive. There are many ways to bring families together around shared interests. The more you get to know everyone, the better you will understand how to build on those shared interests.

> I was pleased to participate in my first "Grandparents' Picnic" at the elementary school. I met my granddaughter on the school lawn, and we set up our blanket and the lunch foods I brought. Before she took a bite, my granddaughter jumped up and ran off. Where did she go? Well, soon she returned with three boys from her second-grade class. She noticed they were standing alone against the brick school wall because they didn't have grandparents to participate. We were able to all fit on my blanket and we had quite a lively conversation about superhero movies. Can you think of ways the school might have planned this event with more sensitivity?

In many schools each teacher and specialist operates individually to interact with parents – and in some schools teachers are asked not to contact parents but to go through the principal or head master. But for the family this results in them feeling like they are getting lots of info that may be repetitive or disconnected – even conflictful. Think how you would feel if you received uncoordinated, overwhelming info. It would be better to get streamlined, cohesive info – showing that the senders were collaborating and working in unison with some kind of plan – and that would ease communication on both sides.

Be prepared to answer questions from families who have concerns about their child's well-being, behavior, or learning. Many will look to their child's teacher as an expert in education and child development. They may view the teacher as a trusted partner who knows their child and can offer advice. At other times, you may need to have difficult conversations with families about concerns you may have about the same topics. Objectivity, empathy, respect, and openness on both sides will support effective discussions. Here are some helpful strategies:

- Use reflective listening – repeat the person's question or comment to be sure you have understood it correctly.
- Answer briefly and invite a response from the family member before launching into a lengthy explanation of something only to find that's not what they meant to ask about.
- Use plain language, factual observations, and specific examples rather than generalities and assumptions. Follow up with notes or an email to be sure all sides have a good understanding of what was discussed. Try to use an interpreter, but if not possible, a written summary can be translated. Families should also have the opportunity to reply in their most comfortable language and expect the teacher to have interpretation or translation services available.

> A parent received an email from her young child's teacher saying "I observed on the playground today and noticed that your child, Amelie, was happily playing a jumping game with some of her classmates. She was taking turns, jumping, laughing, and commenting to her friends. I know you had concerns about her social interactions so I thought you'd like to know." Positive messages have big impact.

Information Requested from Families

To support valuable partnerships with families, you should plan regular opportunities to request information from them. In addition to the getting-to-know-you beginnings of your relationship, keep that line of communication open so families can update you on their child's accomplishments, concerns, or changing interests (Buchanan & Buchanan, 2017). You will also want to know as much as possible about changes in the child's home or living situation.

> Heather recently had a very rough day in kindergarten. When Mr. Quentin mentioned this to her mom, he was told that Heather's pet fish had died just before school that morning. Mr. Quentin expressed sympathy and reminded Heather's mom that she could use the school text messaging system or give him a call to let him know about any changes that might affect Heather at school so he could be prepared to offer support.

Supports for Learning at Home

In the early years, there are many ways that families can act as full partners in teaching their child. This is especially valuable when children are DLLs. With so much research pointing to the effectiveness of continued learning of and learning in the home language, the family is a critical resource to fill gaps in what's available at school (NAEYC, undated). Here are some strategies for supporting learning at home:

- Make it very clear that rich, heartfelt conversations, stories, songs, and games are wonderful learning activities that will improve children's success in school. These activities provide additional benefits for children who are DLLs if they occur in the home language.
- Ask families to read to their children every day … and then demonstrate how to read to a young child and talk about books. Send home literacy kits (e.g., bags with books and props for home literacy activities) along with a quick guide or video about how to use them.
- Use text messaging programs to spark home learning.

> Mrs. Li learned how to use the school's new messaging system to send late homework reminders and behavior notices. She thought of some creative ways to make better use of the system, so she started sending messages with a song the children sang that day or a conversation starter. For example, every family got a text message in their own language that said "We got a new class pet today. Ask your child what it is called and what it was eating!" Family members used this message for an informative conversation on the way home.

- Offer a variety of ways for families to learn more about different kinds of activities they can do at home. Some may really enjoy science, but others might like to do art activities or cooking with their child. Respond to their interests and let families know that they can build vocabulary, problem-solving, counting, and many other areas of knowledge and skill in almost any positive family activity. There's no right or wrong choice.
- Individualized Family Service Plans (IFSP), Individual Education Programs (IEP), 504 plans, and Special Educational Needs (SEN) plans are developed for children with identified disabilities to guide the supports, adaptations, and therapies they need to reach their full potential. For young children, family participation in this work is vital and valuable. You can help families understand about positive ways they can extend the benefits of specialized learning supports by practicing them at home. They will likely need ongoing encouragement to keep on track and to help their child keep moving forward.
- Remember that families of young children have many demands on their time and attention. Be careful to frame guidance for home learning activities in ways that are encouraging and respectful, but not punitive or burdensome. It is not effective to create a forced learning situation where families and children experience home learning as a stressful and unrewarding thing. Suggest lighthearted games or optional supports that can be fit into challenging schedules. Always encourage families to read and discuss stories with their children, and show them how to make this a warm and fun activity in ways that are appropriate to the different ages of children. We don't expect a 6-month-old to sit quietly through a whole story – but a few pages and

patting the pictures is a good start that introduces new vocabulary and the purpose of books. Even as children begin to read on their own in first and second grade, they still benefit from the cozy connections they make when a family member reads them a bedtime story in the language that is most comfortable for them.

Families Contribute to the Learning Environment

Families have a lot to offer to their child's classroom and school. The term "funds of knowledge" is often used to describe the wealth of assets each family can contribute to make early education more meaningful and relatable for their child. Each family has expertise in their own language, culture, and the activities and interests of their children. Members of each family may also have skills, talents, or experiences that can contribute to learning at school (NAEYC, undated).

When young children are learning new concepts, it helps for them to use materials they already know about. Familiar items help a child make connections between prior knowledge and the new concept or skill you want to teach. This is especially important for children who are newcomers or children who are DLLs. When children start in a new school or program, the new materials, new language, new rules, new people, new content can all be overwhelming to them. When you ask families to send objects, videos, or stories from home, you make it possible for each child to see something recognizable that they can understand and talk about. Not only does this represent the child's home culture, but it also provides a practical basis upon which the child can make the needed learning connections. For infants and toddlers, ask families to provide photos of favorite people and pets that can be made into a baby-safe photo album. Preschool families might send in cleaned, empty food containers for the dramatic play kitchen area. Kindergarten families might send in kitchen tools that children can use with clay. First grade families might be asked to send in magazines, greeting cards, catalogs, and newspapers in English and their home languages that children can use for collage and letter and word recognition activities.

Here are some examples from the field:

- A grandfather who was a musician visited the classroom and taught children songs in his native language.
- An aunt who lived in a major city had a video chat with her nephew's first grade class in a rural school and she took the children on a virtual walk through her neighborhood.
- Mothers of children in a bilingual preschool class attended English as a Second Language (ESL) classes while their children were in session. As part of their ESL work, they recorded rhymes and chants they remembered from their childhood, translated them into English, and made posters and videos to share with their children's preschool class.
- Parents of a newly enrolled baby provided a video showing how they calm their infant before naptime.
- A kindergartner's fifth-grade brother came to class to show and tell about their family's new pet chameleon.
- A bilingual family member came to the school social worker's office with the newcomer parents of a young student to describe their harrowing refugee experiences and how they worried about the effects this would have on their child's ability to settle in and learn.
- A child who entered preschool not speaking was not responding even when the speech therapist was brought in. A conversation with the family revealed the boy was

very interested in bugs and insects. The speech therapist and teacher worked together to gather some books, puppets, and videos about bugs. They even brought in a small container with some leaves and caterpillars. What they learned from one conversation with the family changed the course of the child's learning as he began to speak with increasing confidence and eventually taught some of his friends some fun facts he knew about bugs.

Connecting with the Community

Your school or program is a vital part of the community. Consider participating in community-wide activities to publicize the success of your school and your students and to celebrate the assets and diversity that are included.

The community can also be a vital part of your school or program (Zacarian, Calderón, & Gottlieb, 2021). You might call on the community to support work by inviting approved bilingual volunteers to join in classroom reading, demonstrations, or to serve as play partners. Provide a video orientation or some training to prepare them for developmentally appropriate interactions with your students and ways to use their language assets to support learning. Other options include reaching out to local organizations that represent the cultures and languages of your group and ask them to contribute stories, games, and learning materials.

Many programs ask employers, health and dental clinics, and other community services to host in-person or virtual field trips to help children learn about their neighborhood friends and leaders. Public libraries participate in the Association for Library Service to Children (ALSC) program called DÍA (Diversity in Action) as a way to highlight diverse languages and resources provided by the local libraries. Many children's librarians have received training and early literacy kits from ALSC that they can use at their home library or bring out to preschools, childcare programs, and schools. Libraries are great community partners for families and educators. They have a mission that is directly in line with your personal and school-wide educational goals, they are designed to support diverse families, and they have access to many different kinds of books and resources in many languages, representing many cultures.

Childcare resource and referral agencies are the organizational hubs of early childhood care and education information in each community. They generally have information for families in multiple languages, workshops and special events for caregivers and teachers, and information about summer camps, after school care, and other services.

Stay informed about the services available in your community so you can connect families with the help or engagement they need. As you develop a strong relationship with each family, you may be the person they come to if they experience a crisis. Be ready with referral information for social services, financial assistance, health care resources, and safety supports. You can also encourage family learning together by sharing updates about free concerts, public library programs, cultural fairs, and nature education opportunities.

Many companies, organizations, and even foreign embassies will respond to requests from educators and supply fun or informative materials to support learning. For example, many larger banks have kits for learning about money. Travel agents might donate posters of the countries that some of your families are from. Dentists might have children's dental care kits to give out.

> A New Jersey Head Start program enrolled a large number of children who had moved to the area from a particular region of Mexico. The Head Start director contacted the Mexican embassy and soon received a package of color posters representing the

> area, some brochures, souvenirs, and children's activity books that had been created by the regional visitor's council. The staff and children learned together about some of the traditions, the landscape, and the unique characteristics of their region.

Community-Based Language Schools

In areas with strong language-based communities, families or houses of worship often establish weekend or part-time language schools. These are intended to help children learn their heritage language if it is not strong at home. We do not have research to identify best practices for these schools. They may be taught by experienced language teachers, or they may be taught by heritage language speakers who have no knowledge about developmentally appropriate practices and effective teaching methods. This is an interesting phenomenon in many communities. It would be helpful for you to know if any of your students are participating in this type of language study so you can offer support for sustaining that learning and connecting it with your lesson plans.

Community and Families Unite for Tribal Language Revitalization

The story of Tribal language revitalization in the United States is very compelling. Many young children were starting life in Native American families that spoke only English. With fewer and fewer young people growing up speaking tribal languages, the communities became concerned that these beautiful languages would be lost. Scientists, educators, funders, and community members joined forces to develop a plan for language revitalization that was only possible if all of these stakeholders worked together. In Native American communities, where respect for Tribal elders is very important, it was a natural solution to involve these community language experts to participate with early childhood programs to bring the languages back to life, and to enliven the use of these languages. They brought stories, games, and music to preschool programs in many locations. Children and teachers all learned new words, songs, stories, and chants. Family members were included in the learning so they could support the Tribal language in their own lives as well as in their interactions with their children. This is a compelling example of how language became the driving force that brought community members together for a common goal (NCCLR, 2014).

Communication Tools and Resources

In your work with diverse families, you will encounter many digital and physical tools as well as a variety of resources to support and enhance communication, understanding, and relationship building.

a   Interpreter – certified, interpreter service, informal staff or family member (must receive training on early childhood uses and confidentiality), live via telephone service.
b   Translator – certified, translation service, informal staff/family member/volunteer, translation software, website, mobile apps.
c   Text message – informal, subscription text updates for families, two-way home-school text message platforms that include translation such as Remind, Talking Points.
d   Email – for two-way communication, allows families to get help with the information sent, used for exchanging photos and videos.

e   Paper – color code for different purposes such as always using green paper for forms requiring payment, repeating sentence forms, standardized icons to enhance meaning.
f   Phone calls – if families prefer voice communication, consider enlisting more experienced bilingual family members from school to act as ambassadors to reach out to new families and make sure they stay informed.
g   Video chat – Zoom, Teams, other forms of digital interactions.
h   Social media – Facebook, Twitter, Instagram.
i   In person meetings – Committee, advisory board, focus group, or informal socialization events such as coffee corner at drop-off time.
j   Written information – Surveys and suggestion boxes.
k   Family – teacher conferences.
l   Classroom video access – programs that allow family members to access closed circuit TV video of what's happening in the classroom.
m   Video collections for families – ReadyRosie.com, ECLKC.

Transitions

Families need support as they transition their child into a new school and/or class. Your school or program should have a solid process to welcome new families and to guide families through transitions. Your plans should mesh with the policies of your program, while adding your own touches. Pay special attention to supports for families who speak different languages.

Create a very simple welcome packet of information to help each family know more about what to expect when their child enters your class. Use photos and simple descriptions. Some teachers even provide QR codes or links to brief videos of class routines and fun activities. Some teachers will interact directly with family members when they drop off their child. Other schools have a centralized drop off procedure or bus transportation, making contact with family members each day impossible. You will need to be prepared for both scenarios.

Families need to know that their child's teacher is ready for their child – that they know enough about the child to make them feel safe, welcome, and comfortable even from the first day. If you don't have contact with the family in-person, a quick phone call or text message to say hello and let them know something positive about their child's first day can be very comforting. It must be so difficult for families of young children to send their child off for the day to an unfamiliar place, knowing their young child may not have the language to communicate what they did or how they felt all day. Be open to the family's questions and suggestions to help their child make the transition.

Language is key to supportive transitions. Remember that a sign saying "hello" or "welcome" in many languages is nice, but once you say hello – that word doesn't give you much more to talk about. Try learning some key words or phrases in the child's home language from the family members. A short list of ten or twenty words that you really need to facilitate communication with the child can make a significant difference in the child's first day. Many teachers learn words for toilet, play, eat, drink, stop, help, good, hurt, and phrases like "how are you?" and "your mom will come back soon." You might learn the word for "bathroom" or "grandma" from a website – but that might not be the term the family uses with their own child. An added benefit to this practice is that it affirms family members' roles as valued partners as you begin your work together to teach their child.

116 *Family and Community*

> Some teachers ask families to create a scrapbook with pictures and messages about things that are important, familiar, and loved by their child. Some even send some craft supplies to support this activity. This can become part of the child's portfolio that is updated regularly and then a passed along to the child's next teacher.

When it is time for the child to transition out of your classroom, here are some things to keep in mind. The school will usually have clear policies about what can and cannot be released to the family or passed along to the next teacher. Sharing information about the child is important, but so is confidentiality. Children may be transferring out of your class to receive specialized services based on language needs or an identified disability. Families may have forms to fill out or agreements to sign. You can be helpful during these transitions by being familiar with these processes and ready to help the families understand their options and responsibilities.

Ideally, the child's current teacher should be invited to meetings regarding the child's next placement. ESL teachers, preschool/nursery teachers, and general education teachers can be valuable contributors to decision-making processes because of their expertise and their familiarity with the child. This also makes them helpful advocates to support the voices of the families in these procedures.

Conclusion

This chapter has described a wide array of opportunities and responsibilities that may fall within your job description as an early childhood educator. Always keep in mind that you don't do this work in isolation. You will be part of a larger community of educators, staff, volunteers, and families working together for the good of all of the children. The NAEYC principles can inform system-wide, research-based planning efforts that should include families in decision-making for the school and for their child, support two-way and reciprocal communications that support diverse languages, and strengthen learning at home. This system-wide approach to engaging with families and the community ensures improved desired outcomes for children and sets families on their path as their child's advocate and the teacher's partner.

Choose Your Own Path Check-In

1. What have you learned in this chapter about working with families and the community that will help you in one of these roles?
2. In a job interview for one of these positions, how would you describe your top priority for engaging with families to support children from all language backgrounds?

Infant/Toddler teacher	Preschool/Nursery teacher	Kindergarten/Reception teacher	Primary teacher
ESL/EAL teacher	Special educational needs teacher	Speech therapist	Physical therapist
Occupational Therapist	Early childhood coach	Education Manager/Supervisor	Director/Headmaster/Principal

Social Media Messages and Discussion Starters

- Most school family engagement plans connect with some or most families. But, it's the families that don't connect that might need you the most. What would you change?
- Flip your family engagement plan. Instead of planning activities, plan for each family what will work for them, what language they prefer, and how they would like to participate.
- Why do some early childhood programs partner with local libraries and others don't? What are some benefits of working with your library to enhance the learning experiences of children in your class?

References

Buchanan, K., & Buchanan, T. (2017) Six Steps to Partner with Diverse Families, *Principal Magazine*, January/February, 46–47.

Cooper, A. (2021) *And Justice for ELs: A Leader's Guide to Creating and Sustaining Equitable Schools*, Thousand Oaks, CA: Corwin.

Gonzalez-Mena, J. (2014) 50 *Strategies for Communicating and Working with Diverse Families*, 3rd ed., Thousand Oaks, CA: Pearson.

Koralek, D., Nemeth, K., & Ramsey, K (2019) *Families and Educators Together: Building Great Relationships that Support Young Children*, Washington, DC: NAEYC.

National Academies of Sciences, Engineering, and Medicine (2017) *Promoting the Educational Success of Children and Youth Learning English: Promising Futures*, Washington, DC: The National Academies Press.

NAEYC (undated) *Principles of Effective Family Engagement*, Washington, DC: NAEYC.

NCCLR (2014) *A Report on Tribal Language Revitalization in Head Start and Early Head Start*, New York: National Center on Cultural and Linguistic Responsiveness, retrieved from https://eclkc.ohs.acf.hhs.gov/sites/default/files/pdf/report-tribal-language-revitalization-2015.pdf.

Vesely, C., Letiecq, B., & Goodman, R. (2017) Immigrant Family Resilience in Context: Using a Community-Based Approach to Build a New Conceptual Model, *Journal of Family Theory and Review*, 9, 93–110.

Zacarian, D., Calderón, M.E., & Gottlieb, M (2021) *Beyond Crises: Overcoming Linguistic and Cultural Inequities in Communities, Schools, and Classrooms*, Thousand Oaks, CA: Corwin Press.

8 Co-teaching, Collaborating, and Working with Specialists

Follow the Chapter 8 Roadmap with These Headings

Introduction	Space for In-Person Collaboration
Partnering with Paraprofessionals	Shared Professional Development
Collaborating with Teachers	Collaboration for Remote Learning
Co-Teaching	Working with Specialists
Collaboration as a Priority for Teacher Educators	Conclusion
Social Media and Digital Connections	

Chapter 8 explains the many collaborative relationships that will make your work stronger as an early childhood educator. You will read about working with paraprofessionals and teachers. Processes and practices for co-teaching and collaborating will be provided. Sections will cover ways of communicating with colleagues via social media, digital connections, and space for in-person meetings. The chapter provides recommendations for shared professional development, working together to support children during remote learning and working with a variety of specialists to ensure all children receive high-quality, coordinated early education.

> **Top Tips for Collaborating, Co-Teaching, and Working with Specialists**
> - When collaborating with other teachers or specialists, plan intentionally to agree on modes of communication that work for all.
> - Many schools hire paraprofessionals or assistant teachers who are bilingual to increase supports for the home languages of children. Extensive training will be needed to prepare bilingual staff for when and how to use their valuable language assets.
> - When specialists work with young children, they may use a push-in, or pull-out, or consultative model. Minimizing disruptions in the children's routine should be a priority when making these plans.
> - Part of the value of working with other educators is learning about their expertise in the field and learning how to enhance and extend the services they are providing to children.
> - Co-teaching may be new to many teachers. Ask your employer to provide guidance and sufficient planning time to do it well.

DOI: 10.4324/9781003089216-8

- Creating long-term professional learning communities can be an effective way for peers to support each other in improving quality and implementing professional development content.
- Music, art, computer, and physical education teachers may seem to operate in their own fields, but in a diverse early childhood program they can increase effectiveness if they co-plan with classroom teachers. Children, especially dual language learners, benefit from repetition and extension of learning so they can practice their new vocabulary. Look for ways to link art projects, songs, computer explorations, and physical games to the content happening in the general education setting at the time.
- Social media forums provide opportunities for educators to learn from and collaborate with colleagues outside of their own school, region, or country.

Introduction

When you chose early childhood education as a career, you planned and prepared for the work you would do with children. But when you enter the field, you will find that a lot of your time and energy will be devoted to working with other professionals. The saying is true: Teaching is like a team sport! There may still be times when you feel isolated or independent in your work, but those times will be balanced with many opportunities to share ideas, plans, practices, insights, and the teaching stage with other adults who are as dedicated to the field as you are. This is a complex and enlivening part of the work that needs a significant place in all teacher preparation programs. The purpose of this chapter is to prepare teachers for collaborations with paraprofessionals, other teachers, and specialists. It will also provide information for paraprofessionals and specialists about preparing to work with classroom teachers.

Partnering with Paraprofessionals

Most childcare and preschool programs have more than one adult with each group of children. This generally includes a lead teacher, or a certified teacher in some cases, along with paraprofessionals who have fewer qualifications than the teacher. Job titles for these positions include teacher aide, assistant teacher, or one-on-one aide. These staff members are needed to meet requirements for adult-to-child ratios. Some programs also hire paraprofessionals who speak the languages of the children and families in the program and represent their cultures. Including children with disabilities may result in a program or school serving children at any age from birth to 8 years adding one or more paraprofessionals to the classroom. A child with a significant disability might be assigned their own one-on-one aide. In some classrooms there are as many adults as there are children.

With this many adults, the lead teacher or classroom teacher is responsible for coordinating the team, but this may not be a formal supervisory role. The teacher is accountable for ensuring equitable access to high-quality education for all children in her care or class. In many states, regulations prohibit paraprofessionals from taking over as a teacher, or they state that only certified teachers can introduce topics and present lessons. This should be clarified for you at the time of your employment. Also, keep in mind that many teachers start their careers with paraprofessional positions, so you may see both sides of this collaboration.

Many schools provide professional development training for teachers while the paraprofessionals stay with the children. Then teachers are expected to impart what they've learned to their team. Ideally, there will be a system in place for this or you might need to plan one. Trainers and/or supervisors should identify which parts of the training must be conveyed to paraprofessionals, and they should provide copies, materials, and allotted time to make this possible. It will be up to you to make sure that every member of your team gets all the information they need.

Changing Roles of Paraprofessionals

In a well-functioning early childhood classroom each adult has a well-defined role and a clear understanding of the shared goals of the classroom. Two key trends are amplifying attention to the potential roles played by paraprofessionals: Growing diversity in the population of young children is awakening childcare programs and schools to the need to build and support a more diverse workforce. Further, there is an increasing awareness that programs and schools need to elevate inclusive programs that support equity and belonging, and that combat bias (Brillante & Nemeth, 2016).

Bilingual paraprofessionals may provide needed home language supports in the following ways, but training is needed for them to be most effective:

- Sustained conversations with children in their home language (training is needed on how to engage in high-quality teaching and learning interactions).
- Facilitating small group or individual story times and learning activities (curriculum training is needed).
- Interacting with families in their home language (training is needed on confidentiality rules and handling difficult conversations).
- Translating and interpreting (this can be a valuable service to the school, but compensation and time should be allotted rather than making this extra work for the lowest paid staff members).
- Gathering observations, anecdotes, and work samples for children's assessment portfolios (training is needed on observing, recording, and collecting information about what children say and do during the day as well as the program's assessment process/tool).

As you can see, the most valuable functions of paraprofessionals will require some kind of professional development, coaching, and supervision, while being careful not to overstep the boundaries of the positions. When some members of your team speak the home languages of the children and families, they run the risk of being the only person who interacts with those children and families. This can be comforting, but also may isolate the child from some of what the rest of the group is doing or what the teacher is saying to them. It also may mean that families become comfortable in the relationship with one member of the team and other members find it difficult to engage with them across language differences. These are all issues that need to be addressed on an ongoing basis in your work.

When paraprofessionals are hired to support special education classrooms or high-needs classrooms, they may come in with the goal of supporting particular children who need a lot of adult support. Some children with significant disabilities are assigned a one-on-one aide to help them with learning, participating, and getting around. Keep in mind that an inclusive classroom is not meant to be a big room, where isolated pairs or groups do separate activities. Inclusion means that children should play and work together, and participate in learning activities as different but equal members of the class. Paraprofessionals need to understand when and how to scaffold to help children get started with a learning task or social interaction, then pull back on the support to encourage the child's independent participation.

The same kind of approach is effective for bilingual paraprofessionals. We know from research that it is not effective for bilingual staff to simply whisper a translation of what the teacher is saying into the child's ear. Children who are dual language learners (DLLs) need some time to focus on what the teacher is saying in English and they need direct, meaningful conversations in their home languages at other times (López & Páez, 2020).

Multiple adults in an infant or toddler room often have the same positions because the program promotes primary caregiving – the practice of assigning each infant or toddler to one specific adult who is principally responsible for caring for that child and communicating with the child's family (Program for Infant-Toddler Care, 2021). In high-quality infant/toddler programs, there should be one or a small number of children engaged directly with a familiar adult who has developed a bond with each of those children rather than one lead teacher presenting lessons to the whole group. While this may be a unique way to arrange a team of adults, it shares the common need for all of the adults to be well-prepared to provide high-quality care for all of the children.

Collaborating with Teachers

There are many ways to benefit from working with other teachers and specialists in early childhood education. For many years, most developed nations, including England and the United States, have prepared teachers with particular specialties for particular types of positions. This created specialized silos that worked independently. Teacher preparation programs have independent departments for each specialty, there are separate certifications, and specialists attend their own conferences and read their own journals. Recently, the trend in schools is to break down the barriers between specialties and bring educators together to combine their knowledge and skills for the benefit of a more inclusive approach to education. If collaboration is the new norm in schools, then it may be time for colleges, universities, and professional organizations to follow suit.

Many of the challenges faced by early childhood educators involve multiple disciplines. Specialists may have become accustomed to working in silos, but children are not quite so neatly categorized. They may have assets and needs that cut across many disciplines as well. Working together in teams may be the best way to bring the input of specialists together to share information, resources, and solutions (Honigsfeld & Dove, 2010).

Collaborative relationships can take many forms. Pair collaborations form when two professionals work together for an entire class or a particular student or category of students. Some programs and schools also set up teaching teams or grade clusters to work together. They may coordinate efforts on a short-term project or special event, or they may have regular meetings to exchange information and updates relevant to their work.

Often, collaborations are created to improve teaching practices rather than to meet the needs of a particular child or children. They may be formed to exchange feedback and collegial support. Personal learning networks (PLNs) are informal groups of like-minded professionals with shared interests and goals, but different areas of experience and expertise. They turn to each other to get feedback on ideas or solutions to problems. They may be part of the same program, or they may find each other on social media platforms or at professional association meetings. Professional learning communities (PLCs) have a more formal structure of members who commit to meeting a specified learning goal together with regular meetings, consulting experts, and homework assignments.

Research has shown this particular approach to shared in-depth learning about research, directed toward real implementation can be very effective in improving teaching practice. These can also be great opportunities for teachers and specialists from different positions to join together in meaningful ways (Thornton & Cherrington, 2019). Some schools build PLCs into contracts and schedules, so that is something to investigate with your employer.

> XYZ Preschool has a professional development plan that involves staff in choosing a topical focus for a year, then assigns teachers in co-learning pairs. These teachers attend professional development together, then observe each other implementing new strategies and provide each other with feedback and support. By visiting each other's class, the teachers get to see different examples of the new strategies at work. This type of professional development offering provides teachers time and purpose to develop valuable professional relationships with each other.

Coaching as a relationship-based approach to professional learning is growing increasingly popular in the field of early care and education. An educator is trained as a coach and enters into a coaching partnership with a teacher to discuss observations, assessment data, and personal needs leading to plans for teacher improvement that is addressed in this collaborative relationship. This is discussed further in Chapter 9.

Collaboration can happen in smaller ways such as sharing lesson plans or activity kits in staff meetings or collected in a supply closet. Some schools compile an internal staff newsletter as a forum for teachers to highlight their creativity with materials, activities, or resources they've developed. It is important for all staff to be included in this type of exchange so all areas of expertise, experience, and innovation can enter the mix.

Co-Teaching

Co-teaching is a unique form of educator collaboration. It involves working together on the whole range of teaching tasks from planning to lessons/activities, to evaluation (Honigsfeld & Dove, 2010). In practice, two people might share a class and responsibilities, but they still may have siloed roles, for example, the ESL co-teacher only stepping up during language arts/literacy lessons and letting the general education teacher take care of everything else or the special education co-teacher in an inclusion class only focusing on the "included" children who have disabilities and delays. It takes time for teachers with different areas of expertise to unite as a coordinated co-teaching team. It takes time each day to allow for effective communication and team building activities, and it takes patience over time for these adjustments to take shape. As their approach becomes more cohesive, co-teaching partners are able to create blended supports that work for children who may have disabilities, or behavior challenges along with language differences or other learning factors.

Co-teachers may find themselves teaching over digital media while children are home. It will be necessary to maintain the collegial relationship with each other, but to take a fresh look at the entire process of co-teaching. We can be sure that it won't be effective for two teachers to sign on and overwhelm children with co-presented lessons or lectures. This will be a time when your work will be most effective if you are each working with small groups and the remaining time is used for extensive planning.

Two-Way Dual Language Immersion

A unique version of co-teaching happens in a two-way dual language immersion class. A well-known study (Barnett et al., 2007) found this approach was more effective than a monolingual English immersion classroom for young children. Many experts and researchers have acknowledged the value of high-quality implementation of this dual language format, but we do not yet have enough research to specify exactly how to set up the model. In general, the classes can be established for any age, birth through primary years. About half the children speak one language and half speak the other language. The children stay together and they all learn some of the time in one of their languages, some of the time in the other language. The goal, which is often well-achieved, is for all of the children to learn and develop equally in both languages to become bilingual and biliterate.

With groups of young children, it is advisable to conduct these classes with a team of co-teachers rather than one bilingual teacher going back and forth between languages. Having each teacher entirely responsible for one language seems to bring the language into focus for the children. They get the benefit of two high-quality language models. The research does not dictate how much time should be spent in each language, but for young children, shorter time periods are better. For example, they might use alternating days or two-day blocks in each language. Some programs even do half a day in one language and half in the other, but it will be important to switch which language happens in the morning or afternoon so children experience all learning activities and routines in both languages. The co-teachers need to plan carefully. Theoretically, the learning should move forward, challenging the children to learn new information in each language each day. It is not meant to be a constant repeating pattern of the same information in each language. Instead, teachers need to plan to use methods that support multilingual learning, such as visuals and demonstrations, to help children progress in all learning domains without much repetition.

Collaboration as a Priority for Teacher Educators

It seems like a bit of a disconnect when we see teacher education graduates taking positions that require extensive and meaningful collaborations, while colleges and universities still operate in isolated departments. For example, some colleges provide English language supports for immigrants who are studying education, but they rarely collaborate between the two departments to bring students English practice using content from early childhood education courses. That would be a significant and powerful step to take. In fact, the Migration Policy Institute report (Park et al., 2015) showed that a potential barrier to bilingual adults progressing to higher paying positions in early childhood education is the lack of support they receive to get degrees in education.

Teacher preparation programs should model the same kinds of cross-discipline collaborations that graduates will see in their employment. Professors should also collaborate to unify and deepen content across disciplines. What are some ways that your courses could provide you with more cross-discipline content and discussion? These recommendations also apply to the professional development you will encounter after you graduate. When you are involved in planning your school's professional development or when you are invited to submit questions or feedback, these are the kinds of suggestions you can make to have your voice heard. This chapter contains models for making this possible.

Social Media and Digital Connections

There are many ways to connect with other professionals online, and more platforms continue to appear. There are ways to interact with and benefit from colleagues from your own program or from all over the world. You might use social media to find one or two like-minded professionals who would suggest solutions or introduce you to their contacts. You might participate in asynchronous collaborations by submitting questions to a group and watching answers come in over time. Or you might join a real-time discussion on Facebook Live, a topical Twitter chat, or a book discussion on an audio platform like Clubhouse. There are broad, general education groups and groups with very narrowly defined focus.

This author cohosts a Twitter chat on education for English/multilingual learners that has been operating weekly since 2010 (#ELLCHAT and #MLLCHAT). Members of this chat have gone on to co-present conference sessions and webinars, or to co-author articles. As with other social media groups, members will announce in-person meet-ups at conferences that help build these valuable collaborations. You might join the Facebook page for a national organization or a subgroup. For example, the American Educational Research Association has a Facebook page for their Bilingual Education Research special interest group where members disseminate information they've found in their current research and discuss ideas for future studies, sometimes meeting new research partners online. You can find many ways to learn more about other disciplines and find new talking partners that can give you insights into areas of expertise that might not be available in your local areas. Publishers host Zoom chats with authors. Experts may be interviewed on Clubhouse. With the advantages of digital connections, you might find yourself collaborating with top experts in the field.

Space for In-Person Collaboration

Early childhood educators are famously adaptable. Many workshops are presented in classrooms with adult teachers perched on chairs designed for 3-year-olds. However, adults learn and think best in respectful and comfortable settings. Schools and programs that promote collaboration should set up appropriate spaces for the most productive work. In addition to adult-sized seating, there should be table space where teams can lay out materials to facilitate their discussions. Privacy is important so partners can speak freely and not disturb others. Big boards are so often needed to show group planning such as flip charts or white boards. Always make sure there is ample storage for files, portfolios, and resources. Digital resources such as file sharing platforms and shared editing capacity will also be helpful. Adequate time for discussions and planning make it possible to use the physical set-ups in meaningful ways.

Shared Professional Development

Collaborations provide early childhood educators with opportunities to learn together, coordinating their funds of knowledge and developing new skills based on this combined foundation. Such collaborations may be addressed nationally; for example, the U.S. Department of Education recommended joint professional development to include preschool teachers in learning about teaching linguistically diverse children (U.S. Department of Education, 2016). This shared experience is considered a priority that can be adopted by collaborations across other ages of children (e.g., infant/toddler teachers, primary teachers) and disciplines as well. Personal professional learning can also be part of this coordinated approach.

Reading material from each other's disciplines can help partners find common ground to address common goals. With the rapid growth of online learning options for educators, there are countless opportunities that fit your agreed-upon goals.

Collaboration for Remote Learning

Significant aspects of our field changed in 2020 with the COVID-19 pandemic. Many schools and childcare centers shut down and teachers had to switch quickly to online learning. According to Honigsfeld and Nordmeyer (2021), "as a result, we have witnessed a seismic shift toward a more collaborative mindset" (p. 2). The authors suggest that new conditions have made social-emotional support even more important in collaborative work. They also outlined a three-step format for co-planning that involves:

1 pre-planning to agree on how and when to meet for planning and collaboration;
2 co-planning time to come up with processes, sequence, and scope of working together; and
3 post-planning to assign the tasks established in the co-planning time.

The importance of this basic process is in its ability to support a continuing structure for work that may be new to the participants and may be happening in unprecedented circumstances.

Working with families is critical in planning for remote learning, as we discuss further in Chapter 7. In these circumstances, family members might function as co-teaching partners. Honigsfeld and Nordmeyer (2021) suggest that changing our wording to talk about "learning at home" instead of remote or virtual learning may help children feel more comfortable. This terminology also indirectly honors the contributions of family members by crediting the strengths of learning at home with participation of teachers rather than remote learning that is transmitted by teachers.

Paraprofessionals can play an important role during remote learning if the work of each adult is carefully planned. For example, bilingual assistants can provide much needed conversational support and explanations in the home languages of children and families. Those with experience working with children who may have behavior challenges or challenges dealing with remote learning can provide more personalized interactions, commenting on the child's work and engaging them with personal attention.

When working with professionals from different disciplines, it is important to clearly uphold the principles of developmentally appropriate practice (NAEYC, 2020). This means working together to provide meaningful experiences in the child's home language that are fully connected with the overall curriculum and plans for learning activities. Real materials should be provided to the children or found at home. Lessons should be linked to each other rather than appearing as disconnected learning opportunities. Young children with diverse languages, experiences, and abilities will need to see how their play and learning activities are tied together with shared vocabulary and concepts so they can use prior learning to build new learning. As co-teaching partners, family members also need to be able to see and support those patterns and connections.

Working with Specialists

Table 8.1 is intended to support both the specialists in early childhood education and the classroom teachers/carers that work with them. These mutually beneficial relationships elevate the work of all parties by combining their broad ranges of expertise.

Table 8.1 Suggested topics for collaboration

Position	What they do	Ideas from this book to support collaborative work in early childhood
Special Education Teacher or Special Educational Needs & Disabilities	Certified to teach children with disabilities and developmental delays	Learning about typical language and developmental milestones Adapting special education curriculum for children who are DLLs Using culturally relatable materials
Occupational Therapist	Help children develop small motor skills for writing, self-care, using fingers and hands for schoolwork, social interactions – everyday activities	Connecting with and supporting children who are DLLs Partnering with diverse families
Physical Therapist	Help children develop large motor physical skills, balance, and coordination so children can learn to move more independently	Connecting with and supporting children who are DLLs Partnering with diverse families
ABA – Applied Behavior Analysis therapist	Uses positive reinforcement to address social, communication, and learning skills – most often with children with autism	Connecting with and supporting children who are DLLs Importance of supporting home language Partnering with diverse families
English as a Second Language teacher/EAL	Certified to help children learn to speak, understand, read, and write in English – ESL in U.S. EAL in U.K.	Learning about typical language and developmental milestones in the early years Consulting with general education teacher and supporting general education curriculum Learning about developmentally appropriate practices in the early years
Bilingual Education teacher	Certified to teach in English plus another language	Learning about typical language and developmental milestones in early years Coordinating with and adapting general education curriculum Learning about developmentally appropriate practices in the early years
Speech/language therapist	Help children develop expressive and receptive vocabularies, diagnose and treat speech, language, cognitive/communication disorders	Learning why supporting both home language and English is important Including the child's interests and culturally relevant materials Partnering with diverse families
Reading specialist	Teacher with additional training/certification to help struggling readers	Connecting with and supporting children who are DLLs Supporting early literacy in home language and English, biliteracy
Children's librarian or school librarian	Purchasing and organizing books for children; researching and curating digital, video, and other types of materials; and teaching children early literacy skills and about library use	Learning about the importance of authentic home language materials Supporting racial equity, anti-bias, and linguistically and culturally authentic resources

(*Continued*)

Table 8.1 (Cont.)

Position	What they do	Ideas from this book to support collaborative work in early childhood
Physical education teacher	Body management, sportsmanship, and sports	Learning about typical language and developmental milestones in the early years Learning/using strategies for connecting with children who are DLLs, home language supports Learning about developmentally appropriate practices in the early years
Music teacher	Vocal and instrumental music	Typical language and developmental milestones in early years Strategies for connecting with children who are DLLs, home language and culture supports Developmentally appropriate practices in the early years
Foreign language/world languages teacher	Teaching a new, non-majority language to children	Learning about typical language and developmental milestones in the early years Consulting with general education teacher and supporting general education curriculum Learning about developmentally appropriate practices in the early years
Drama teacher	Teaching about acting and expressing, and creating backdrops and costumes	Learning about typical language and developmental milestones in the early years Strategies for including children with diverse experiences, cultures, abilities and languages (DECAL) Learning about developmentally appropriate practices in the early years
Gifted and talented teacher	Teaching children with top scores on typical assessments	Learning about why supporting home languages is important Strategies for including children with DECAL Learning about developmentally appropriate practices in the early years
Computer/technology teacher	Organizes computer/tablet choices, apps, and software, and teaches children how to use them safely	Learning about typical language and developmental milestones in early years Strategies for including children with DECAL Learning about developmentally appropriate practices in the early years
School social worker	Supports children and families with social-emotional needs and connects them with community resources	Learning about culturally and linguistically responsive interactions Considering DECAL
School psychologist	Evaluates children for psychological services and special educational needs; provides counseling to children and supports teachers	Learning about culturally and linguistically responsive interactions Considering DECAL

(*Continued*)

Table 8.1 (Cont.)

Position	What they do	Ideas from this book to support collaborative work in early childhood
Guidance counselor	Helps children with adaptation and adjustment concerns	Learning about culturally and linguistically responsive interactions Considering DECAL
School nurse	Cares for the health needs and injuries of children	Learning about culturally and linguistically responsive interactions Considering DECAL

Push-In and Pull-Out Supports

One model for providing specialized supports to young children is called "push-in." This means a specialist will come to the classroom and pull the child or children aside within the room to work on skills. This method is commonly used in early childhood programs. It may be used by speech or other therapies as well as English as a Second/Additional Language specialists. This means one child might be visited by more than one specialist.

This method may be chosen so that one specialist can move from place to place to provide direct services to children in different classrooms or buildings. Some specialists like to have the time to see a child in their classroom setting, interacting with other children, while also having time to work with them one-on-one (Honigsfeld & Dove, 2010). But this may be somewhat disruptive to the classroom routine or distracting to the focus child and the other children.

Another way for specialists to provide services is through "pull-out" or "stand-alone" meetings with the child. The specialist schedules a time and place to bring the child out of the classroom for an entirely private session. While this is even more disruptive for the child, some specialists appreciate this opportunity to devote total focus to a particular child with no distractions (Honigsfeld & Dove, 2010). Young children who experience multiple languages, or behavior challenges, may benefit from a break from the busy classroom atmosphere.

In both cases, the specialist may be accustomed to using a specially designed curriculum for students based on their Individual Family Service Plan (IFSP) or Individualized Educational Program (IEP) or on data about the child's language proficiency and needs. Young children may need a stronger connection to their classroom curriculum or approach to facilitate cognitive connections that ensure learning and practice.

When these methods are assigned by the school or program, collaboration between the teacher and specialist will be needed to maximize the effectiveness of the intervention. Where possible, both partners (teacher/carer and specialist) need to work out a mutually agreeable schedule. They also need to share information about the curriculum and the individual child's interests and progress. An effective collaborative program model in early education must have an intentional assessment component. This may include formal and informal approaches to assessment. "The ultimate goals of assessment are to enhance the effectiveness of all teachers' classroom instruction and to ensure improved student achievement" (Honigsfeld & Dove, 2010, p. 174).

The role of some specialists is to provide enrichment to students in the area of their special talent or background. Children may go to the school library, music room, art room, or gymnasium. In other cases, the specialist has an itinerant position and brings the enrichment supplies to the students. These enrichment specialists are also important partners in early childhood education, though their own preparation may not have included developmentally appropriate practices for teaching young children. Sharing your curriculum and lesson plans with these specialists can be very helpful so their contributions fit the needs of your children more appropriately.

Consultation Options

Traditionally, and still true for older grades, therapies and support from specialists has been provided through direct services to the child. Greater attention to developmentally appropriate practices in the early years has given rise to new ways to think about what works. While older children can benefit from learning new vocabulary, concepts, and skills during meetings with a specialist once a week, younger children need more frequent repetition and opportunities to actively use their new learning right away to retain it. Specialists in ESL/EAL teaching, reading specialists, and some kinds of therapies can have the desired effect when the specialist consults with the classroom teacher instead of or in addition to meeting directly with the child. The specialist can suggest everyday changes that will help the child in question or instruct the teacher on how to use specific techniques under particular circumstances. This allows the teacher to implement these supports at different times of day, in different learning contexts. It also reduces the frequency of disruptions a child might experience if they need to stop what they are doing to meet with a specialist. These consultations should include a tracking and documentation mechanism so all parties know what is happening and what progress is being made.

Closer Look at Specialists

We've talked about the processes and formats for collaboration and co-teaching in early childhood. Now, let's take a closer look at the work of people that may collaborate with you. Remember, this book is designed to serve as a cross-disciplinary textbook. It has many features that are useful for specialists in a variety of areas, along with guidance about how this information can enhance collaborative work in early childhood education.

In general, any adult who will work with children aged from birth to 8 years will be most successful if they follow developmentally appropriate practice (NAEYC, 2020), understand and support the general education curriculum and the current activities of the children, recognize the importance of supporting home languages and cultures and English, and work across disciplines to create a more seamless, coordinated learning experience for each child. Table 8.2 shows some conversation starters to facilitate interactions between teachers and specialists.

Table 8.2 Cross-discipline conversation starters

If you are a general education teacher or early childhood teacher, here are questions to ask specialists	*If you are a specialist, here are questions to ask general education teachers and early childhood teachers*
What is the child's official diagnosis or identification – and what does that mean?	Do you agree with the language plan, EHC plan, IFSP, or IEP? What would they change?
Can you explain the reasoning behind the language plan, IFSP or IEP functional goals?	What is set in your curriculum and what is flexible and adaptable?
What in the child's IFSP or IEP might be flexible or adaptable?	What additional information do you know about the child that will enhance understanding of the diagnosis or identification?
What do the specialists want to accomplish with this child? And why?	What is the most important thing you want to see supported within the specialist's work with the child? Why?

If you are a general education teacher or early childhood teacher, here are questions to ask specialists	If you are a specialist, here are questions to ask general education teachers and early childhood teachers
What do you suggest I read or view to learn more about it?	What should I read or view to learn more about it?
How often can you meet or touch base?	How often can you meet or touch base?
How can we work together in support of the general education curriculum?	How can we work together in support of the general education curriculum?
What are your plans for measuring the child's progress?	What is your plan for measuring the child's progress?
What can the classroom teacher do to maintain or extend the activities and interventions you plan for this child?	What can the specialists do to maintain and extend the activities and lessons you currently have planned for this child?

Conclusion

There are so many ways that collaboration and co-teaching enhance your work with young children and enhance your development as a professional. To benefit from all of these contributions, it takes clear, purposeful planning, communication, and follow-through.

Diverse colleagues can contribute to thinking and planning that enriches classroom experiences by adding diverse perspectives, cultural assets, and creativity that are responsive to the needs and experiences of children. They can ensure that each child gets the responsive attention they need to thrive in early childhood education and prepare for success as they grow and develop.

Choose Your Own Path Check-In

Age/setting (need to fill this in)	What would you add or bring to each of these spaces to facilitate collaboration conversations?
Infant care center	
Toddler play room	
Outdoor learning environment	
Family childcare home	
Open preschool/nursery classroom	
Kindergarten/reception classroom	
Academic primary classroom	
Space for individual or small group therapies	
Family education space	
Virtual learning	
Remote learning home environment	

Social Media Messages and Discussion Starters

- Early childhood educators have to collaborate with each other in most settings. What do you wish your colleagues knew about working with young children that might not have been included in their coursework?
- Do you work in a school that employs bilingual paraprofessionals or assistant teachers? What kinds of professional development do they receive to support effective use of their multiple languages in supporting early learning? What do you think they should know?

References

Barnett, W.S., Yarosz, D.J., Thomas, J., Jung, K., & Blanco, D. (2007) Two-Way and Monolingual English Immersion in Preschool Education: An Experimental Comparison, *Early Childhood Research Quarterly*, 22 (3), 277–293.

Brillante, P., & Nemeth, K. (2016) Preparing and Supporting Paraprofessionals for their Critical Roles in Early Childhood Education for Diverse Learners, *Early Years: The Journal of the Texas Association for the Education of Young Children*, 37 (2).

Honigsfeld, A., & Dove, M. (2010) *Collaboration and Co-Teaching: Strategies for English Learners*, Thousand Oaks, CA: Corwin Press.

Honigsfeld, A., & Nordmeyer, J. (2021) Teacher Collaboration During a Global Pandemic, *Education Leadership Special Report*, 77, 47–50.

López, L.M., & Páez, M. M. (2020) *Teaching Dual Language Learners: What Early Childhood Educators Need to Know*, Baltimore, MD: Paul H. Brookes.

NAEYC (2020) *Developmentally Appropriate Practice Position Paper*, Washington, DC: NAEYC.

Park, M., McHugh, M., Zong J., & Batalova, J. (2015) *Immigrant and Refugee Workers in the Early Childhood Field: Taking a Closer Look*, Washington, DC: Migration Policy Institute.

Program for Infant-Toddler Care (2021) Six Program Policies Anchor our Work, retrieved from www.pitc.org/about.

Thornton, K., & Cherrington, S. (2019) Professional Learning Communities in Early Childhood Education: A Vehicle for Professional Growth, *Professional Development in Education*, 45 (3), 418–432.

U.S. Department of Education (2016) *Non-Regulatory Guidance: English Learners and Title III of the Elementary and Secondary Education Act (ESEA), as amended by the Every Student Succeeds Act (ESSA)*, Washington, DC: U.S. Department of Education.

9 Professionalism

Follow the Chapter 9 Roadmap with These Headings

Introduction	Professional Roles with Families and Community
Foundations of Knowledge and Skills	Cultural Humility and Focus on Equity
Professional Learning and Development	Working as a Bilingual Educator
Working Within an Integrated System of Early Care and Education	Working with Children who Speak Languages You Don't
Professional Ethics	Ability to Adapt and Change
Teacher Dispositions	Conclusion

Chapter 9 introduces the range of topics that support your effectiveness and growth as a professional in the field of early childhood education. The chapter introduces key foundational knowledge and skills needed to enter the field as well as strategies for getting the most benefit from your participation in professional learning and development. Your role within an integrated system of early care and education will be discussed along with the professional ethics and teacher dispositions involved. You will revisit discussions from Chapter 7 from the perspective of professionalism in working with families and the community to support educational equity through cultural humility. Significant sections will address how bilingual educators work with their language assets and how professionals should work with children who don't speak their language. The chapter concludes with a meaningful discussion about the personal qualities and efforts every professional needs to adapt and change and to stay current in the field.

Top Tips for Fostering Professionalism

- Top national reports reveal a shared view of what early childhood educators need to know to be successful: child development and language development, curriculum, observation and assessment, working with families, and understanding cultural and linguistic diversity – all topics that are covered in this book.
- Language development and cultural and linguistic diversity are topics that are least likely to be covered in teacher preparation courses for early childhood fields, yet they are some of the most important topics for success in the field.
- Sustained professional development with a clear purpose is important for quality improvement, but educators need to make a personal commitment to active participation and implementation as well.
- Research shows that Professional Learning Communities work well to support improvements in classroom practice.

DOI: 10.4324/9781003089216-9

- Teacher success is based on more than what you do in your classroom – it is also based on how you maximize your role within the school community.
- Professional dispositions and professional ethics highlight the importance of your beliefs and attitudes in your work. It's not just about skill.
- Taking a cultural humility approach when learning about the cultures of the families in your program is the best path to infusing authentic cultural representation into children's learning.
- Early childhood educators need two kinds of guidance for working with children who are dual language learners: guidance for bilingual teachers whose language matches the child's language, and strategies for when your language and the child's language do not match.

Introduction

This chapter focuses on the skills and knowledge educators need to succeed as professionals in an increasingly diverse and demanding field. While you may describe your plan in terms of working with children, your true impact will be on the connection you make with each individual child. Readers of this book may be preparing for many different kinds of positions that support early learning and development. In your work with young children, you have the privilege and responsibility to create the foundation for all future learning and success. The importance of this position was the subject of the seminal report on this topic, *Transforming the Workforce*: "Indeed, the science of child development and early learning makes clear the importance and complexity of working with young children from infancy through the early elementary years, or birth through age 8." The research also highlights young children's need for consistency and continuity across time as they grow, and across systems and services. But, the report found that most of the systems that support young children are actually fragmented (National Institutes of Medicine & National Research Council, 2015, p. 1). Another key finding in the report was that positive relationships that facilitate high-quality learning interactions are most important for early learning. "Conversely, adults who are underinformed, under-prepared, or subject to chronic stress themselves may contribute to children's experiences of adversity and stress and undermine their development and learning" (National Institutes of Medicine & National Research Council, 2015, p. 4).

The Alliance for A Better Community in collaboration with the National Council of La Raza compiled a report specifically to guide the field on what competencies are needed to be an effective teacher of children who are dual language learners (DLLs). "Children have the right to receive high quality, linguistically and culturally competent education" (AABC, 2012, pp. 10–11). The report established that effective teaching for children who are DLLs should be based on the assumption that all children have strengths, assets, and knowledge to bring to any learning situation. Since we know that most early childhood educators will work with at least some children who are DLLs, these qualities should apply to all.

When educators work in fragmented silos, they have information that others don't see, and they need information that others don't provide. Each person is operating with only a portion of the knowledge they need to fully support the progress of each child. When educators work together, their work is more effective and efficient. This is certainly a case where it's better to work smarter, not harder. Just as children benefit when professionals from different disciplines work together, teacher candidates benefit when their colleges and universities integrate the information they need across disciplines that explore child development and early childhood education. In fact, this is one of the recommendations from the *Transforming the Workforce* report based on review of the research (National Institutes of Medicine & National Research Council, 2015).

The synergy that children need comes not from duplicating work but from sharing and working more efficiently. There are certain aspects of professionalism that affect all of these jobs. In 2020, NAEYC released their critical update: Professional Standards and Competencies for Early Childhood Educators (NAEYC, 2020).

1 Child development and learning in context …
2 Family–teacher partnerships and community connections …
3 Child observations, documentation, and assessment …
4 Developmentally, culturally, and linguistically appropriate teaching practices …
5 Knowledge, applications, and integration of academic content in the early childhood curriculum …
6 Professionalism as an early childhood educator.

(NAEYC, 2020, pp. 9–10)

Based on the *Transforming the Workforce* report, they worked extensively with members and stakeholders from the field to define the key competencies needed by early childhood educators. When combined with the recommendations of the AABC, you can see that research and views of experts come together to form a unified picture of what professionalism means in our field. The goal of this book is to provide you with background in all of the areas recommended in these national reports on teacher competencies.

You will read about a foundation of knowledge and skills about language acquisition, child development, and early education curricula are covered in Chapters 2, 4, 5, and 6. Working with families and the community is the topic of Chapter 7. Observing, screening, and assessing children to inform personalized learning plans that meet individual needs is addressed in Chapter 5. Cultural humility, culturally and linguistically competent methods, and focus on equity appear in Chapters 1 and 5. Working within an integrated system of early care and education in Chapters 3, 8, and 10. And, of course, this chapter addresses professional learning and development (giving and taking; writing and publishing), and a sense of professional ethics.

Foundations of Knowledge and Skills

We rely on the vast and growing body of research to inform the work of all professionals who have contact with young children. Many times, the research professionals read comes from their silo – their subset of the field. For example, librarians read early literacy research in library journals, speech pathologists read about early literacy in speech and hearing journals, and teachers read about early language and literacy in education research journals. So, they are all talking about early language and literacy, but they may never read the same resources. And yet, we know that your work can be more successful if you break down those barriers and collaborate with peers across disciplines. This is especially important for your shared work with children who are DLLs.

One key point that has been found repeatedly in research across the field is this: research shows that supporting each child's home language and embedding it in meaningful learning experiences throughout the day is a necessary and effective approach (Banse, 2019). This is one of the strongest conclusions we have in a growing body of research, so it is important that all people who work with young children share this piece of foundational knowledge and use it to support the children in a cohesive way across disciplines.

In her review of the research, Banse realized that some educators believe the best way to support progress in English is to teach or support children only in English – but the research does not support that belief. When some professionals support home language and others avoid it, children experience a disjointed and less effective learning day.

Professional Learning and Development

Being a professional involves steady pursuit of growth and progress in your work. This commitment is what sets professionals apart from workers. There are many avenues for you to participate in professional development, but they will only make a difference in your work if you are prepared to make a change.

One of the most powerful and yet challenging aspects of becoming an excellent early childhood educator is that everyone has some experience in the field that results in preconceived notions about how to do the job. You have all been children, interacted with children, and heard other people talk about what's right or wrong for caring for children. Even now, as you are taking courses, you may have some experience working with children. And, since you chose this career path, we can assume you enjoy working with young children and believe you will be good at it.

Effective teaching requires being willing to reflect on your practices and be ready to adapt and improve as you go along. This can be an exciting and enlivening part of the job, but it can also be difficult at times. Sometimes, preparing to make a change means becoming aware that something you are currently doing might not be the best way. But how can you change if you cling to every practice, choice, or plan you make? Constant Hine (2019) makes the case that you can work your way through difficult changes by changing your attitude about the change itself. If you change your perceptions about the feedback you receive and see it as a positive opportunity for growth, it will be easier to adjust to new ways and enjoy the results of your growing work.

A great place to start is by making a professional development plan for yourself. In the same way that a comprehensive, cohesive, and responsive curriculum ensures young children will be successful learners, a comprehensive, cohesive, and responsive professional development plan can be the best approach to your own learning and development. It can tie together all the ways you learn new concepts and skills and guide you in choosing professional learning options to integrate with your plan for the most successful outcomes in your own work.

Here are the items to include in your personal professional development plan that would be included in foundational knowledge and skills:

- *Topics that reflect your interests.* Engage in self-reflection. Take time to identify topics that really interest you – ones you already feel good about or that you are excited to learn about. These topics might reflect your particular talents, activities that have worked well for you in the past, or something you feel is important to teach to children.
- *Topics you might avoid, but need to learn more about.* Sometimes, the topics that are most difficult for you may be the topic you really need to add to your work. If you love math and always look for math workshops, that won't help you get any more comfortable teaching science. You may have attended a workshop on a topic that you did not like – but don't let the poor quality of a particular event turn you away from a needed topic. There are other ways to learn it.
- *Topics that are needed by your employer, funder, and/or state.* There may be topics you are required to learn for your employer, or due to funder requirements or state regulations.

For example, a new health regulation may come into effect and all staff have to learn about it. Or, a Head Start program might have gathered data showing they are not fully in compliance with a requirement for Head Start funding, so all staff need to attend training to improve.

- *Data from your observations, coaching, supervisory reviews, and/or child assessments.* What you learn from classroom/teacher observation measures, such as CLASS (Classroom Assessment Scoring System), ECERS3 (Early Childhood Environmental Rating Scale), FCCRS (Family Childcare Rating Scale), ITERS3 (Infant Toddler Environment Rating Scale), Q-CIIT (Quality of Caregiver-Child Interactions for Infants and Toddlers), ECCO (Early Childhood Classroom Observation Scale), and CASEBA (Classroom Assessment of Supports for Emergent Bilingual Acquisition). What the aggregated results of child assessments show, e.g., trends that indicate a need to improve instruction in one area or another (Melhuish & Gardiner, 2018).

- *Near-term plans for improving your work with the children in your current group.* There will be times when you need to learn information or strategies to address changes or needs related to the children you are working with at the time. For example, you might have a new group of children who speak a language unfamiliar to you. A topic might come up in your curriculum that is new to you. You might be assigned as an English as a Second Language/Additional Language teacher to support a group of 4-year-olds and you might need some new information about how to integrate your supports with what's happening in the general education classroom.

- *Long-term plans for improving your work overall.* A cohesive professional learning plan enables you to work steadily toward future goals. Long-term goals might address skills and knowledge you need for your current position, or they might include further learning and certifications you would need to move to new positions. Many educators pursue graduate coursework because it is tied to increases in salary. This can also increase your knowledge and skills and prepare you for career advancement.

- *Specific goals for using what you learn in your work.* Professional learning will only make a difference in your professional work if you plan for how you will use it. This is an intentional process that requires you to be an active participant in any professional learning, whether you choose it or not. It also depends on your commitment to making time and finding the energy to learn. For most positions in early education, the days are long and tiring. While this is the reality, all educators still need to keep current in the field. Make the time to read whole articles, not just the headlines. Pay attention throughout a full webinar and take notes. And, because this is a lot to ask hardworking educators, you might also advocate with your employer to provide release time or other supports to ensure all staff participate actively in professional learning.

- *Options for acquiring the knowledge you seek.* Collaborate across disciplines and settings. Invite preschool teachers to school district training. Invite family childcare providers to a preschool/nursery teacher training. Invite speech and physical therapists to family childcare training. There are innumerable options, and those have been captured in the next section. One important component of your plan will be continuity. Research has shown that haphazard one-shot workshops have little or no effect on an educator's practice. The greatest benefit of developing your own professional development plan is that you can attach all your time spend on professional learning to your specified goals. Look for options that include preparation, learning, follow-up, and follow-through. One exception to this recommendation is when you want to learn a specific skill or activity. For example, you might attend a presentation at the local bank to get resources and activity ideas to introduce counting and money to your students in different languages. This could be accomplished and implemented based on just one workshop.

- *Colleagues with whom you will share and discuss your professional learning.* Recent research showed that teachers who attended online training experienced decreased confidence when they did not have a coach with whom to discuss the training. Apparently, viewing a training alone made teachers focus on what they were not doing well, but teachers who viewed the same training and had a coach to discuss how they could use the training had a more positive experience (Roberts et al., 2020). With so many ways to read, listen to, view, or interact with professional learning on your own and at your convenience, you might miss opportunities to engage in training or workshops with colleagues that give you time to have conversations about what you are learning. To amplify the benefits of professional learning, be sure to include some discussions with your coach, mentor, or colleagues. For example, meet for dinner after a training day. Get on a Zoom chat with friends from different schools who are interested in hearing about your workshop. These are valuable parts of your professional learning that make a difference in how you will use and benefit from what you learned. Also, if you have learned and tried something new, it can be rewarding and enriching to present what you learned to co-workers. Does your program have a newsletter for staff that could be a place to exchange teaching ideas and activities that are relevant to your curriculum?
- *How you will document, review, or record what you've learned and use it to adjust your plan.* Every educator should maintain a portfolio with details about every professional learning task they have completed. Your portfolio may be used to support your case for a raise, promotion, retention, or tenure. Your portfolio will also be discussed with your mentor, coach, and supervisor. Most states have a statewide early childhood workforce registry that allows participants to build a digital portfolio of all the different kinds of professional learning they have experienced from many sources. The National Workforce Registry is an organization that supports the state registries to ensure they are most helpful and effective. Their website (www.registryalliance.org) can help you learn about the process and what you need to know in your position.

Some schools and programs have their own staff professional development systems that ask you to enter details on a website. You may need both the local and the state registries. To enter information into a registry, you will need to be careful to get all required information. If you attend a presentation, you may need a course number, a certificate, the signature of the presenter, the citation of a book or article with a summary of how you plan to use it, or more. Your position or certification may require you to compile documentation that you completed a certain amount of professional development to renew or maintain your qualifications. Registries make it possible to enter the information once, then submit it for these different requirements.

Be an Informed Consumer

Become an informed consumer of professional learning. Learn how to evaluate sources of professional learning for accuracy and value. There are many ways to get free professional development. Some are not worth the trouble, and others are high quality. The important thing is to not just go for the cheapest option without evaluating the quality of the information you'll receive. Some professional development courses and conferences are expensive and may cost thousands. Is it possible to obtain the same level of learning for less money locally or virtually? Find out if your employer will provide funding for your professional learning. Review the qualifications of presenters and authors. You may enjoy and benefit from hearing or reading from fellow educators, but they may share content that is based on their own experience and dispositions that might not support your own professional development plan. The more you know about foundational knowledge and research in the field, the more you can benefit from appropriate suggestions from peers. Just because a person has been a teacher for a long time doesn't mean their advice follows research and/or policy. Always read an entire description or article. Headlines and titles can be notoriously inaccurate. You might see a workshop about addressing cultural and linguistic responsiveness and find out it is only talking about one particular language or culture. You might read the title of an article highlighting a great new teaching tool, only to find out that the article itself is actually pitching a product for sale.

Many publishers and educational supply companies provide training, workshops, webinars, articles, and other professional learning. These can be high quality resources, or they might just be pushing one product. Try to find out as much information as you can before engaging.

> Be a critical reader of research: Check the sample size and applicability (e.g., a study about children who are developing skills in French and Arabic might not apply to your work with children speaking English and Spanish). Evaluate the authors (e.g., have they published more than one article on this topic? Have other researchers replicated the findings?)

Ensure that your professional learning is woven into or connected with professional learning needs, services, and goals for your organization. A synergistic early childhood education system should be set up to coordinate the professional learning of all staff. Ideally, your employer will have a policy and procedure in place to guide each staff member's professional development plan, supporting both system-wide and individual growth and development. It is nearly impossible to expect high quality implementation of newly learned skills, knowledge, or strategies unless there is meaningful follow-up and support from supervisors and the school as a whole. Encourage coaches and supervisors to participate with you in professional learning opportunities. When discussing your choices for your own professional learning, ask them about implementation. Will they encourage you to try new ideas? Will they give you feedback about how you are doing? Will there be time for you to receive coaching/mentoring support for your new learning?

Here are some sources for professional development:

- Synchronous vs. asynchronous online training.
- Courses at 2- and 4-year colleges and universities – Courses leading to advanced degrees, bon-credit courses, and workshops offered by the college or university.
- One-shot workshop.
- Online course with multiple sessions.
- Reading a book or article.
- Active participation in social media for professionals. This doesn't mean that social media is, by itself, educational. Social media can be used to get suggestions for topics you might want to explore further. Don't accept a tweet or repost it without reading it. Many times titles fail to accurately reflect the content of an article or blog, and you might be re-sending a message that you did not intend.

- Participants at national conferences often tweet or post about what they are learning. You can follow them and pick up some great ideas and resources without paying to attend the conference. And, you may have a lot to share with colleagues locally or all over the world. Conferences might be virtual, in-person, or hybrid. They might also be international, national, regional, state, or local. Attend or follow conferences through social media that connect you to other organizations and specialties.
- Products made and sold or given away by educators on sites like Pinterest or Teachers Pay Teachers.
- Products, blog posts, webinars, and workshops by catalog companies.
- Professional learning supports from the publisher of the curriculum you use.
- National organizations and their local chapters. They have content on their websites for free or purchase, along with newsletters, white papers, briefs, position statements, and other resources.
- Online teacher resource sites such as National Geographic and Teacher channel.
- YouTube channels provided by educators (e.g., Teaching at the Beginning, www.youtube.com/channel/UCKQ5FgGVIFpdt36_sv9FL-Q).
- Facebook groups or pages, Facebook live events conducted by reputable sources.
- New platforms like Clubhouse and Spaces on Twitter.
- I want to highlight the 2010 movie documentary *Babies* (www.focusfeatures.com/babies).
- Also, the unrelated new series from Netflix that is also called *Babies* (www.netflix.com/title/80117833).
- Viewing recorded webinars vs participating live to interact and ask questions.
- Reviewed articles that have to be approved, reviewed, and finalized by editors vs. blog posts which anyone can write and require no oversight or review by anyone.
- Podcasts – recorded interview, presentations, or discussions.
- Vlogs – video blog posts.
- Book club – in person, on social media, or at work.

You might also find new information to spark your work in surprising places. Here are some ideas. Look for workshops at local museums and public libraries. Nonprofit organizations such as YMCA that host a speaker series. Look for author talks at bookstores or online. Find nature education inspirations at state and national parks, wildlife preserves, and zoos. Learn a new language by reading children's stories in those languages and practicing the words and phrases with colleagues. Create a lunch and learn group to practice conversations in languages other than English.

Professional Learning Communities and Personal Learning Networks

These are options for working with a group of colleagues to build and share knowledge and expertise. Professional learning communities (PLCs) bring a specific group together to agree on a focused learning goal, and to work together over a period of time to read, discuss, and/or invite guest speakers to support pursuit of that goal (Thornton & Cherrington, 2019). Your personal learning network (PLN) is not so formal. Your PLN is anyone in the field who you turn to for advice, resources, or answers to questions. Every early childhood professional should identify, nurture, and rely on their PLN.

Working with Coaches and Mentors

Many, but not all, early education systems have a formalized coaching/mentoring system established to support every educator. They may use a research-based formalized coaching system like Practice-Based Coaching that comes with guides for coaches and coachees. In other settings you might develop a less formal, but still valuable, relationship with a coach or mentor. The most notable feature of a successful coaching activity is that it must function as a collaborative partnership between two professionals. It is not ideal for your supervisor to also be your coach. Your coach should not be someone who has control over your job. You must be able to speak freely and share concerns and mistakes as well as celebrating successes.

The collaborative coaching partnership assumes that both partners have valuable knowledge about effective teaching practices and that the coachee has the ability and willingness to reflect on their practices. Coaches might want to see video examples of the teacher's work or meet in-person or virtually to talk about how things are going. Ideally, they review data and the coach supports the teacher to make their own goals for improving practice. With those goals in mind, the coach may make focused observations or ask the teacher to record videos of their teaching practices to address those goals. These observations and videos make it possible for the teacher alone, and for teacher and coach to reflect, discuss feedback, and plan for growth and improvement. Coaching interactions should be purposeful and goal driven. When the partners identify a need that is not one of the coach's strengths, they might agree to learn together via a professional development resource. Then the role of the coach becomes a familiar support as the teacher takes responsibility for implementing new practices they learned about together.

The quality of the relationship between coach and coachee is vital to the success of the process. For that reason, teachers and coaches should be able to switch until they find people who partner well together. But this is more than a shoulder to lean on or someone to talk to. The coach or mentor should play a strong role in empowering the teacher to improve. Both partners must keep good records of their process to document baseline findings and observable changes as the process continues.

Taking Care of Yourself and Your Career

For anyone who has a demanding career, there can be a lot of work and a lot of stress. Successful professionals find ways to manage stress, maintain life balance, and stay fresh and motivated to get better all the time. As part of your professional development, consider working in time for mindfulness and relaxation practices such as yoga or meditation. Attending conferences and workshops, convening with colleagues, and striving for advancement are also ways to maintain that spark of enthusiasm for your valued and valuable profession.

Working Within an Integrated System of Early Care and Education

No educator works alone. Your work will be supported, challenged, and enlivened by your relationships with many others who have a hand in the early learning experiences of the children in your care. In any position, you will encounter different languages, races, cultures, and backgrounds of colleagues, children, and families. Successful early childhood educators of the future will build their careers through personal values, professional relationships, a willingness to keep learning and improving, and an open approach to this work.

Young children experience success when the different parts of their lives work together (National Institutes of Medicine & National Research Council, 2015). Whether there is formal co-teaching or a quick touch-base, shared information and coordinated strategy is the pathway to effective outcomes for young children. This is especially true when children do not speak the majority language. Children who are DLLs are highly capable and yet they have more demands on their learning experiences due to language differences. The more coordinated and cohesive their early learning experiences are, the more they can put together learning connections that help them progress as they should.

With the growth of linguistic and cultural diversity in many areas educators in all positions should have some background knowledge and skills to ensure that their work provides equitable access to learning for all children. This process can be enhanced when professionals rely on each other to support their knowledge and skills. A critical factor in providing consistent support for children from birth through age 8 is the ability of care and education professionals to work in synergy with other professionals both across settings within the care and education sector and in other closely related sectors, especially health and social services (National Institutes of Medicine & National Research Council, 2015, p. 11).

We will now take a closer look at a seminal report in our field, by the National Institutes of Medicine and the National Research Council. Here are the key elements that the *Transforming the Workforce* team of experts identified in their extensive reviews of the research (they are the actions that affect learning and development outcomes for all children):

- Be prepared to support diverse populations.
- Participate in a professional development system that both introduces and provides ongoing support for key competencies.
- Engage with coaches and mentors who support highly effective teaching.
- Develop teaching environments that enable effective practices.
- Align systems and policies to support high-quality teaching that is culturally and linguistically responsive.

(National Institutes of Medicine & National Research Council, 2015)

While *Transforming the Workforce* focuses on all early childhood education and includes children who are DLLs, another seminal review of research, *Promoting the Educational Success of Children and Youth Learning English: Promising Futures* (National Academies of Sciences, Engineering, and Medicine, 2017), reports on all levels of education for children and youth who are learning English and includes attention to the early years. And the joint policy statement from the U.S. Department of Health and Human Services and U.S. Department of Education (2016) adds a focus on teaching young children who are dual language learners. These significant reports share a message that focuses on how each educator in any position has to work with others and within a broader school or system. Research supports this integrated view rather than placing the burden on each educator in isolation. Here are some ways you might collaborate with colleagues as part of this system. You might meet face-to-face to plan for a particular student, or have a team meeting to support each other, or engage in a video chat. Some colleagues stay in touch via email to share notes or plans with a collaborating teacher or written notes in a notebook that follows the student. Some use recorded voice message with a brief reminder, suggestion, or observation. Some programs and districts have project management software allowing collaborating teachers to enter notes that other team members can view, add to, or change. Colleagues might share in some professional learning to build their combined knowledge and skill, such as attending a book club on a shared topic or attending each other's professional development.

Colleagues have enjoyed participating in a lunch-and-learn or after school discussion of a relevant article. One of you might do a brief presentation at a staff or team meeting to share something you learned via personal professional development. You could also reach colleagues by writing a short article for the staff newsletter or creating a video to demonstrate a strategy you use with children who are DLLs. Consider setting up a professional lending library of lesson kits including stories in several languages, multilingual songs, props, supplies, and talking points.

> Mr. Robert designed a great project for his diverse reception/kindergarten class who were doing virtual learning. He read a story about city buildings in English to the whole class, then read the same story in home languages to small groups. He emailed a link to the story so families could enjoy it multiple times at home. He invited the children to work with family members to find items in their homes they could use to build a city. Children of all languages found familiar, culturally relevant objects such as cans or boxes of food, or small boxes. Some participated in building while on video chat with the teacher. Others needed a break and built it later and sent a photo to the teacher to show what they built. Then Mr. Robert sent text messages to the families in their home language via the school's system asking them to support their child in drawing or designing a new city. Children then showed their creations and talked about them with great excitement. This project lasted for more than a week and touched many benchmarks across most of the domains. So, Mr. Robert created an outline of how he ran all the parts of this project, along with links to the videos and messages he created for families, and copies of the books he used and some building materials that could be used for in-person learning. This boxed project was made available in the school's teacher library.

Another option for you to share important strategies would be to create a demonstration video showing families how to read aloud with their children or how to play a learning game to support children who are DLLs, then share the video with others on your team. Prepare to contribute when plans are made for children who have disabilities. Classroom teachers and ESL/EAL teachers should participate in plans for creating an Individualized Education Plan for special educational needs to give input about supporting the child's first and second languages.

Most importantly, as a professional who is a member of a system and an entire field, you need to know where to go for the most credible information and leadership in your field. To learn more about policies and regulations that guide your work:

- Federal departments
  - Department of Education.
  - Office of Special Education Services OSEP.
  - Every Student Succeeds Act ESSA.
  - Health and Human Services – childcare.
  - Health and Human Services – Head Start.
  - Out of school care.
  - English Language Acquisition.
  - U.K. Department of Education.
- State offices that regulate these categories will also have rules and resources that you'll need to know about:
  - Education.
  - Special education.

- English language development.
- Childcare.
- Family childcare.
- Health and safety.

Balancing multiple overlapping regulations may add complexity to your work. You will also have rules you have to follow for your curriculum. Rules may also be imposed by different funding sources that affect your school. And, if your program is involved in becoming accredited, there will be additional requirements to follow. As a professional, these are all things you should know about, but your work within an integrated system will provide the support you need.

Stay connected with the early childhood field in general. You can join professional organizations now with relatively low-cost student fees and decide which ones meet your needs going forward. Many professional associations have learning and leadership opportunities for teacher candidates such as conference scholarships, research fellowships, and young professional advisory boards. Look for ways to meet other early-career members like you as well as experienced members who might welcome you to co-author an article or co-present a workshop. National and state conferences sometimes offer discounts or free admission to volunteers who help out – another great way to get involved and meet colleagues to add to your PLN.

Professional associations that offer free resources and websites as well as an array of supports for professionals:

- NAEYC – National Association for the Education of Young Children
- TESOL – Teachers of English to Speakers of Other Languages
- NABE – National Association for Bilingual Educators
- American Montessori Association
- ILA – International Literacy Association
- AERA – American Educational Research Association
- NHSA – National Head Start Association
- CDA – Council for Professional Recognition
- ASCD – Association for Supervisors and Curriculum Developers
- DEC – Council for Exceptional Children Division for Early Childhood
- Childcare Aware of America
- British Council
- OMEP – World Organization for Early Childhood Education
- UNIDOS – U.S. formerly National Council of La Raza
- ALSC – Association for Library Service to Children (part of the American Library Association)
- Zero to Three
- WIDA
- National Association for Elementary School Principals
- ACTFL – American Council of Teachers of Foreign Languages and NNELL – National Network for Early Language Learning
- NCTE – National Council of Teachers of English
- SRCD – Society for Research in Child Development
- NBCDI – National Black Child Development Institute
- NAFCC – National Association for Family Childcare
- Waldorf Schools of America
- NAREA – North American Reggio Emilia Association

- Nursery World, UK
- NCELA – National Center for English Language Acquisition
- ACEI – Association for Childhood Education International
- ASHA – American Speech, Language, Hearing Association
- Forest School Association

Professional Ethics

Most professions have codes of ethics. There are a few statements to guide our work. NAEYC has a comprehensive code of ethics for early childhood educators (NAEYC, 2011). This statement is organized in categories of ethical responsibilities for children, families, colleagues, and the community at large. The focus is on doing no harm, protecting privacy, and working with an assumption of respect. A code of ethics with more clinical components can be found at the American Speech and Hearing Association (2016).

Categories of ethics that apply across disciplines state that early childhood professionals must:

- Do no harm.
- Collaborate with and support colleagues.
- Partner with and support families.
- Be honest.
- Maintain confidentiality.
- Be careful in using social media and digital connections.
- Provide all services equitably without discrimination against any person or group.
- Commit to ongoing professional learning and improvement.
- Communicate openly and effectively.

Teacher Dispositions

Everyone who becomes a professional working with young children has developed ideas and feelings about how that work should take shape. These factors help teachers develop dispositions about their work. Dispositions are the beliefs, commitments, and values that will influence you as you make plans and decisions about your work with children, families, and colleagues. When you are aware of your dispositions and are able to articulate your views, then your teacher dispositions act as a philosophy that guides you in your work. In this 2012 report from the National Council of La Raza, the experts identified teacher dispositions needed for success as a teacher of diverse young children:

1. Commit to developing your competency and knowledge level about teaching young children who are DLLs.
2. Practice cultural responsiveness to be effective in your work with diverse children, families, and colleagues.
3. Maintain awareness of the factors outside of school that affect early learning experiences for diverse young children, and commit to nurturing young children and their families with recognition of the realities of their linguistic and cultural experiences.
4. Develop a flexible and responsive approach to handling ambiguity, conflicting guidance, and complex decisions within the complicated sphere of work with diverse young children.

(AABC, 2012, pp. 43–44)

Professional Roles with Families and the Community

We covered the topic of working with families and the community in Chapter 7. We add it to this chapter on professionalism because this aspect of your work is mentioned in the major reports that guide our field. This is a vital component of your commitment to working with young children. Educators of older children are generally not asked to work as closely with families as early childhood professionals will be. In your professional role, you will get to know each family, develop a family engagement plan that includes ways to interact with each and every family, provide information for families and the community, see information and resources from families and the community, and develop valuable partnerships.

Cultural Humility and Focus on Equity

In Chapter 1, we provided a lot of information about terms and practices supporting equity. This topic re-emerges in this chapter because it is such an important component of professionalism in early childhood education. Cultural humility might be considered a teacher disposition. In a general sense, it is a practice of openness to learning about the languages, cultures, and experiences of others without assuming any kind of superiority. Cultural humility can help you be more open to learning the whole range of knowledge and skills you'll need as a progressive early childhood educator (NAEYC, 2020). It will also pave the way to an attitude of acceptance for a variety of professional learning experiences. This attitude of acceptance can contribute to your effectiveness within a diverse and integrated educational system where diverse viewpoints, people, and positions have to work smoothly together. Cultural humility is a characteristic of ethical conduct and it certainly is important in supporting work with all families (Brown, Vesely, & Dallman, 2016; Vesely, Brown, & Mehta, 2017).

Other terms apply to this discussion. Supporting the languages and cultures of young children and families is considered a "social justice" issue. A specific component of this is "language justice." As a professional working with young children, you have an obligation to support equitable access to learning for all young children. There really are no shortcuts or options that allow some children to get more or better educational foundations than others. Here is the definition of "language justice" from the American Bar Association website:

> Language justice is an evolving framework based on the notion of respecting every individual's fundamental language rights – to be able to communicate, understand, and be understood in the language in which they prefer and feel most articulate and powerful.
>
> (ABA, 2021)

How does this statement apply to your work? How does it inform your understanding of the importance of each person's language?

It is your obligation as a professional to ensure equitable access to learning so that each child and every child benefits from:

- Access through content and comprehension of information.
- Access through relationships that engage and nurture learning.

- Access through agency and the confidence they are able to make decisions and impact their environment.
- Access through belonging that is a response of the people and the environment to help a child feel represented, and to help them feel seen and heard.

Not only will you be responsible for ensuring that your practices support equitable access to learning in all four categories, but you should prepare to serve as an advocate. Since you will have strong, well-informed relationships with each child and their family, you may be called upon to serve as an advocate for that child and family to get needed services within and beyond the school, to work against unfair practices, and to advocate for all your children in the community. A full understanding of and commitment to the values of bilingualism and biliteracy must be supported as you apply research findings to the increasingly diverse student populations of the future.

Working as a Bilingual Educator

When you are able to fluently read, write, and speak in two or more languages, your language assets will add a great deal to your work as an early childhood educator. You might seek certification as a Bilingual Educator. This requires coursework and language assessment. With these credentials, you would be assigned to a bilingual education class where you would teach children who speak your non-English language, using a combination of English and your other language. How much and when these languages will be used are decisions that depend on the students you have, the state or national regulations that are in force, and the decisions made by your school. You may be given a curriculum for bilingual education or you may be given the general curriculum and asked to make your own language adaptations. For young children who are very new to English, you may teach as much as 90% of the time in the non-English language to be sure the children fully understand content, vocabulary, and skills. Even so, you will also begin making connections between familiar language and English. As the children progress, you will gradually add more English, though most bilingual education classes remain at a balance of up to 50% in each language. If you are given a transitional bilingual education class, your goal would be to do as much as possible to support the children's learning so they can get ready to transfer to monolingual English class. A maintenance bilingual education class is intended to support continued learning in both English and the home language.

You will have the responsibility of keeping up with your non-English language, being sure to serve as a high-quality language model. It is a good idea for you to read as much as possible about your work in your non-English language so you can also continue to learn and grow.

While you need specific certification to teach bilingual education, there are many mays to use your language skills to support children who are DLLs in general education classes. In this case you would be a teacher who happens to be bilingual. You should be intentional to plan how and when to use English and your additional language for teaching and for interacting with families. You will need to search for and adapt resources and learning materials to support your lesson plans (Nemeth, 2009).

Working with Children who Speak Languages You Don't

Whether you speak one language or several, you will likely encounter children who speak a language that doesn't match the languages you know. The strategies for teaching non-matching languages revolve around providing some supports for each child's learning in their home language and supports to help children understand and engage in content you present in a language other than theirs. Even when you do not speak a child's language, they still need some home language experiences during the day (Banse, 2019). These strategies are described in Chapter 5. They focus on making sure children can comprehend lessons and activities with the help of nonverbal communication, meaningful visuals, and props with intrinsic meaning. It is also recommended that you find ways to involve family members and volunteers who speak the languages of the children (Nemeth, 2009).

Ability to Adapt and Change

This aspect of professionalism was never more apparent than the experiences of the COVID-19 pandemic and the sudden shutdowns of schools and services. Every person who worked with young children in any capacity instantly found their work had changed and their new ways of working required them to use new tools, methods, schedules – and yet they were expected to keep following their curriculum and ensure equitable access to learning for all. Very young children at home are not able to participate in virtual learning without a dedicated adult present. Early primary years children face additional challenges when suddenly deprived of contact with friends and familiar routines.

However, the pandemic was not the only source of major change. Many areas experienced natural disasters like the hurricanes that destroyed programs and infrastructure in Puerto Rico or major political changes like Brexit. We have learned so much about setting priorities for preparedness within schools and systems, and for individual educators. As a professional, you also carry personal responsibility to be aware of the challenges educators have faced and the solutions they have developed so you can learn from them. Among the many lessons learned, one thing is certain: Part of your preparation will need to include practicing with virtual learning and new ways of using materials, tools, and engagement strategies!

But perhaps the most useful thing educators from all corners of the field have learned is that they do have the strength, capacity, and disposition to keep doing their best to help children learn and grow in the face of massive, unexpected changes. That ability to adapt and change is the true mark of an early childhood professional.

Conclusion

Being an early childhood educator is about being a lifelong learner. Professionalism focuses on what you express as much as it does on what you take in and learn. Participation in the field outside your particular classroom is both a responsibility and a reward of this professionalism.

Choose Your Own Path Check-In

Consider how people in these positions might work together. Use this form to spark your thinking as you prepare for your career. You might also use this in conversation with others to build those important professional collaborations.

Title	Which of these positions have you worked/will you work with in some way? What do you want to know about their work?	How could they benefit from reading research about supporting each child's home language?	What topic do you know about that you wish each of these positions knew too?
Infant/toddler teacher or caregiver			
Childcare teacher			
Classroom teacher/general education			
Preschool/nursery teacher			
Paraprofessional, teacher aide, assistant teacher			
Reading specialist			
Kindergarten/reception teacher			
Primary years teacher			
Librarian			
EAL/ESL teacher			
Bilingual education teacher			
Teacher who is bilingual			
Special educational needs teacher			
Social worker/family worker			
School psychologist			
Physical therapist			
Occupational therapist			
Teaching coach/mentor/master teacher			
Speech therapist			

Social Media Messages and Discussion Starters

- What is your favorite professional learning resource?
- What have you learned via social media about early childhood education?
- What is one competency that you think will be absolutely necessary for early childhood educators in the next 10 years?

References

AABC (2012) *Dual Language Learner Teacher Competencies (DLLTC) Report*, Los Angeles, CA: Alliance for a Better Community.

ABA (2021) Language Justice During COVID-19, retrieved from www.americanbar.org/groups/young_lawyers/projects/disaster-legal-services/language-justice-during-covid-19/#:~:text=What%20is%20language%20justice%3F,feel%20most%20articulate%20and%20powerful.

American Speech and Hearing Association (2016) Code of Ethics, retrieved from www2.asha.org/Code-of-Ethics.

Banse, H. (2019) Dual Language Learners and Four Areas of Early Childhood Learning and Development: What Do We Know and What Do We Need to Learn?, *Early Child Development and Care*, 191 (9), 1347–1360.

Brown, E.L., Vesely, C.K., & Dallman, L. (2016) Unpacking Biases: Developing Cultural Humility in Early Childhood and Elementary Teacher Candidates, *Teacher Educator's Journal*, 9, 75–96.

Hine, C. (2019) *Transformational Coaching for Early Childhood Educators*, St. Paul, MN: Redleaf.

Melhuish, E., & Gardiner, J. (2018) *Study of Early Education and Development (SEED): Study of Quality of Early Years Provision in England (Revised)*, London: U.K. Department of Education.

NAEYC (2011) *Code of Ethical Conduct and Statement of Commitment*, Washington, DC: NAEYC.

NAEYC (2020) *Professional Standards and Competencies for Early Childhood Educators*, Washington, DC: NAEYC.

National Academies of Sciences, Engineering, and Medicine (2017) *Promoting the Educational Success of Children and Youth Learning English: Promising Futures*, Washington, DC: The National Academies Press.

National Institutes of Medicine & National Research Council (2015) *Transforming the Workforce for Children Birth Through Age 8: A Unifying Foundation*, Washington, DC: The National Academies Press.

Nemeth, K. (2009) *Many Languages, One Classroom: Teaching Dual and English Language Learners*, Lewisville, NC: Gryphon House.

Roberts, A.M., LoCasale-Crouch, J., Hamre, B.K., & Jamil, F.M. (2020) Preschool Teachers' Self-Efficacy, Burnout, and Stress in Online Professional Development: A Mixed Methods Approach to Understand Change, *Journal of Early Childhood Teacher Education*, 41 (3), 262–283.

Thornton, K., & Cherrington, S. (2019) Professional Learning Communities in Early Childhood Education: A Vehicle for professional Growth, *Professional Development in Education*, 45 (3), 418–432.

U.S. Department of Health and Human Services & U.S. Department of Education (2016) *Policy Statement on Supporting the Development of Children who are Dual Language Learners in Early Childhood Programs*, Washington, DC: U.S. Department of Health and Human Services and U.S. Department of Education.

Vesely, C.K., Brown, E.L., & Mehta, S. (2017) How Home Visits Transform Early Childhood Preservice Educators' Attitudes for Engaging Families, *Journal of Early Childhood Teacher Education*, 38 (3), 242–258.

10 What Administrators, Supervisors, and Instructors Need to Know

Follow the Chapter 10 Roadmap with These Headings	
Introduction	Family and Community
Features of this Book	Collaboration, Co-Teaching, and Working with Specialists
Language Development	Professionalism
Getting Started	System-Wide Planning for Early Education
Curriculum	Conclusion
Meeting Individual Needs	
Environment and Materials	

Chapter 10 is designed to revisit the content of Chapters 1–9 from the point of view of school leaders, teacher preparation instructors, and professional development providers. It summarizes the key messages that users of this book will seek to implement in their work in early childhood education. This chapter will summarize key features of this book and direct leaders to the terms to be used. The focus of this book on the core understanding of language development will be explained. Guidance for early childhood educators on getting started on their careers is presented so leaders can participate in this support. Sections on early childhood curriculum, meeting individual needs, and setting up the learning environment will be addressed. This chapter will also describe the systems approach needed to fully engage with families and the community. This chapter will cover the roles of administrators and instructors in supporting collaboration and co-teaching across disciplines for early learning. Finally, it will address notions of professionalism and system-wide planning for successful early childhood education.

> **Top Tips for What Administrators, Supervisors, and Instructors Need to Know**
>
> - When leaders participate with teachers in professional development, new knowledge is more likely to be used for quality improvement.
> - Plan onboarding of new teachers and specialists that provides detailed information about your school traditions, staff expectations, and the curriculum models in use.
> - When welcoming bilingual teachers, specialists, and paraprofessionals, provide special orientation about how and when they should use their multiple languages.
> - Involve staff in curriculum selection and be sure to choose models that adequately and appropriately support cultural and linguistic diversity.

DOI: 10.4324/9781003089216-10

What Leaders Need to Know 151

- Do more to support early childhood educators in their efforts to meet the individual needs of young children, as research shows this to be the most effective approach for the early years.
- Culturally and linguistically appropriate materials and environments provide a necessary backdrop to effective early childhood education. This requires more than making a quick purchase from catalogs once a year.
- Teachers need to work directly with families, but they don't do it alone. Consider school-wide supports such as time off, paid interpreters, comfortable spaces to make it easier for teachers to meet and work with families.
- Teachers also need to work with each other and with specialists. The school should provide extra co-planning time, shared professional development, and communication tools to make these collaborations effective.
- Supporting teacher professionalism is an investment in the future of the school.

Introduction

This chapter will serve two purposes. First, it will summarize and frame the key messages of the other chapters with the understanding that leaders need to share the same updated knowledge base as their staff in order to provide effective supervision and to program implementation. Second, teachers need to see how their work is part of a program-wide or school-wide system that enables successful outcomes for all children.

While this book is written as a text for teacher education courses across multiple disciplines, the success of its impact depends on how much school and program leaders know about what their new teachers and specialists are learning so they can build a system that supports their well-informed work. This chapter is provided so that a teacher or specialist can give it to their boss to start a conversation about shared knowledge and goals for that employee and for the whole school. This is also here to support early childhood educators as they work toward advancement in their positions. Most particularly, this book is written with language at the center of every topic. In this way, we pave the way for a more equitable and just system of education. For example, did you know: More than half of the immigrants in the early childhood workforce work in family childcare homes or the lowest paying jobs in childcare or schools. A significant factor is found in the rarity of finding adequate supports for diverse languages and backgrounds in teacher education programs. This may be followed by professional development providers who are also not prepared to make sure their content and guidance are accessible to diverse audiences (Park et al., 2015). Most principals report that their teachers seem inadequately prepared to teach children from diverse language backgrounds even as the diversity of languages is growing (Mitchell, 2019). This shortfall should lead to greater scrutiny of coursework for school leaders as well as the relevance of content provided by professional development and curricular supports.

Features of this Book

Early childhood educators absorb a great deal of information as they prepare for their professional work and it is important that the people who train them, supervise them, and support them have access to the same knowledge so they can operate from a shared understanding of early childhood development and learning.

These roadmaps provide a quick summary of the content that you can find in every chapter of this book. You are encouraged to view these roadmaps as components of a complete picture of early childhood education and then to locate particular topics that are of interest to you currently. They illustrate the competencies recommended by NAEYC for early childhood educators (NAEYC, 2020). To support early childhood educators in developing the six areas of competency, leaders and instructors must be well-informed on:

- Child development and learning (including language development) in relation to the child's background and experiences.
- Relationships with families and the community.
- Ways of getting to know individual needs and progress of each child through observation and assessments.
- Supporting effective teaching that is developmentally, culturally, and linguistically appropriate in support of equitable access to learning.
- Specific knowledge about early learning standards for each age being taught as well as the selection and implementation of developmentally, culturally, and linguistically appropriate curriculum.
- The elements of professionalism for early childhood educators as individuals and within the environment of the school or program.

(NAEYC, 2020)

As an early childhood education leader or future leader, consider how these elements are embedded in your work.

Follow the Chapter 1 Roadmap with these Headings

The Focus of this Book
Important Terms
Features of this Book
Early Childhood Educator Competencies for the Future

Language Development

To understand language development is to understand the underpinnings of early learning in all domains. This chapter provides depth of knowledge that informs the "why" behind effective teaching practices and learning outcomes.

Follow the Chapter 2 Roadmap with These Headings

Introduction	Research to Practice
Language Development	Language Learners are Not All the Same
Developing Additional Languages	Speaking One Language Does Not Make Us the Same
Language Across Learning Domains	Language and the Future

Getting Started

This chapter provides a detailed guide for people who are preparing for a career in early childhood education and suggestions for how to begin their work. At every step, teachers need to interact with leaders and instructors as they find their place within the system and the field as a whole. Consider how the school could update their onboarding practices with these goals in mind.

Follow the Chapter 3 Roadmap with These Headings

Introduction	Things to Address in the Early Days
Before you Graduate	Setting Up a New Classroom
Getting a Job	Planning for Students to Get Started
Beginning a New Position	Preparing to Greet Each Child

Curriculum

Research shows that early learning outcomes are best achieved in the context of a high-quality curriculum that is culturally and linguistically appropriate. Planning and implementation of curriculum must involve coordination between leaders and educators.

Follow the Chapter 4 Roadmap with These Headings

Introduction	Addressing Government Standards and Benchmarks
Components of a Curriculum	Lesson Plans and Activities
The Role of Language and Culture in Curricula	Developmental Theories Influence Lesson Plans
Elements of High-Quality Curriculum	Measuring Curriculum Fidelity
Curriculum Options	Anti-bias Curriculum
Is it a Curriculum or an Approach?	Engaging Families in Extending Curriculum
Curriculum for Learning Domains	Curriculum Trends for the Future

Meeting Individual Needs

Along with high-quality curricula, research points to the importance of understanding the individual needs and progress of each child, from birth to age 8, and supporting personalized approaches and curricular adaptations to meet those needs. Consider how the school plans for meaningful and responsive professional learning and collaboration to support this work by educators.

Follow the Chapter 5 Roadmap with These Headings

Introduction	Disabilities and Delays
Teaching Individual Children	Supporting Each Child Through Transitions
Conversations for All	Challenging Behaviors
Personalizing in Remote Learning	Racial Equity and Anti-Bias Practices
Getting to Know Individual Children	Experiences of Stress and Trauma
Screening, Evaluation, and Assessment	Conclusion
How Schools Ensure Individual Needs Are Met	

Environment and Materials

Successful early childhood education depends on making the right choices for setting up the environment and providing materials for learning. Along with high-quality teacher practices, these are the components that make curricula and personalized learning supports work. Consider how the purchasing policy and budget of the school or program could be more responsive to the demands of a high-quality approach to early learning.

Follow the Chapter 6 Roadmap with These Headings

Introduction	Learning Connections and Technology
Designing Learning Environments	A Welcoming Entrance
Health and Safety	Furnishings and Learning Centers
Universal Design	Learning Outside the Classroom
Culturally Responsive Environments	Strategies and Practices to Enhance the Learning Environment
Following Children's Interests	
	Conclusion

Family and Community

Effective partnerships with families and with members of the community are critical for early childhood education, but they are not just the responsibility of each educator. Consider what supports are built in to school policy, budget, and planning to build these important relationships and to foster success for each teacher.

Follow the Chapter 7 Roadmap with These Headings

Introduction	Connecting with the Community
Communicating with Families	Communication Tools and Resources
Supports for Learning at Home	Transitions
Families Contribute to Learning Environments	Conclusion

Collaboration, Co-teaching, and Working with Specialists

Key reports that summarize research on early childhood teacher preparation have identified the need for cross-discipline collaboration and co-teaching as areas that need to be improved (National Institutes of Medicine & National Research Council, 2015). Consider the role of school leaders to provide scheduling, space, and professional supports to facilitate the integration of this work.

Follow the Chapter 8 Roadmap with These Headings

Introduction	Space for In-Person Collaboration
Partnering with Paraprofessionals	Shared Professional Development
Collaborating with Teachers	Collaboration for Remote Learning
Co-Teaching	Working with Specialists
Collaboration as a Priority for Teacher Educators	Conclusion
Social Media and Digital Connections	

Professionalism

It is the responsibility of each early childhood educator to understand and practice professionalism in all of their work, but the tone is set by instructors and leaders who prepare and support these educators. Consider how the written and unwritten policies and practices within the school or program enhance professionalism and identify areas that need improvement.

Follow the Chapter 9 Roadmap with These Headings

Introduction	Professional Roles with Families and Community
Foundation of Knowledge and Skills	Cultural Humility and Focus on Equity
Professional Learning and Development	Working as a Bilingual Educator
Working Within an Integrated System of Early Care and Education	Working with Children who Speak Languages You Don't
Professional Ethics	Ability to Adapt and Change
Teacher Dispositions	Conclusion

System-Wide Planning and Implementation

Teaching does not happen in isolation. Early childhood educators are part of a local system and a larger state or national system. For the work of each educator to be successful with each young child, it is the job of the administrator to build and strengthen the system by coordinating all of its parts. This is necessary to respond to a range of rapidly moving trends such as increasing diversity, changing funding priorities, and major shifts in policy and practice. Starting with a focus on language provides a hub on which to attach all the other features of your system-wide plan for early childhood education.

Much of each teacher's success depends on how well their employer handles the components described in Chapter 3 Getting Started. With a system-wide plan for a good start, educators can turn their attention to fully understanding and implementing curricula and adapting to meet the needs of each individual child. The establishment of a high-quality teaching and learning environment is also critical to ensure that culturally and linguistically responsive surroundings make it possible for each child to reach their potential (NAEYC, 2020). Supporting your early childhood education staff to work with each other across disciplines and to flourish as a professional in the wider context are also critical components of systems planning that enable successful outcomes for all children. Here are the areas of coordination that need to be addressed in the school's systematic approach:

- Recruiting, onboarding, and supporting staff.
- Creating an integrated plan for professional development that is:
    - Respectful of participants.
    - Based on data.
    - Integrated across content areas to meet identified goals.
    - Accessible in multiple ways to meet individual needs of learners.
    - Tied to plans for implementation, coaching, and supervision support.

- - Provided by presenters who are familiar with the school's curricula.
  - Provided by presenters who are prepared to address their content in context of cultural and linguistic responsiveness.
  - Also supportive of individual pursuits and collegial sharing.
- Purchasing materials and designing spaces for high-quality early childhood education that is developmentally, culturally, and linguistically appropriate.
- Focus on two-way communication with multiple options to engage with every family.
- Selection of high-quality curriculum that is developmentally, culturally, and linguistically appropriate and is supported for implementation with fidelity.
- Choice of assessments, plans for adapting for linguistic differences, and training for all staff as needed.
- Plans for facilitating transitions of children into, through, and out of your school or program.
- Intentional supports for the health and wellness of all members of the school community.

School leaders might hire consultants to support any aspect of this system-wide engagement. When hiring professional development providers, make sure they will tailor their content to the curriculum your teachers are using, and that they will provide strategies that are developmentally appropriate and respectful of cultural and linguistic diversity.

Conclusion

Early childhood educators have so much talent, knowledge, and commitment. They should expect nothing less from the people who teach them, hire them, and support them as professionals. When teachers and specialists learn in different college/university departments, and when their coursework does not match what their instructors and employers have learned, the resulting mismatch can cause great damage to the potential for successful educational outcomes. This book has attempted to overcome this issue by tying all the threads of early childhood education together. It is the work of the users of this book that will really make the difference now and for the future.

Choose Your Path

For your reflection:

Age/setting	What is something your strengthened leadership system can improve about each of these settings, that you learned about in this book?
Infant care center	
Toddler play room	
Outdoor learning environment	
Family childcare home	
Open preschool/nursery classroom	
Kindergarten/reception classroom	

Age/setting	What is something your strengthened leadership system can improve about each of these settings, that you learned about in this book?
Academic primary classroom	
Space for individual or small group therapies	
Family education space	
Virtual learning	
Remote learning home environment	

Social Media Messages and Discussion Starters

- To teacher preparation instructors: How do you stay in touch with changing demographics of schools where your students will work?
- To directors, principals, and headmasters: When you arrange professional development for your early childhood educators, how much time do you spend learning what they learn?
- To early childhood educators: What is one thing you wish your supervisor would change to make it easier for you to do your job effectively?

References

Mitchell, C. (2019) Overlooked: How Teacher Training Falls Short for English-Learners and Students with IEPs, *Education Week*.

NAEYC (2020) *Professional Standards and Competencies for Early Childhood Educators*, Washington, DC: NAEYC.

National Institutes of Medicine & National Research Council (2015) *Transforming the Workforce for Children Birth Through Age 8: A Unifying Foundation*, Washington, DC: The National Academies Press.

Park, M., McHugh, M., Zong J., & Batalova, J. (2015) *Immigrant and Refugee Workers in the Early Childhood Field: Taking a Closer Look*, Washington, DC: Migration Policy Institute.

Index

Note: *italicised* page references indicate illustrations; **bold** ones indicate tables

30 million words 20–21
504 plans 111
adaptations 42, 43, 52, 62, 69, 86, 92, 111, **128**, 147, 155
administrators 150–157
Advancing Equity in Early Childhood Education 4
advocacy 103, 108
African American boys 13, 78
after-school clubs 75
Alliance for A Better Community 133
alphabet knowledge 18, 50
American Academy of Pediatrics 36, 93
American Bar Association 145
American Council of Teachers of Foreign Languages (ACTFL) 143
American Educational Research Association (AERA) 124, 143
American Montessori Association 143
American Speech, Language, Hearing Association (ASHA) 144
analysis/prediction questions *19*, 20
anecdotes 74, 106, 120
anti-bias 5, 40, 41, 56–57, 60, 78, **126**, 153; *see also* bias
Applied Behavior Analysis (ABA) **126**
art 18, 51, 82, **91**, 98, 99, 100, 105, 111, 119
assessments 29, 32, 42, 43, 47, 60, 61, 66, 73–74, 80, 92, 95–96, 122, 128, 136, 152, 156; and the curriculum 47, 52, 56, 74, 106; event-based 42; formal 5, 42, 74, 128; formative 42, 74; informal 5, 42, 74, 128; NAEYC standards 5, 6, 134; and paraprofessional staff 120; portfolio 42, 74, 106, 120; progress reports 106–107; summative 42; tools for 45, 52, 106
assistant 4, 52,65, 118, 119, 125 *see also* paraprofessional
assistive technologies 76, 92
Association for Childhood Education International (ACEI) 144
Association for Library Services for Children (ALSC) 113, 143

Association for Supervisors and Curriculum Developers (ASCD) 143
attachment theory 55
autism spectrum disorder 76
autonomy vs. shame and doubt 53

babies 10–12, 18, 20–21, 22–23, 36, 63, 70, 84, 87, 90, 95, 98
Babies (movie documentary) 139
Babies (Netflix series) 139
background knowledge 19, 50, 105
background noise 85, 101
Backward Design of curricula 42
Bank Street 47–48
Banse, H. 22, 135
Basic Interpersonal Communication Skills (BICS) 20
before-school clubs 75
behavior, challenging 75, 78, 125, 128, 153
belonging, sense of 21, 22, 51, 61, 87, 101, 103, 107–108, 120
benchmarks 40–42, 45, 49, 52, 74, 142 153
bias 4, 25, 37, 38, 56–57, 78, 88, 107, 120; *see also* anti-bias
Bilingual Education Research special interest group 124
Bilingual Educators 3, 29, 30, 74, **126**, 132, 143, 146
bilingual staff 56, 65, 75, 107, 118, 120, 121, 123, 125, **126**, 133, 150
bilingualism 3, 23–24; balanced bilinguals 24; emergent bilinguals 3, 12, 20, 24, 51–52, 136; sequential bilinguals 23; simultaneous bilinguals 23
Black Indigenous People of Color (BIPOC) 3
Blocks 2, 19, 84, 88, 90, 91, 96, 98, 123
Books 10, 30, 32, 35, 37, 41, 42, 45, 47, 65,69, 76, 77, 83, 84, 87, 88, 91; baby-safe 10; board-books 96; class-made 96; fiction 16; non-fiction 16; picturebooks 18; photobooks 64; wordless 57, 97
book areas 96
book clubs 139, 141

book knowledge 19, 50
Bowlby, J. 55
Brazelton, T. Berry 55
The British Council 51, 143

Calderón, M.E. 79
Chard, S. 48
Chen, J. 43
child-centered approaches to curricula 46, 47–48
Childcare Aware of America 143
CLASS (Classroom Assessment Scoring System) 70, 95, 96, 136
Classroom Assessment of Supports for Emergent Bilingual Acquisition (CASEBA) 136
classrooms 4, 31, 83–102; areas within 18, 34, 96–98; displays 33, 56, 68, 83, 84, 86, 87, 89, 93, 95, 97, **97**, 100, 101; entrances 33, 65, 82, 86, 94–95, 154; furnishings 65, 67, 82, 85, 95–98, 154; health and safety 85, **97**, 154; labels in 18, 34, 82, 86–87, 96, 97, **97**; setting up 28, 33–34
closed-ended questions **19**, 20
Clubhouse 124, 139
co-teaching 118, 122–123, 125, 154
coaching 122, 137, 139–140, 141
code-switching 13–14, 75
cognates 22
Cognitive Academic Language Proficiency (CALP) 20
Cognitive 22, 40, 77, 126, 128; cognitive ability 15; cognitive competence 75; cognitive development 16–17, 53–54, 64; cognitive domain 50
Colker, L.J. 32
collaboration 118–131, **126–128**, 133–134, 136–137, 140, 144, 147, 151, 154
Colorin Colorado 51
communities 5–6, 29, 62, 103–104, 108, 113–114, **127**, 134, 144, 145, 152, 154; culturally responsive materials from 83, 90–91, **91**; language resources in 29, 31, 90–91, 104, 113, 114
competencies 1, 5–6, 133, 134, 141, 152
comprehensive curricula 46–47
concrete operational stage of cognitive development 54
conferences 78, 94, 124, 137–138, 139, 143
confidentiality 104, 116, 120, 144
consequences 55
constructivism 54
consultants 156
consultation options 129
consultative models 118
conversations 10, 23, 34, 36, 70–71, 77, 100, 121, 125, 139; "conversation compass" 19–20; with families 33, 72, 105, 106, 110, 112–113, 120; importance of 8, 13, 14, 18, 19–21, 60, 64, 70–71, 111, 121; prompts for 19–20, **19**, 57, 65, 82, 89, **91**, **97**, 111, **130**; *see also* questions
Council for Exceptional Children Division for Early Childhood (DEC) 74, 143
Council for Professional Recognition (CDA) 143
COVID-19 pandemic 4, 34, 35, 57, 79, 106, 125, 147
cozy spaces 96
crafts 98, 116
Crago, M. 25
The Creative Curriculum 47
cultural humility 4, 78, 87–88, 132, 133, 145–146, 155
Cultural Items and Language Use Checklist 89
cultural responsiveness 4, 43, 68, 74, 79, 85, **127, 128**, 138, 141, 144, 156; environments and materials 43, 57, 82, 87–89, **88**, 90–91, **91**, 142, 154, 155
Cummins, J. 16, 20, 68
Curenton, S. 19–20
curricula 5, 16, 40–59, 67, 68, 84, 85, 106, **126**, 143, 146, 153, 154; and administrators/leaders 150, 151, 152, 153, 155–156; antibias 40, 56–57; and assessments 47, 52, 56, 74, 106; Backward Design 42; child-centered approaches to 46, 47–48; collaborating with colleagues 120, 125, **126, 127**, 128, 129, **130**; comprehensive 46–47; emergent 44–45, 56; evidence-based 44; fidelity to 40, 56, 153, 156; hidden 4, 56; NAEYC standard 6, 29, 41, 134; research-based 44; supplemental 46–47; teacher-directed 44–45, 46

DECAL (different experiences, cultures, abilities, and languages) 60, 62, 67, **127–128**
decontextualized language 16
delays 15, 60, 65, 67, 72, 73, 74, 76, 77, 153
Derman-Sparks, L. 57
Developmentally Appropriate Practice (DAP) 4, 31, 43, 48, 53, 54, 90, 99, 114, 125, **126–127**, 129
dialects 25
"differentiated instruction" 60
digital technology 17, 23, 33, 34, 35, 50, 64, 68, 86, 89, 92–94, 114, 115, 122, 124, **126**, 137; *see also* social media
disabilities 60, 62, 65, 67, 72, 73, 74, 76, 77, 86, 92, 119, 120, **126**, 142, 153
displays 33, 56, 68, 83, 84, 86, 87, 89, 93, 95, 97, **97**, 100, 101
dispositions, teacher 132, 133, 138, 144, 145, 155
diversity 51, 68, 87, 120, 132, 141, 150, 151
Diversity in Action (DÍA) 113
documentation 5, 6, 29, 30, 63, 72, 75, 87, 129, 134, 137, 140
Dombro, A.L. 21
dramatic play 18, 66, 97–98, 99, 112, **127**
Draw and Tell 94

dual language learners (DLLs) 2, 3, 5, 8, 29, 49, 50, 52, 74, 85, 92, 108, 112, 119, 121, **126–127**, 133, 134, 140–141; definition 2, 24; and digital technology 94, 141–142; and home language support 5, 8, 11, 12, 14, 19, 20, 21, 22, 50, 64, 68, 93, 111, 118, 120, 121, **126–127**, 134–135, 146–147; two-way dual language immersion 3, 123

Early Childhood Learning and Knowledge Center website 44, 115
Early Language and Literacy Classroom Observation (ELLCO) 95
Early Years Foundation Stage 49, 52
echoing 13, 17, 64
Education, Health, and Care (EHC) Plan 73, **130**
Edwards, J.O. 57
ego integrity vs. despair 53
email 68, 89, 91, 92, 105, 110, 114, 141, 142
emergencies 32–33
emergent bilinguals 3, 12, 20, 24, 51–52, 136
emergent curricula 44–45, 56
engineering 17, 50, 98
England 2, 23, 52, 67, 73, 106, 121; *see also* United Kingdom (U.K.)
English as a Second Language (ESL) 3, 51–52, 74–75, **126**, 128
English as an Additional Language (EAL) 2, 3, 51–52, 74–75, **126**, 128
English language learners (ELLs)/English Learners (ELs) 3
entrances 33, 65, 82, 86, 94–95, 154
environment and materials 82–102, 154
Environmental Rating Scales 95, 136
equitable access 61–62
equity 2, 38, 58, 61, 120, 132, 134, 145–146, 155; language equity 25; racial equity 60, 78, 79, **126**, 153
Erikson, E. 53, 54
Espinosa, L. 22
ethics 36, 104, 132, 133, 144, 145, 155
evaluations 37, 38, 73, **127**, 153; *see also* assessments; screening
event-based assessments 42
Every Student Succeeds Act (ESSA) 142
evidence-based curricula 44
expressive language 10, 12, 13, 23, 24, 99, **126**
extended projects 48

Facebook 94, 115, 124, 139
families 20–21, 25, 32, 33, 34, 36, 56, 57, 79, 103–117, 145, 152, 154; definition 4; engagement with 5–6, 26, 31, 35, 36, 46, 60, 61, 62–63, 66, 71–72, 82, 88–89, 90, 91, **91**, 103–117, 120, **126–127**; and remote learning 125; and technology 58, 71–72, 93, 114–115, 142
Family Childcare Environmental Rating School (FCCERS) 95
Family Childcare Rating Scale (FCCRS) 136
family engagement plans 57, 104, 117, 145

feedback 11, 19, 29, 37, 56, 70, 121, 135, 140
fidelity to curricula 40, 56, 153, 156
field trips 32, 99, 112, 113
food and eating 43, 85, **88**, 89, **91**, 97–98, 142
Forest Schools 49
formal assessments 5, 42, 74, 128
formal operational stage of cognitive development 54
formative assessments 42, 74
Fred Rogers Center 92
furnishings 65, 67, 82, 85, 95–98, 154

Gardner, H. 55
Garrity, S. 5
generativity vs. stagnation 53
Genesee, F. 25
Gerber, M. 55
gestures 12, 70, 90
gifted and talented, teachers for **127**
Goins, C.M. 57
Goodman, R. 108
Gottlieb, M 79
grammar 14, 46
Great Britain 66; *see also* United Kingdom (U.K.)
greetings 36, 65, 67–68, 94–95, 103, 107, 115
group sizes 69

Hart, T. 20
Hattie, J. 41
Head Start 2, 24, 37, 44, 73, 105, 113, 142
health and safety 82, 85, **97**, **128**, 143, 154
health and wellness 18, 51
hidden curricula 4, 56
HighScope 47
Hine, C. 135
Hirschler, J. 51
holidays 32, 49, 89, 109
home language 3, 5, 16, 17, 18, 43, 46, 71–72; and bilingual staff 65, 118, 120, 121, 125; and the classroom environment 34, **97**, 107; and cognates 22; educators use 34, 64–65, 69–70, 77, 115; and infants 10, 11, 12, 64, **91**, 93, **97**; language Isolation 108; language transfer 21; primary grades 14, 112; supporting 5, 8, 11, 12, 14, 19, 20, 21, 22, 50, 64, 68, 93, 111, 118, 120, 121, **126–127**, 134–135, 146–147; surveys 36, 105; vocabulary bridging 19, 69
home visits 105
Honigsfeld, A. 125
Huynh, T. K. 14
hybrid learning 34, 35, 57, 92

identity vs. role confusion 53
immigrants 3, 24, 79, 108, 123, 151
inclusion 89, 120–121; inclusive 33, 57, 69, 74, 83, 93, 104, 109, 120–121
Individualized Education Programs (IEPs) 52, 73, 74, 111, 128, **130**, 142
Individualized Family Service Plans (IFSPs) 52, 73, 74, 111, 128, **130**

industry vs. inferiority 53
Infant Toddler Environmental Rating Scale (ITERS) 95, 136
infants/infant settings 9–12, 18, 20–21, 34, 36, 43, 55, 57, 69, 74, 85, **91**, 99, 105, 112, 121; assessments 74, 106, 136; classrooms 84, **91**, 94, 95, 96, **97**, 98, 112; and technology 71, 93; working with individual children 61, 62–64; *see also* babies; toddlers/toddler settings
informal assessments 5, 42, 74, 128
informal language 8, 16, 20, 24
information, presenting 69–70
initiative vs. guilt 53
Instagram 115
International Literacy Association (ILA) 143
interpersonal intelligence 55
interpreting 25, 31; *see also* translating/interpreting
intimacy vs. isolation 53
intrapersonal intelligence 55

Jablon, J. 21
Jam Board app 93
jobs, securing 30–31

Kagan, S.L. 43
Katz, L. 48
kindergarten 15, 18, 37, 45, 47, 49, 66–67, 73, **91**, 95, 96, **97**, 98, 106, 110, 112, 142
kinesthetic intelligence 55
Koralek, D. 32
Kuhl, P. 23

L1/L2 language 3
labeling: children 3, 37, 55, 86; in classrooms 18, 34, 82, 86–87, 96, 97, **97**
language: decontextualized 16; definition 1, 9; expressive 10, 12, 13, 23, 24, 99, **126**; informal 8, 16, 20, 24; oral 13, 14, 19, 50, 70; receptive 10, 11, 12, 13, 24, 99, **126**; *see also* translating/interpreting
language development 1, 5, 8–27, **19**, 46, 61, 64, 70, 73, 75, 104, 132, 152
language isolation 108
language justice 25, 108, 145
language matching 3, 133
language transfer 21
leaders 106, 150–157
learning domains 8, 16–19, 40, 41, 46, 49–52, 123
learning styles 55
lesson plans 40, 42, 43, 48, 52–55, 70, 91, 114, 122, 129, 146
Letiecq, B. 108
libraries 91, **91**, 96, 104, 108, 113, **126**, 139, 142
listening 55, 106; by children 11, 14, 21, 23, 46, 50, 69; to children 20–21, 45, 78, 79, 104; reflective 110
literacy supports 96–97, **97, 126**

maintenance language education 3, 146
majority languages 3, 24, 51, **127**
makerspaces 50, 98
math 16, 17, 50, 51, 56, 71, 98
Mazzeo, D. 62
mentors 32, 137, 139–140, 141
metalinguistic awareness 13, 51–52
Migration Policy Institute 123
minority language 3, 24
Montessori 47–48, 83, 143
mother tongue 3
motor development 16, 17, 85, 95, 98, **126**
multilingual learners (MLs) 3, 9, 42, 58, 123, 124
multiple intelligences 55
music 18, 43, 47, 55, 83, 87, **88**, 89, 91, 98, 99, 105, 112, 114, 119, **127**; *see also* singing/songs
My Story app 94

names, pronouncing 36
narrate 10, 13, 71, 94; narrating 13, 64
National Association for Bilingual Educators (NABE) 143
National Association for Family Childcare (NAFCC) 143
National Association for the Education of Young Children (NAEYC) 4, 30, 31, 92, 116, 143, 144, 152; assessments 5, 6, 134; curricula 6, 41, 43; Developmentally Appropriate Practice (DAP) 4, 31, 43, 54, 90; standards and competencies 5–6, 29, 134
National Black Child Development Institute (NBCDI) 143
National Center for English Language Acquisition (NCELA) 144
National Council of La Raza 133, 144
National Council of Teachers of English (NCTE) 143
National Head Start Association (NHSA) 143
National Institutes of Medicine and the National Research Council 141
National Network for Early Language Learning (NNELL) 143
National Workforce Registry 137
Native Americans 114
naturalistic intelligence 55
Nature Schools 49
newsletter 57, 109, 122, 137, 139, 142
nonverbal communication 9–10, 12, 64, 65, 70, 77, 78, 83, 86, 147
Nordmeyer, J. 125
North American Reggio Emilia Association (NAREA) 143
nursery 64–66, 85, **91**, 93, 94, 95, **97**, 98, 116, 136, 144
Nursery World, UK 144

observations 5, 6, 29, 60, 70, 72, 95, 136, 152
occupational therapy 66, **126**
Office of Planning, Research, and Evaluation 89, 92

online learning *see* remote learning
open-ended questions 19, 20, 70
oral language 13, 14, 19, 50, 70
outdoor learning 49, 82, **91**, **97**, 98
outdoor play 17, **91**, 99

Padlet website 93
pandemics 47; *see also* COVID-19 pandemic
Pandey, A. 105
Paradis, J. 25
parallel talk 13, 51
paraprofessionals 118–131, 150, 154
parents evenings 106–107
peer interactions, children 15, 20, 23, 42, 51, 68, 70, 71, 84, 86, 87
person first language 2–3
Personal learning networks (PLNs) 121, 139, 143
personalization 37, 52, 56, 60–80; for remote learning 60, 71–72, 125
phonological awareness 19, 21, 50
photos 17, 34, 64, 69, 87, **88**, 91, 94, 98, 101, 112; of culturally and linguistically relevant items 83, **88**, 89, 142; families, communications with 92, 93, 114, 115; and field trips 99
physical education 105, 119, **127**
physical therapy 38, 47, 68, 105, 116, **126**, 136
Piaget, J. 53, 54
Pinterest 139
play 17, 20, 34, 42, 43, 46, 49, 53, 66, 89, 95, 96–98; language in 17, 21, 36, 37, 70, 71, 76, 83, 99; outdoor 17, **91**, 99; play areas 86, 96–98
playground speech 16
podcasts 94, 139
portfolio assessments 42, 74, 106, 120
portfolio, professional 137
Positive Behavior Supports (PBS) 75
poverty 2, 66, 79
Practice-Based Coaching 139–140
pre-teaching key vocabulary 68, 71–72
prediction questions **19**, 20
preliteracy 18–19
preoperational stage of cognitive development 54
preschoolers/preschool settings 13, 19, 23–24, 34, 37, 44, 48, 49, 64–66, 71, 73, 77, 93, 96, 105, 112, 124; assessments 42, 74, 106; classrooms 94, 95, 96, **97**, 98; culturally responsive materials 89, **91**, 112, 114; online learning 23, 35
primary grades 14, 20, 23, 37, 43, 46, 48, 52, 67–68, 69, 71, 75, 84, 93, 99, 106, 147; classrooms 67, 94, 95, 96, 100; culturally responsive materials 68, **91**, **97**; family contributions to learning 112
professional development 28, 32, 52, 56, 94, 106, 119, 120, 122, 123, 124–125, 135–140, 150, 155–156
professional learning communities (PLCs) 119, 121–122, 132, 139

Professional Standards and Competencies for Early Childhood Educators 5–6, 29, 134
professionalism 5, 6, 29, 37, 132–149, 151, 152, 155
progress reports 106–107
Project Approach 47–48
project-based learning (PBL) 19, 46, 48, 142
project management software 141
Promoting the Educational Success of Children and Youth Learning English: Promising Futures 141
psychologists **127**
psychosocial development 53
pull-out supports 118, 128–129
push-in supports 118, 128–129
Pyramid Model 48

Quality of Caregiver-Child Interactions for Infants and Toddlers (Q-CIIT) 136
questions 19–20, **19**, 65, 66, 69–70, 90; analysis/prediction **19**, 20; closed-ended **19**, 20; open-ended **19**, 20, 70

racial equity 60, 78, 79, **126**, 153
Rao, V. 90
reading skills 49–50, 111, **126**
ReadyRosie.com 115
reception 15, 18, 37, 49, 66–67, **91**, 95, 96, **97**, 98, 142
receptive language 10, 11, 12, 13, 24, 99, **126**
records *see* documentation
reflective listening 110
Reggio Emilia 47–48, 83, 143
regulations 85, 119, 135–136, 142–143, 146
Reid, J.L. 43
Remind (text messaging platform) 114
remote learning for children 11, 23, 34, 35, 57, **91**, 92, 93–94, **97**, 125, 142, 147; and families 71, 72, 94, 125, 147; field trips 99, 112, 113; personalization 60, 71–72, 125
remote learning for teachers 94, 124–125, 137, 138, 139, 140
research-based curricula 44
Response to Intervention (RTI) 75
Risley, B. 20
Rosproy, T. 35

scaffolding 54, 55, 69, 70, 121
science 16, 50, 51, 98, 99
Scott-Little, C. 43
screen time 35–36, 71
screening 15, 37, 60, 61, 66, 67, 73, 153
self-talk 13, 51
sensorimotor stage of cognitive development 54
sequential bilinguals 23
Sheltered Instruction Observation Protocol (SIOP), 52
sign language 10, 22–23, 30, 68–69, 86
silent period 15
simultaneous bilinguals 23

singing/songs 10, 11, 15, 32–33, 37, 47, 57, 63, 64, 88, 90, **91**, **97**, 100, 105, 111, 114, 119, 142
Skinner, B.F. 55
social emotional learning/development (SEL/SED) 17, 47, 51
social justice 56, 58, 108, 145
social media 32, 92, 104, 115, 119, 121, 124, 138–139, 144, 154
social media messages and discussion starters 4, 6, 26, 38, 58, 80, 101, 117, 131, 148, 157
social workers 105, **127**
Society for Research in Child Development (SRCD) 143
Spaces (on Twitter) 139
spatial intelligence 55
special education 30, 37, 66, 67, 73–74, 75, 76, 92, 105, 120, **126**, **127**, 142
Special Educational Needs (SEN) 73, 111
specialists 4, 33, 37, 67, 71, 74–75, 98, 105, 106–107, 118–131, **126–128**, **130**, 150, 151, 154
speech therapy 66, 68, **126**, 128
STEM (science, technology, engineering, and math) 16–17, 98
stereotyping 3, 4, 72
Stetson, C. 21
stories/storytelling 13, 14, 18, 20, 36, 43, 50, 57, 71, 90, 94, 96, 100, 111–112, 142; families and communities supply 43, 112, 113, 114; technology for 34, 92, 94, **97**
Strader, William H. 14
strength-based approaches 79
stress 15, 24, 25, 45, 60, 61, 62, 65, 72, 79, 95, 108, 133, 140, 153
summative assessments 42
supplemental curricula 46–47

Talking Points (text messaging platform) 114
teacher-directed curricula 44–45, 46
Teachers of English to Speakers of Other Languages (TESOL) 143
Teachers Pay Teachers 139
Teams 115
technology 16, 17, 23, 26, 28, 34–35, 50, 58, 82, 92–94, 98, **127**, 154; adaptive 92; assistive 76, 92; *see also* remote learning for children
telegraphic speech 15
text messaging 34, 63, 68, 89, 92, 105, 109, 110, 111, 114, 115, 142
toddlers/toddler settings 12–13, 23, 30, 32–33, 34, 36, 43, 69, 98, 99, 105, 112, 121; assessments 74, 106, 136; classrooms **91**, 94, 95, 96, **97**, 98, 100; remote learning 71; and technology 56, 71, 93; working with individual children 61, 62–64; *see also* infants/infant settings
tokenism 83, 88, 107
Transforming the Workforce 133, 134, 141
transitional education 3, 146
transitions 76–77, 115–116, 153, 154, 156
translanguaging 75; *see also* code-switching
translating/interpreting 23, 25, 29, 31, 33, 68, 69–70, 73, 87, 92, 94, 104, 107, 108, 110, 114, 120, 121, 151
trauma 5, 25, 61, 62, 79, 108, 153
tribal languages 3, 104, 114
trust vs. mistrust 53
turn-taking 10, 70
TV 11, 23
Twitter 94, 115, 124, 139
two-way dual language immersion 3, 123

UNIDOS (US, formerly National Council of La Raza) 143
United Kingdom (U.K.) 2, 23, 49, 52, 66, 67, 73, 93, 106, 121; Department of Education 52, 142
United States (U.S.) 1, 2, 3, 23, 24, 31, 35, 36, 49, 52, 66, 73, 75, 89, 93, 106, 114, 121; Department of Education 37, 92, 93, 124, 141; Department of Health and Human Services 92, 141
universal design for learning (UDL) 5, 48, 58, 62, 82, 85, 86–87, 154

Vesely, C. 108
video 34, 37, 47, 64–65, 69, 91, 98, 113, **126**; chat 11, 23, 35, 93, **97**, 99, 106, 107, 112, 115, 141, 142; coaching, use in 140; colleagues, collaborating with 141–142; for culturally and linguistically relevant items 83, 112; families, communications with 15, 32, 36, 72, 92, 93, **97**, 104, 106, 107, 108, 111, 112, 114, 115, 142; and field trips 99, 112; in lessons 16, 53, 69, 71–72, 87, 93–94; passive viewing 11, 23; and remote learning 35, **97**; vlogs 139
virtual learning *see* remote learning for children
vocabulary: pre-teaching key vocabulary 68, 71–72; vocabulary bridging 19, 69
volunteer 16, 22, 29, 31–32, 34, 52, 65, 73, 99, 113–114, 116, 143, 147
Vygotsky, L. 54

Waldorf Schools of America 47–48, 143
WIDA 52, 73–74, 143
Williams, C. 20
World Organization for Early Childhood Education (OMEP) 143

Yen, S.-C. 108
YMCA 139
YouTube 94, 139

Zacarian, D. 79
Zero to Three 12, 143
zone of proximal development 54
Zoom 115, 137